THE
STYLISH
LIFE

FOOTBALL

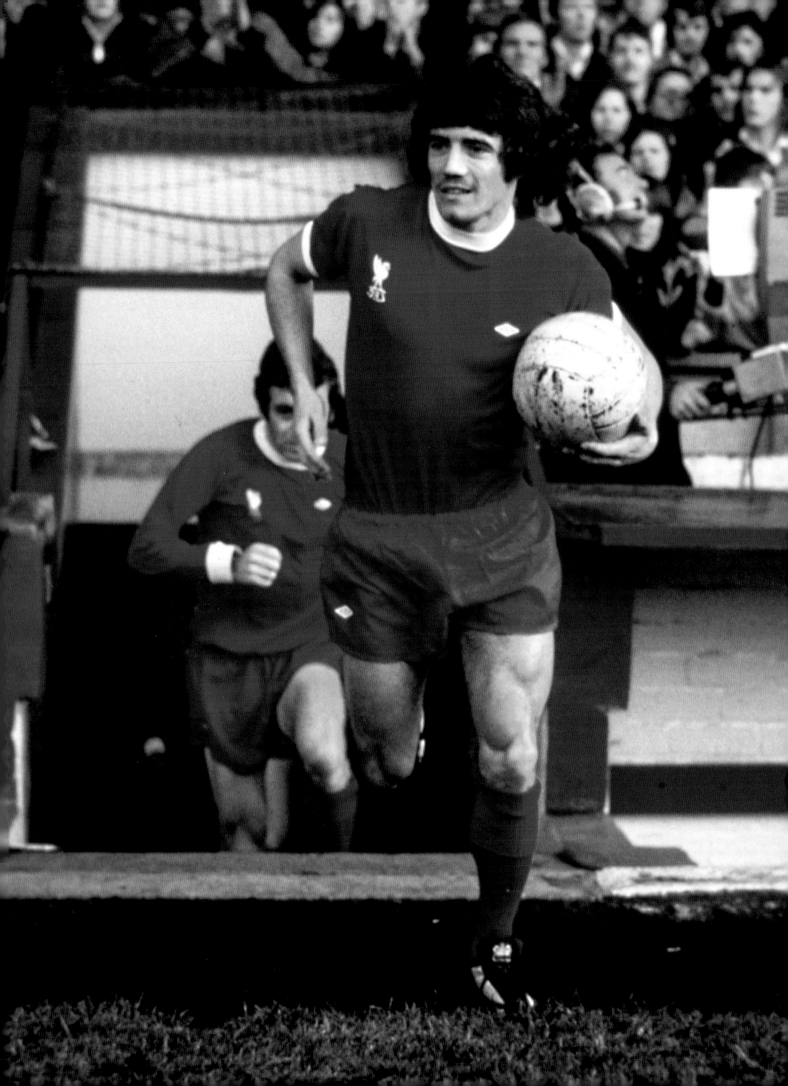

THE
STYLISH
LIFE

FOOTBALL

Introduction by Jessica Kastrop

Texts by Ben Redelings

teNeues

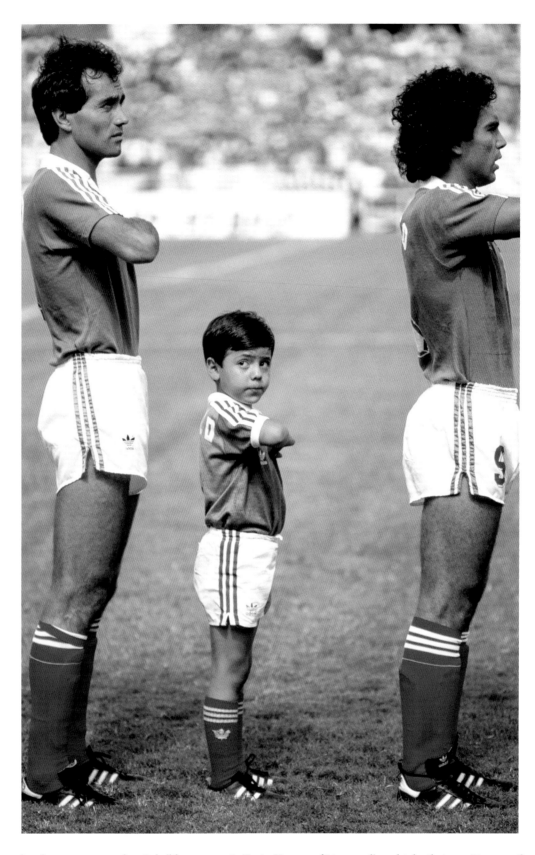

Tension is building: the players run onto the pitch (like on page 2, Kevin Keegan of Liverpool) and take their positions on the centre line (above, full of pathos: Fernando Quirarte, Hugo Sánchez and a dutiful young escort).

CONTENTS

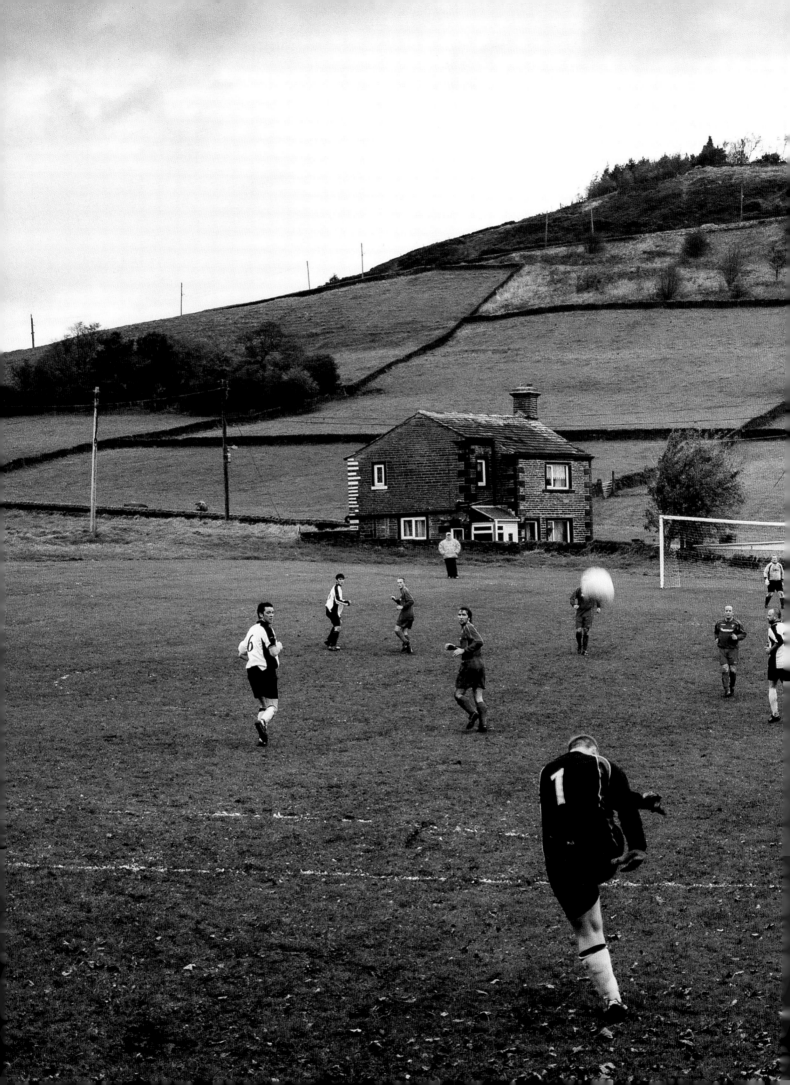

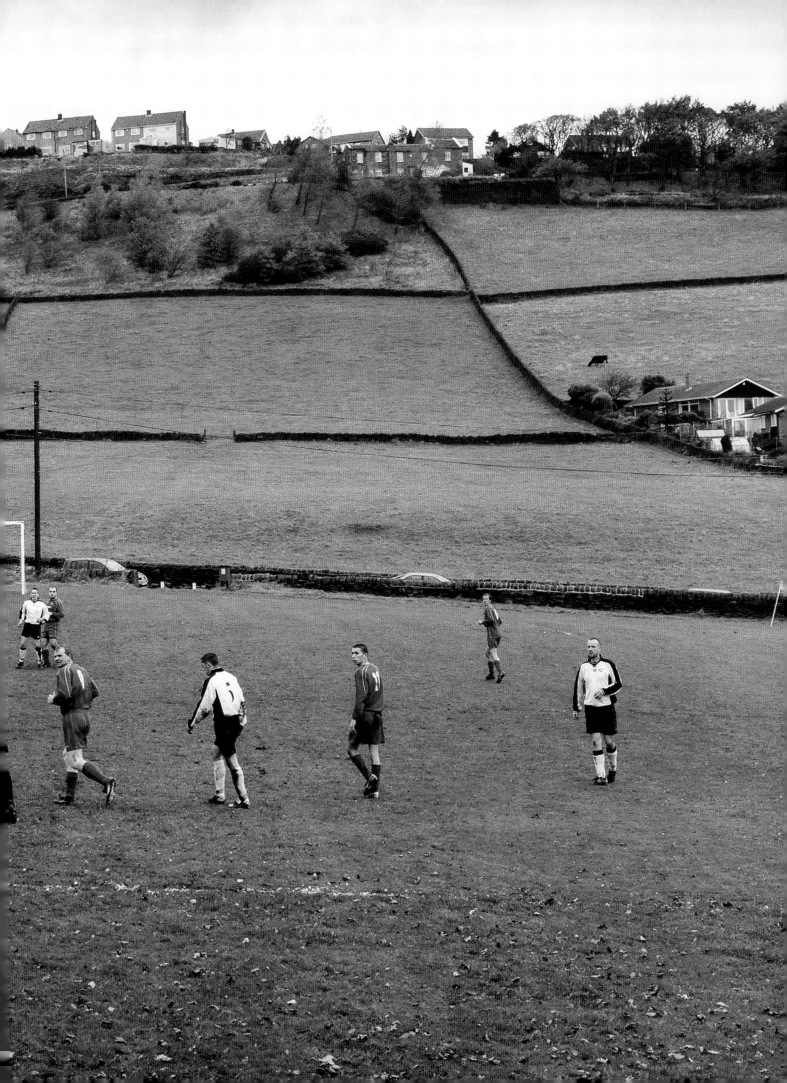

INTRODUCTION

JESSICA KASTROP

"Performance on the pitch – that's what it's all about." This verdict of Borussia Dortmund's legendary striker, Alfred Preißler, is one of football's most popular quotes in Germany, ranking him with Éric Cantona, Brian Clough and other footballing greats. His comment still largely applies today, though besides the sliding tackles, dribbles and free kicks, a fascinating parallel culture has grown up around the sport. The one-of-a-kind blend of romantic myths, magical places, working class people and tradition paved the way for modern heroic sagas that were written afresh every weekend. Football is culture and football is art.

Photographers, artists and writers make football topical. Take Manuel Vázquez Montalbán, for instance, a writer and Barcelona supporter who once said that the modern person incessantly changes everything – from marital partners to *Weltanschauung*. The football club is the only constant here, and your loyalty to it endures from childhood and beyond. Che Guevara, who rooted for his home club Rosario Central, even went a step further. The revolutionary – nowadays himself part of Pop Culture – declared, "Football is not just a simple game. It is also a weapon of the revolution."

When the focus at this point is on the sport's over-importance, one of football's priceless figures rapidly comes into play. Diego Maradona, who is almost worshipped like a god back in his home Argentina, once in a critical condition had to be rushed by his personal doctor to a clinic. But nobody wanted to accept him. The reason was, "We don't want to be the hospital where Maradona dies..."

Today's heroes always turn up smart; they are like projection screens for a host of desires and yearnings. No other game has developed on so many levels. Players become fashion icons and stadiums emerge as design temples – football defines an attitude towards life. It's almost a global lifestyle.

The players' kit for away games has now been upgraded and the fashion is for finer fabrics – the 'shell suit' is now frowned upon by the majority of Champions League managers. The beauty about the big showcase fixtures: everything is always to play for, no matter if one expects the best or the worst. Even if Gary Lineker once defined football like this: "22 men chase a ball for ninety minutes and at the end, the Germans always win." Today, the game on the pitch still inspires hope. Even if David fails a hundred times against Goliath, there'll certainly be a breakthrough some time. It's a wonderful allegory of life. Amidst all the glamour, ultimately, the saying still goes: "performance on the pitch – that's what it's all about."

Into the pleasure field: the goal keeper in Hans van der Meer's brilliantly atmospheric photograph (Warley, England, 2004) seems to aim his goal kick not only up the pitch but right over the adjacent slope (pp. 6/7).

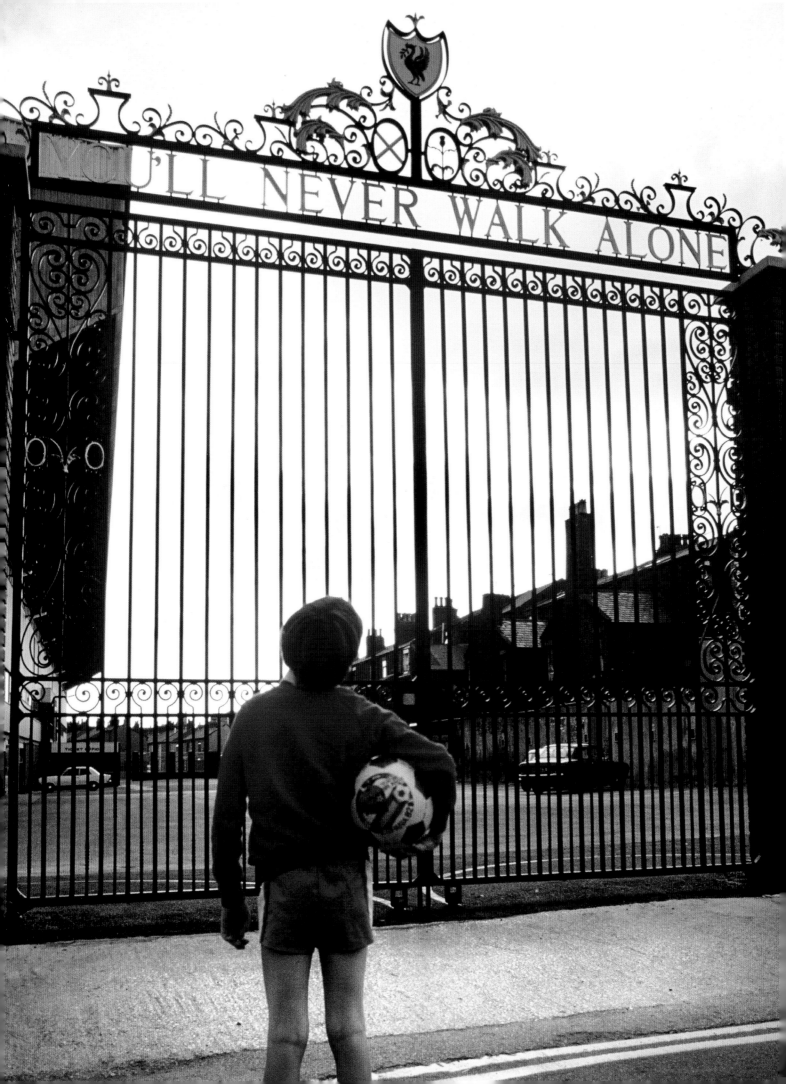

PLACES

"Of all the unimportant things, football is the most important," Pope John Paul II once said – and he's right. Over one billion people around the globe now follow the World Cup finals. No other sport rivals football's popularity. The game's simplicity is the main attraction: a ball, two goals and a handful of players are the basic elements that fuel the fascination of this amazing sport. Children all over the world chase after a round leather ball along stony streets, across dusty fields and in narrow backyards even now. But surrounding this simple game there are temples of passion – vast arenas with capacity for 100,000 or more fans. Week in, week out, history is written inside these mythical places!

It all began at Scotland's oldest football club, Queen's Park. Hampden Park, the club's home ground, is considered the world's first football stadium. It was here that, 150 years ago, football embarked on a long journey, culminating in the event for the masses that we are familiar with today. During this period some unique football grounds have emerged like Brazil's Maracanã Stadium in Rio de Janeiro, or London's legendary Wembley Stadium. Many stadiums were redeveloped and modernized over the years, while some of them were engulfed by the tide of history. Some landmarks remain, like the famous clock from the old Wankdorf stadium in Bern, Switzerland. Here, during the 1954 World Cup the teams could tell the time from this clock. Today, it has pride of place in the square in front of the new stadium.

"Walk on with hope in your heart...": *the love of football, like so many other of life's passions, begins with a sense of longing and dreams for the future...*

Football and its venues have continually evolved over the years. But it took a tragic disaster to introduce a radical rethink by all nations. On 15 April 1989, 96 people lost their lives at the dilapidated Hillsborough Stadium in Sheffield. Since then professional football has experienced the most intensive period of change in its history. Surprisingly, one country, where football was traditionally less popular, set the example for this change. The organization of mainstream sports in the US, as well as managing the big stadiums like popular leisure venues had already fascinated Paul Breitner, one of Germany's 1974 world champions, since the early 1980s: "Football made in the USA – for us that's Hollywood, Mickey Mouse, glitz and glamour; it's a well staged comedy. We smile about it all. But many of us haven't worked out that football will soon look exactly the same where we are. Yes, our approach to football has to go the American way. The 'Operetta League' – that's our future." In fact, this future was already upon us in the early 1990s!

Football's general rise in social status is primarily reflected in increasingly impressive grounds, with hotels close by and shopping centres that offer football merchandise. International top architects like Jacques Herzog or Norman Foster devise the architectural schemes to build new high-tech temples, while designers like Giorgio Armani or companies like Pininfarina create the décor and interiors for the VIP areas. High society's elite now gathers here. Football has become a major social event; it's the playground of the beautiful people.

Mythical venues

Maracanã

Several years after his winning goal in the final match of the 1950 World Cup, Uruguay's Alcides Ghiggia once said, "Only three people have ever silenced 200,000 people at the Maracanã with a single gesture: Frank Sinatra, Pope John Paul II and I." 199,854 fans watched this match – the highest number of spectators on record. 74,738 fans still followed the 2014 World Cup final in the modernized Maracanã Stadium.

Anfield

Liverpool's home ground is a living legend. "The Kop", formerly the largest and most iconic standing terrace was redeveloped in 1994 as an all-seater area. In the 1960s, the fans here tuned up for the first time to sing what later became their anthem, "You'll Never Walk Alone". José Mourinho is full of respect when he claims that even now, "Anfield is the only stadium that can score goals itself!"

Camp Nou

A tour of the Camp Nou stadium currently features among the most popular tourist attractions in Barcelona. Over two tiers inside the vast ground the blue seats bear the yellow lettering of the club's motto, "Més que un club" ("more than a club"). With a capacity of 99,354 spectators, this is Europe's largest stadium. Typically, at Spanish clubs a roof covers just a small seating area.

Signal Iduna Park

Dortmund's *Südtribüne* (South Stand) is legendary. During Borussia Dortmund home games there is standing capacity for 25,000 fans. *The Times* highly recommended the ground of the multiple *Bundesliga* winners, "Borussia Dortmund's ground is a classic. Two huge end terraces (and they are terraces, with the use of safe standing) that fling noise down at the playing area with deafening intensity. This place was built for football and for fans to express themselves. Every European Cup final should be held here. The best atmosphere on the Continent on a game-to-game basis."

Football is everywhere at any time: on the streets, in the school playground or in the stadium – and from the cradle (or child's buggy) to the grave (or fan cemetary); the next two double-page spreads show iconic images by football photographers Stuart Roy Clarke (pp. 14/15) and Gerrit Starczewski (pp. 16/17).

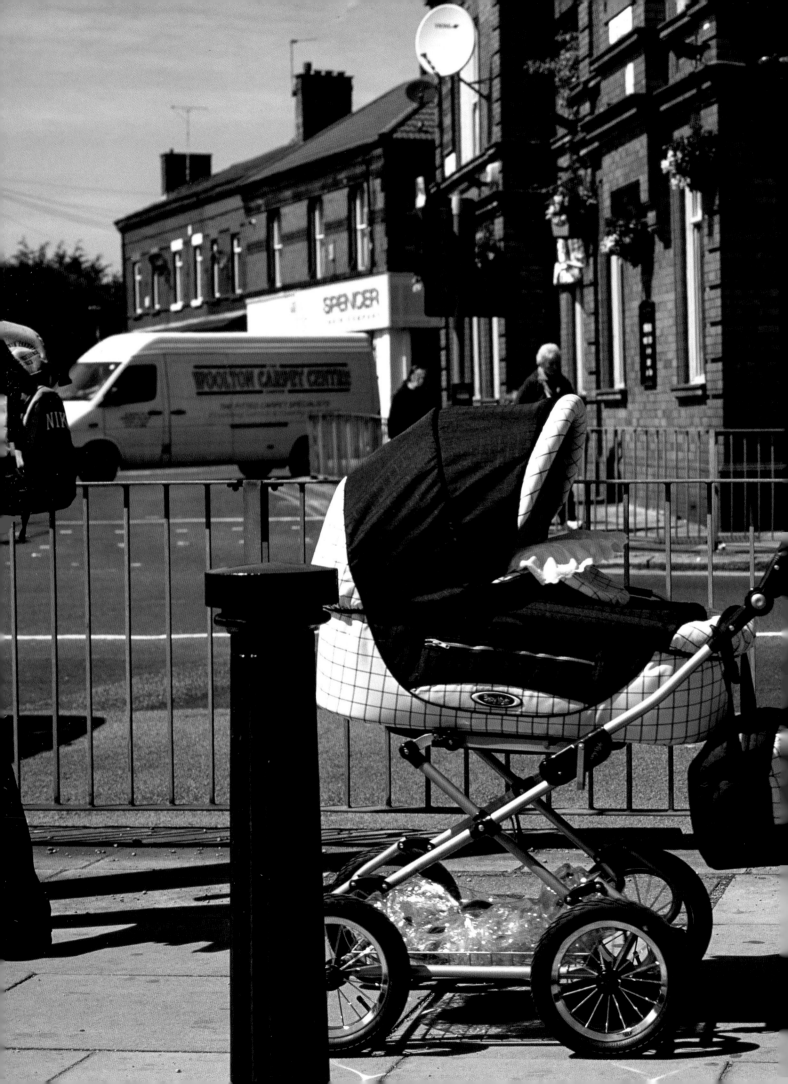

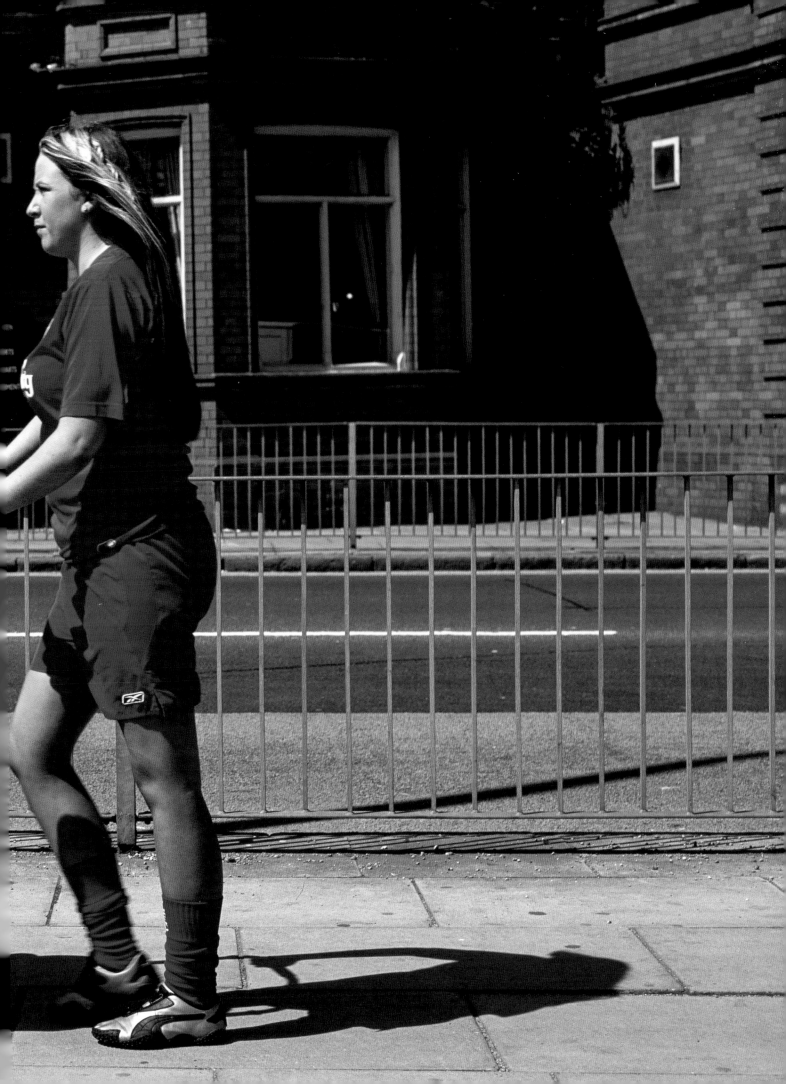

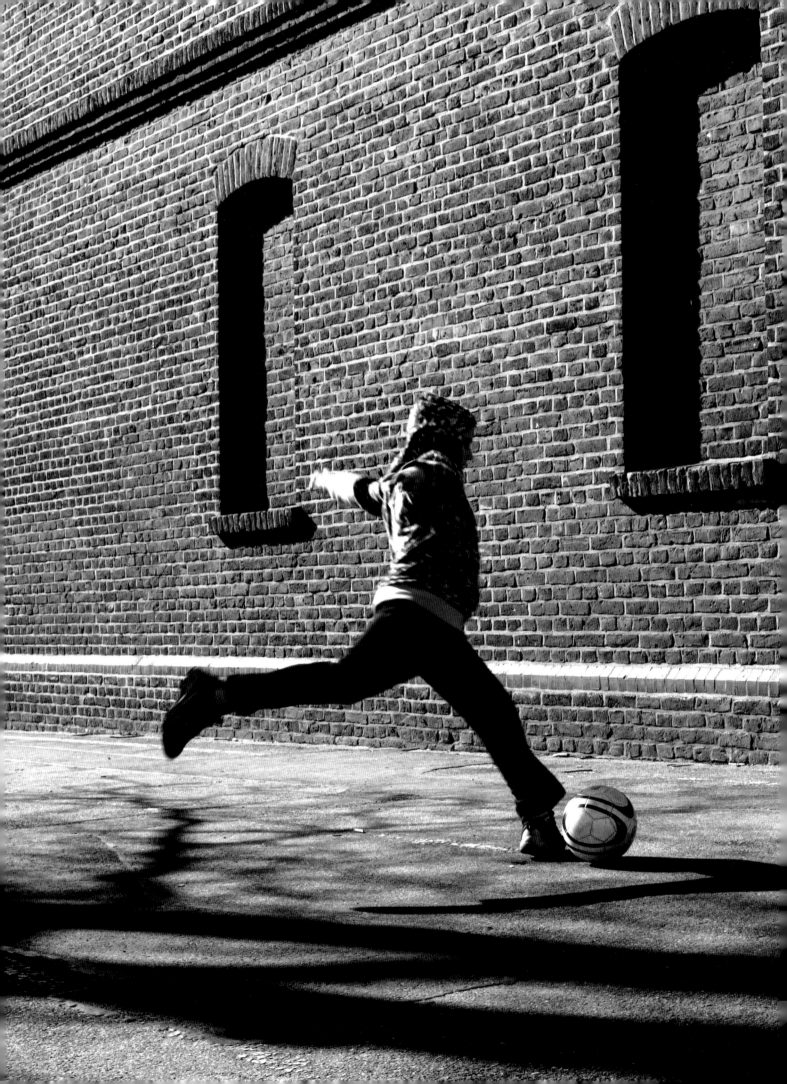

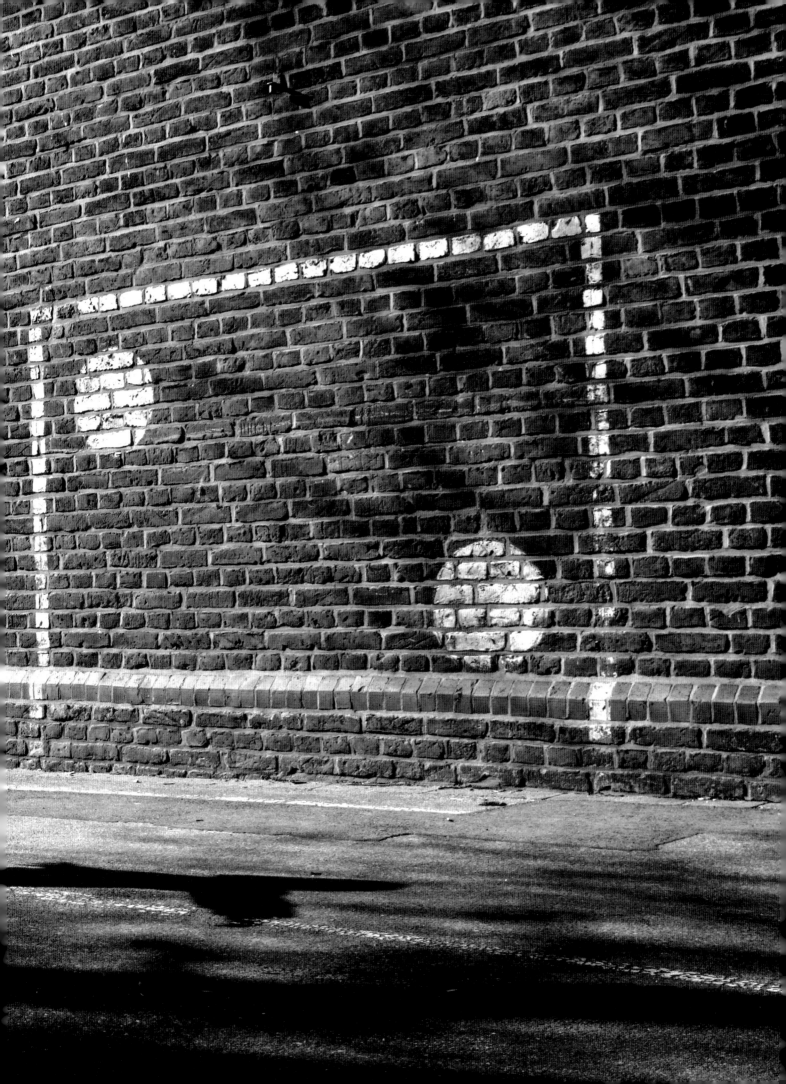

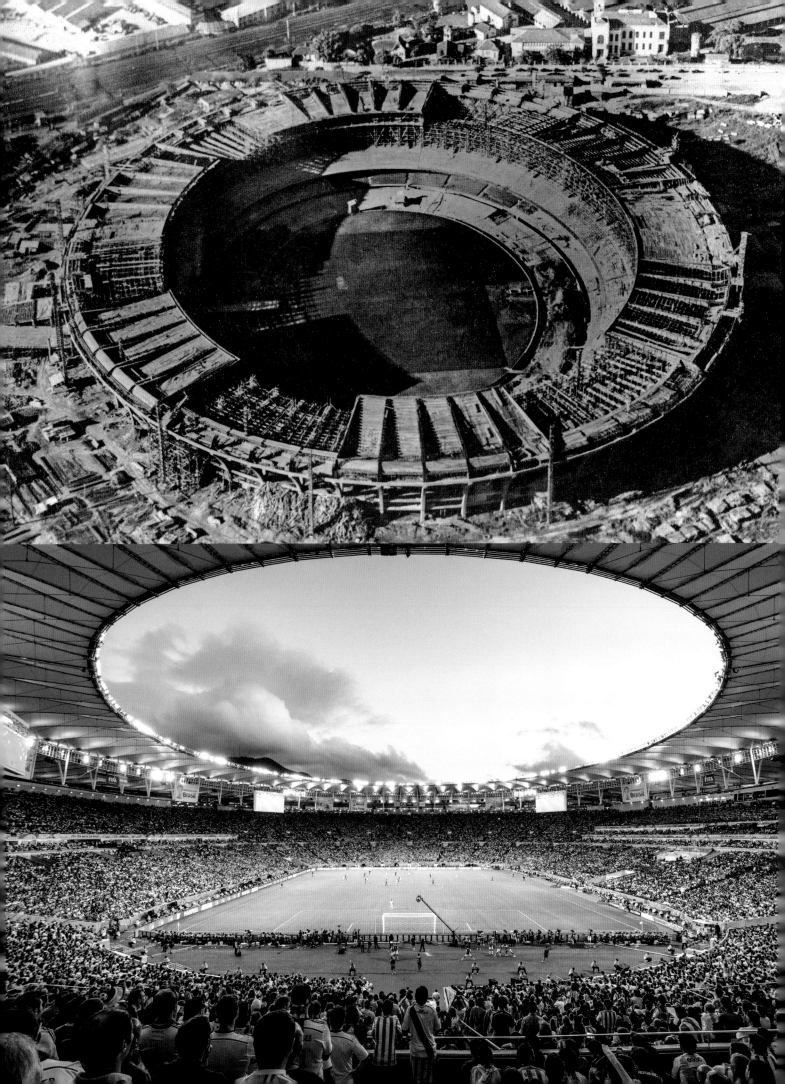

Where legends are made: the Estádio do Maracanã under construction (top left) and at the World Cup Final 2014 (bottom left); a place where countless myths were born; the place where after Brazil's defeat against Uruguay in the 1950 World Cup, according to Uruguayan writer, Eduardo Galeano, there was the "loudest silence in football history"; a sublime place – but not for the substitutes, who had to sit on the bench below ground, like in the photo below of the 1974 Brazil vs. Bulgaria match.

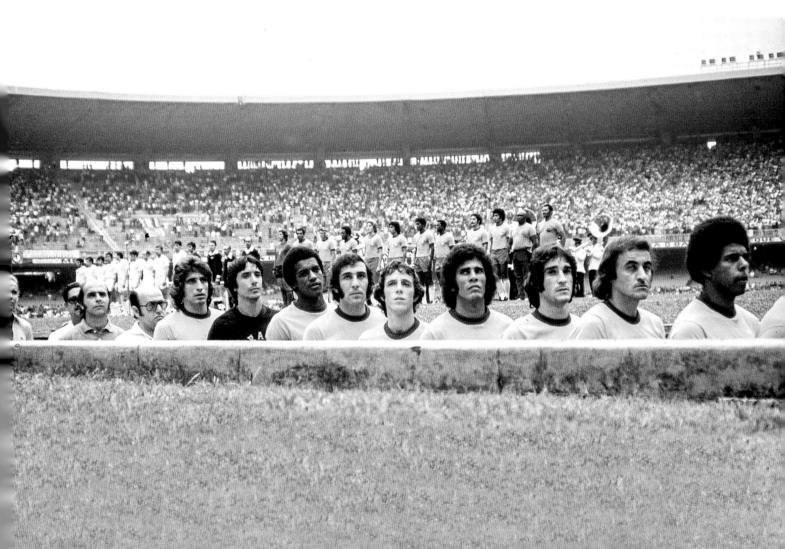

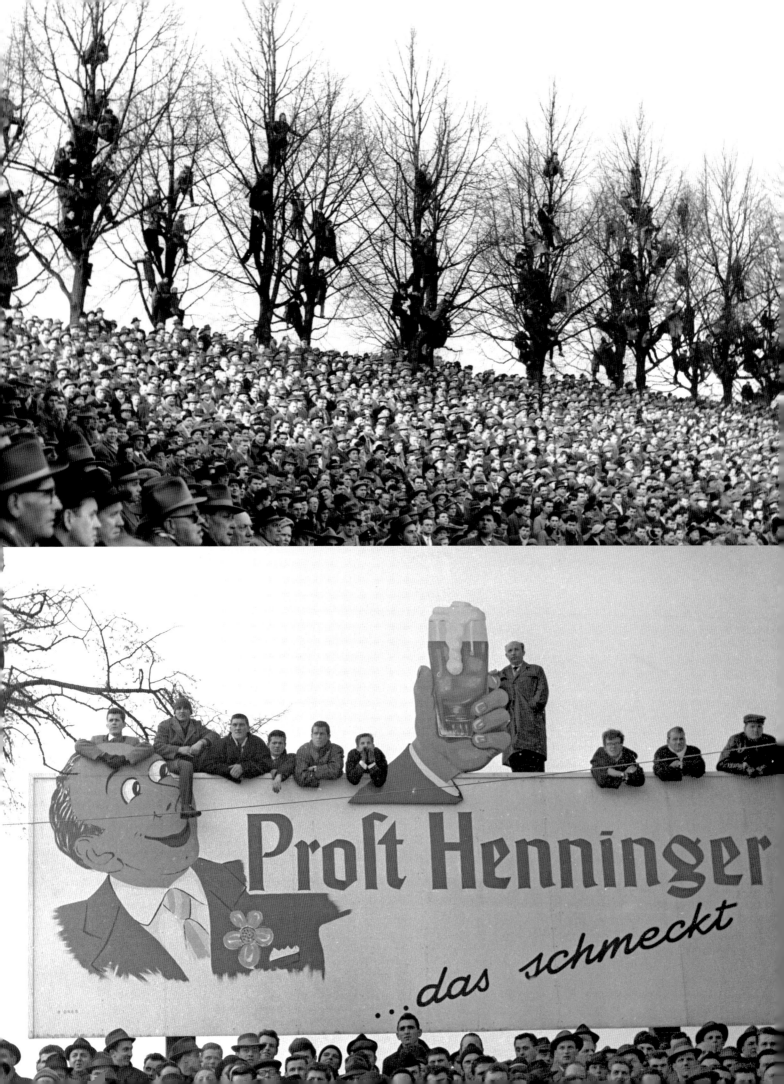

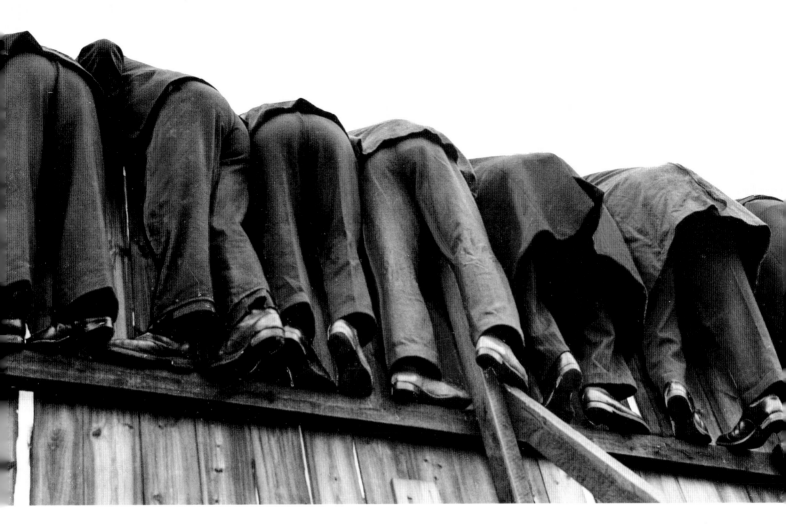

Not right in the middle, but still present: to see a live match it's not essential to be inside the stadium, as resourceful fans prove in Nuremberg 1959 (top left), in Frankfurt 1963 (bottom left) and in London 1935. Behind the wooden barrier in the image above, the London derby between Chelsea and Arsenal was being played – 82,905 spectators turned up to watch, the second highest number of fans attending an English football league match.

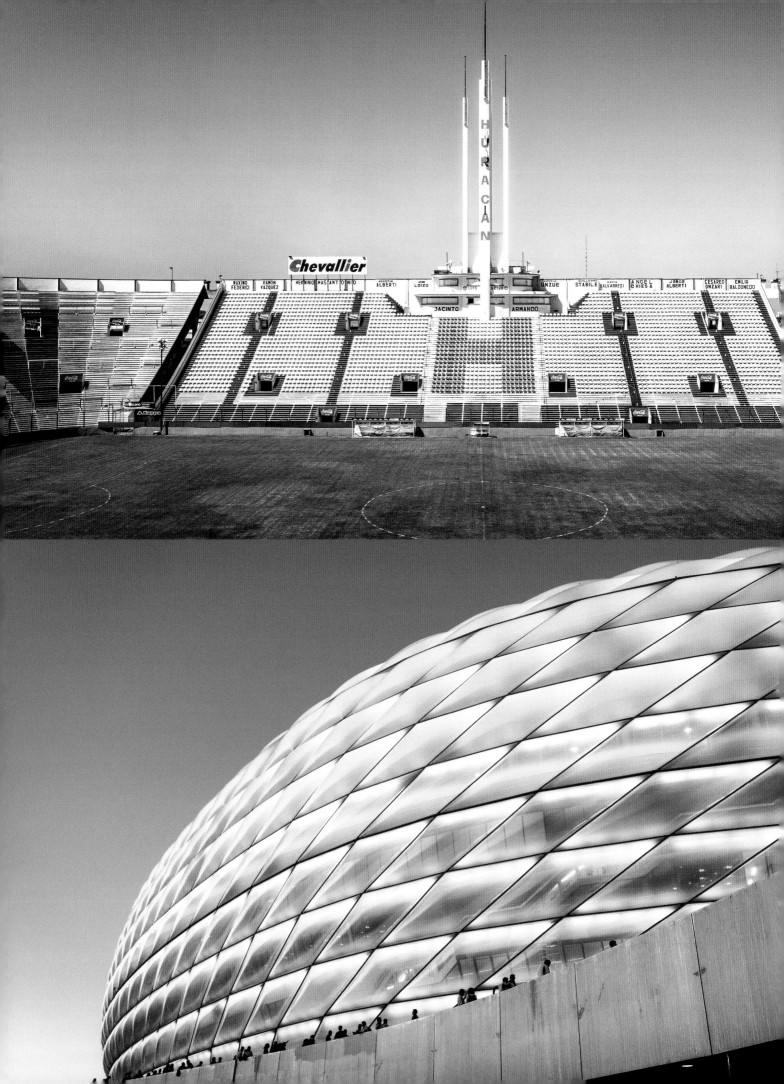

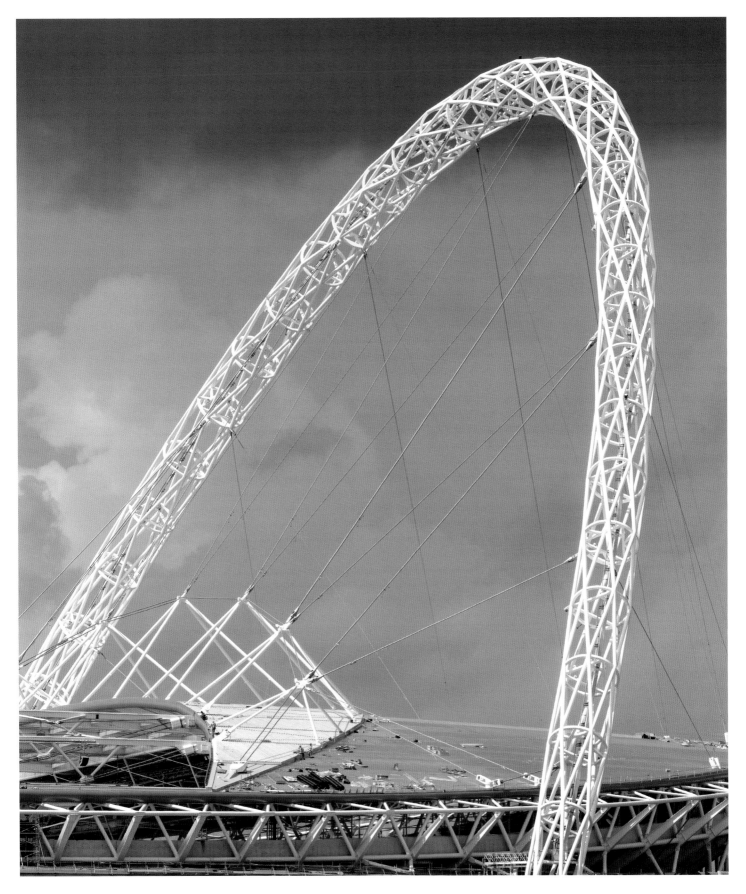

Architecture in football's temples: the Estadio Tomás Adolfo Ducó (colloquial name: "El Palacio", top left) in Buenos Aires, the Allianz Arena in Munich (bottom left, both photos by Reinaldo Coddou H.) and the new Wembley Stadium in London (above); internationally famous architects like Sir Norman Foster (Wembley) or Herzog & de Meuron (Allianz Arena) created the designs.

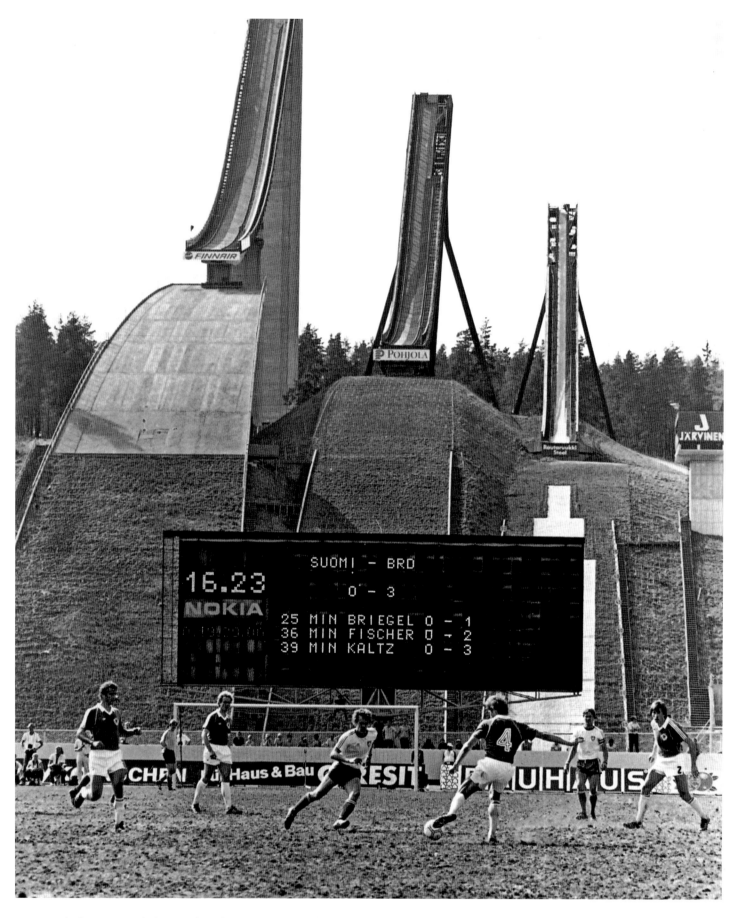

Settings: the home ground of Arsenal until 2006 (top right) did not offer monumental backdrops like the stadiums in Lahti (above) with ski jump runs, or Cape Town (bottom right) with Table Mountain and the Lion's Head; but the location in the heart of London's residential suburb of Highbury certainly still had its charm.

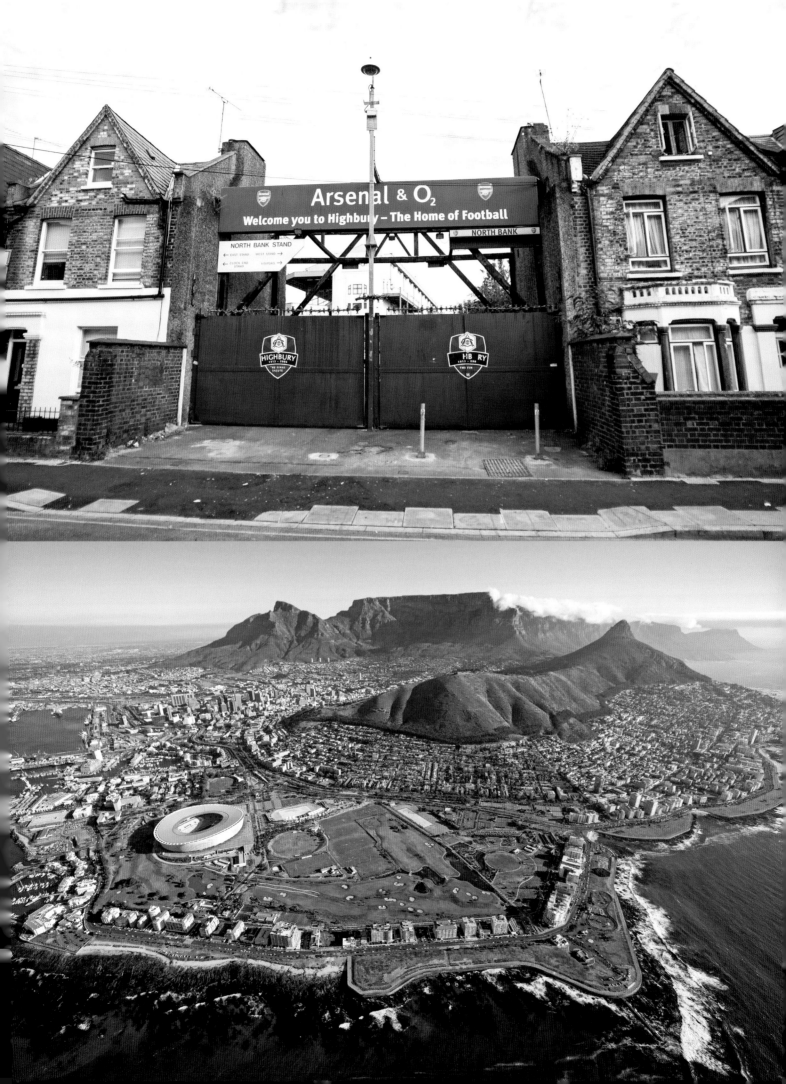

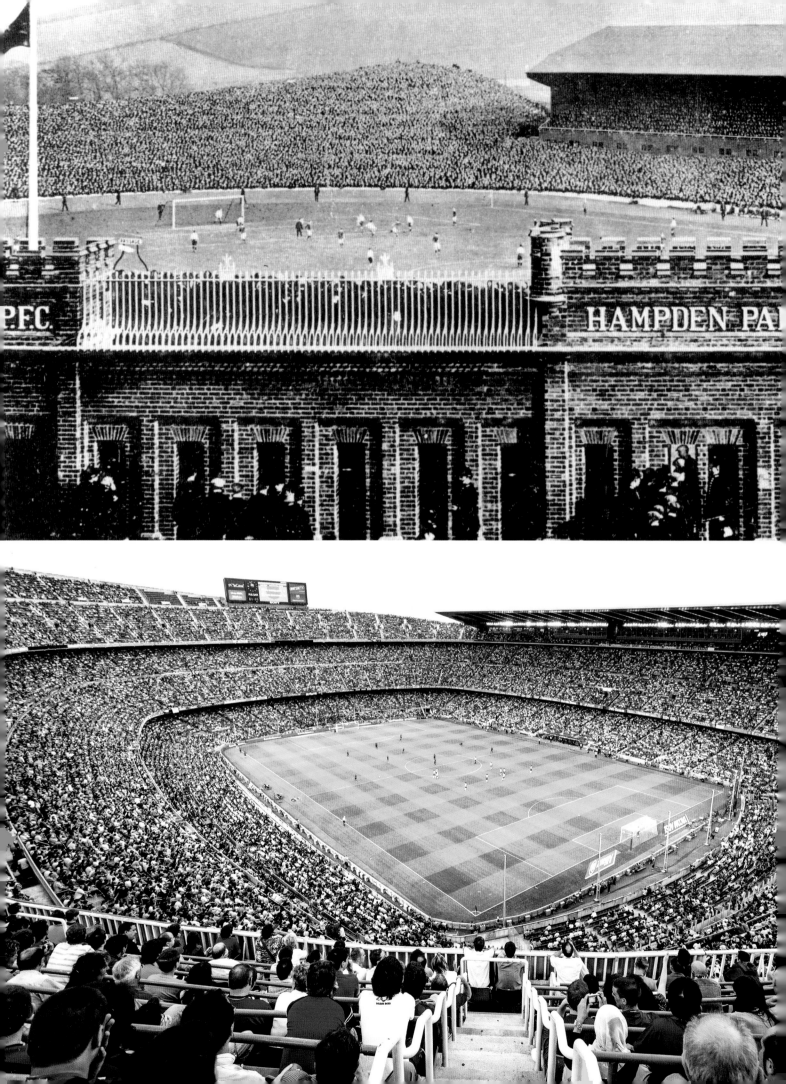

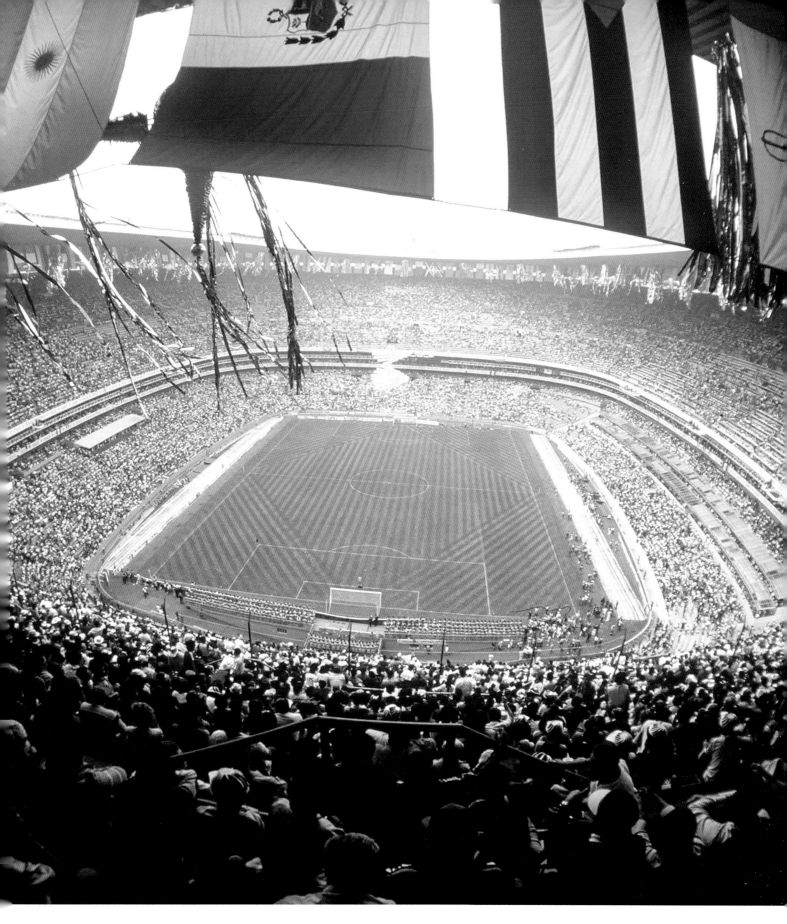

Football for the masses: Hampden Park in Glasgow (top left, during a friendly between Scotland and England in 1910; spectators: 105,000), Estadio Azteca in Mexico City (above, during the opening ceremony at the 1986 World Cup; spectators: 100,000) and Camp Nou in Barcelona (bottom left; during the Barcelona vs. Espanyol derby in 2007; spectators: 90,000).

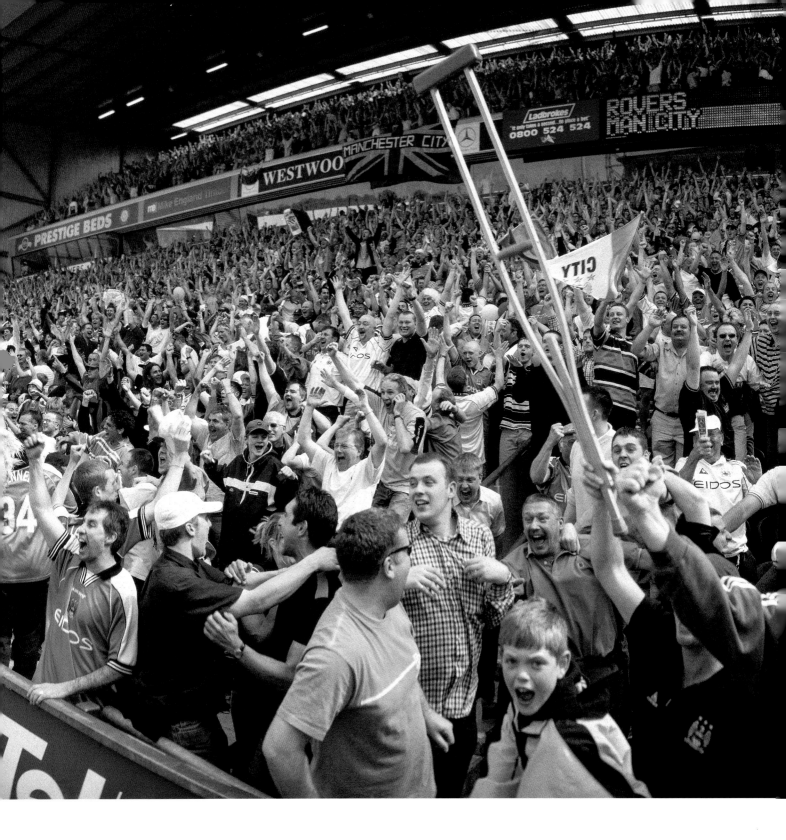

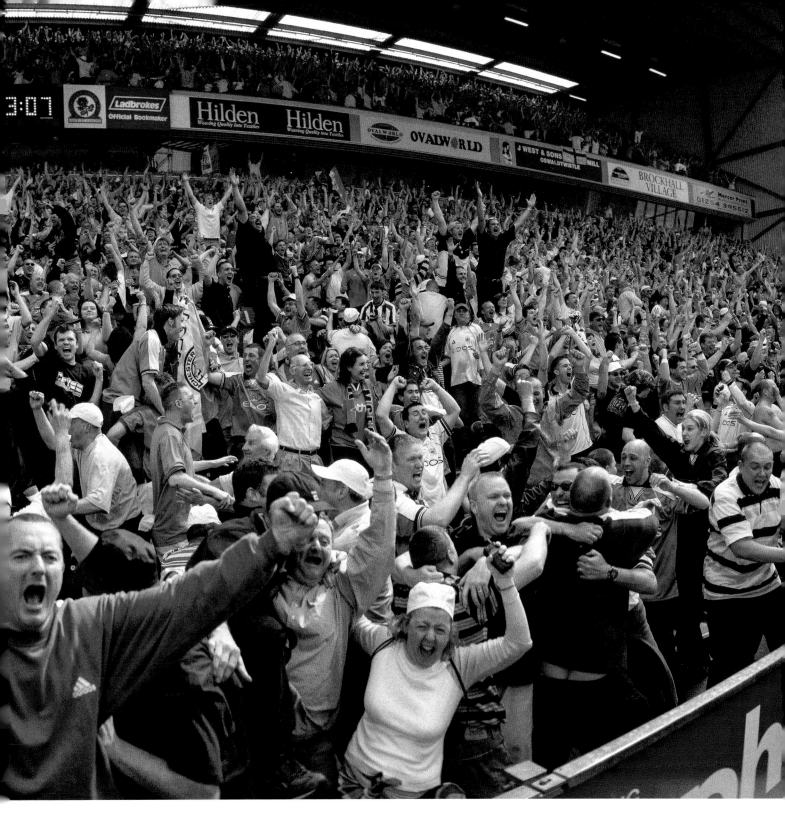

Passion of all kinds: football unleashes unbridled enthusiasm, like among Manchester City fans in 2000, photographed by Stuart Roy Clarke from behind the goal; understandable, as the 4:1 victory against Blackburn Rovers signalled the club's return to the Premier League after a miserable decade, including relegation to the Third Division...

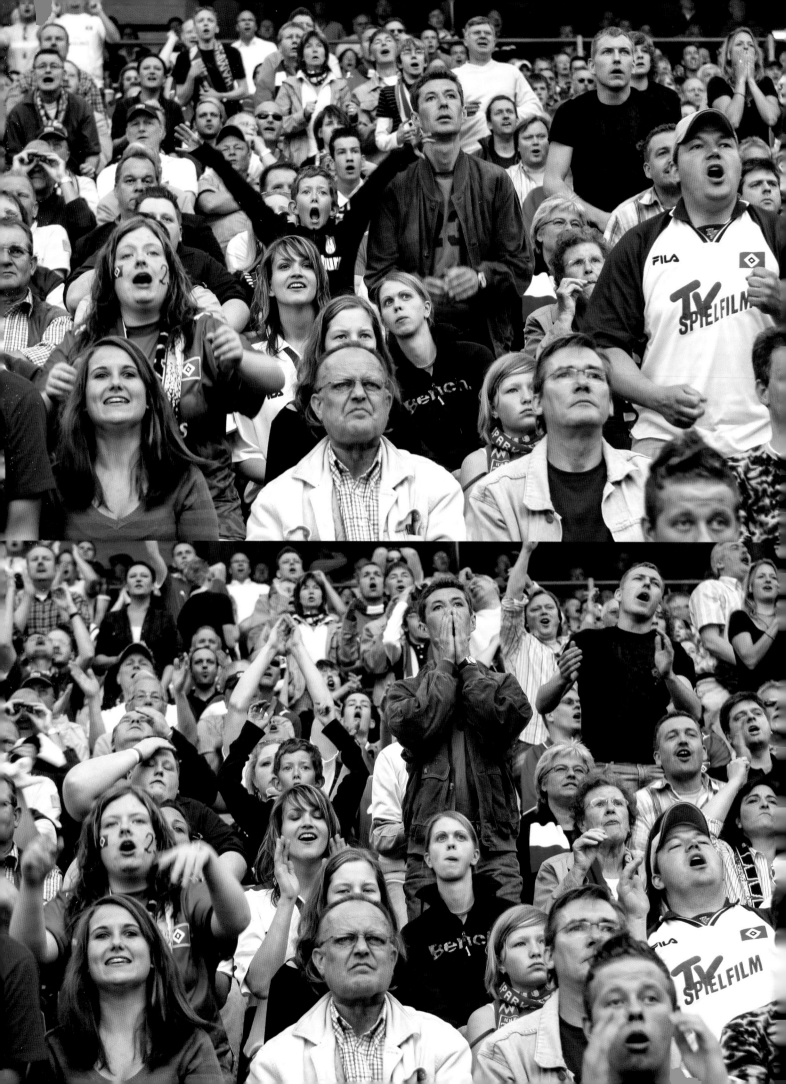

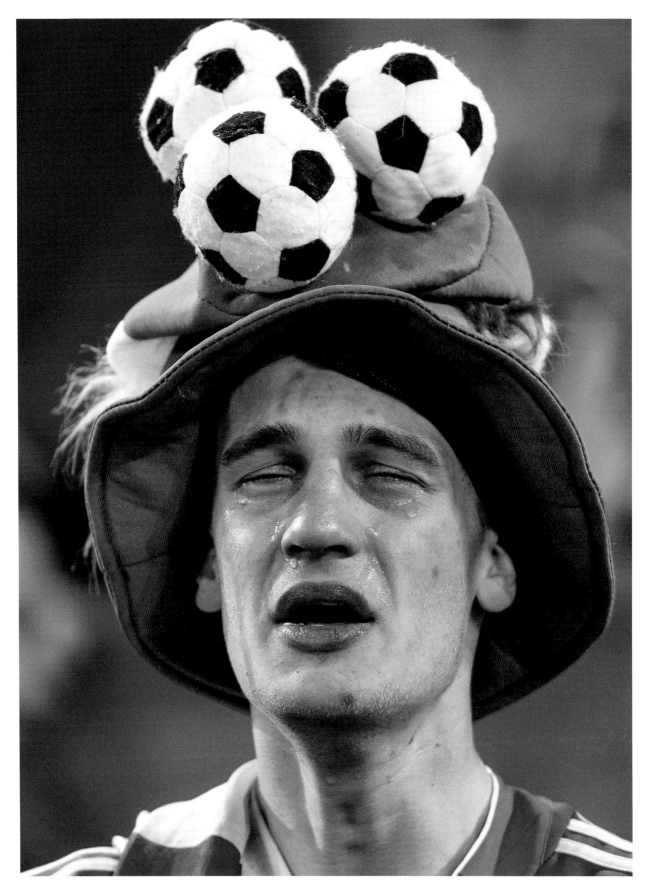

...Football conjures hope and disappointment, as among Hamburg fans (left, in a before-and-after study by Gerrit Starczewski), yet also deep sadness, like that of a French fan (above) after the 0:2 defeat against Italy in Euro 2008.

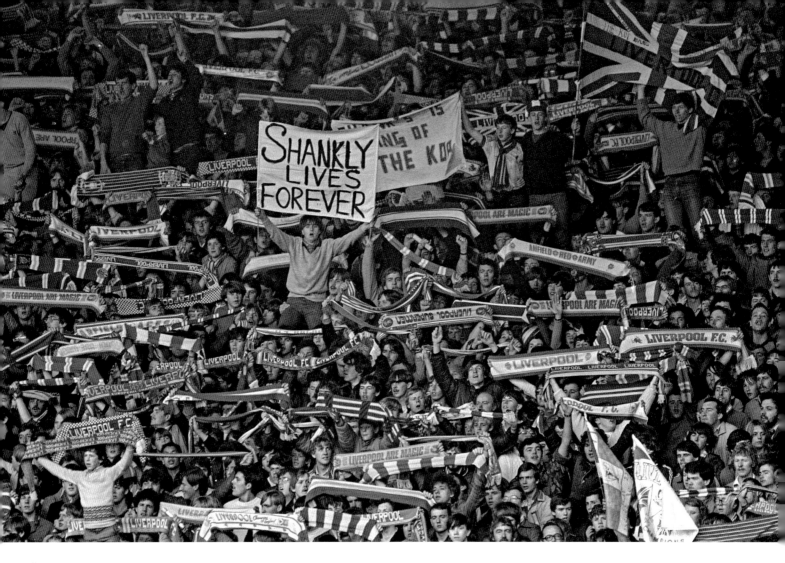

The 12th man: fans in three of the world's most atmospheric stadiums: Liverpool's Anfield (above, 1981), La Bombonera in Buenos Aires (top right) and Borussia Dortmund's stadium (bottom right) with the famous "yellow wall", impressive even in "idle mode"; in his novel, I Furiosi, Italian author, Nanni Balestrini, captures the fascination of being on the terraces for the first time: "...but what I actually remember is not the match. What really impressed me was the spectacle of the fans. I didn't manage to watch the game properly any more because the chanting impressed me and all the things happening here in the stand."

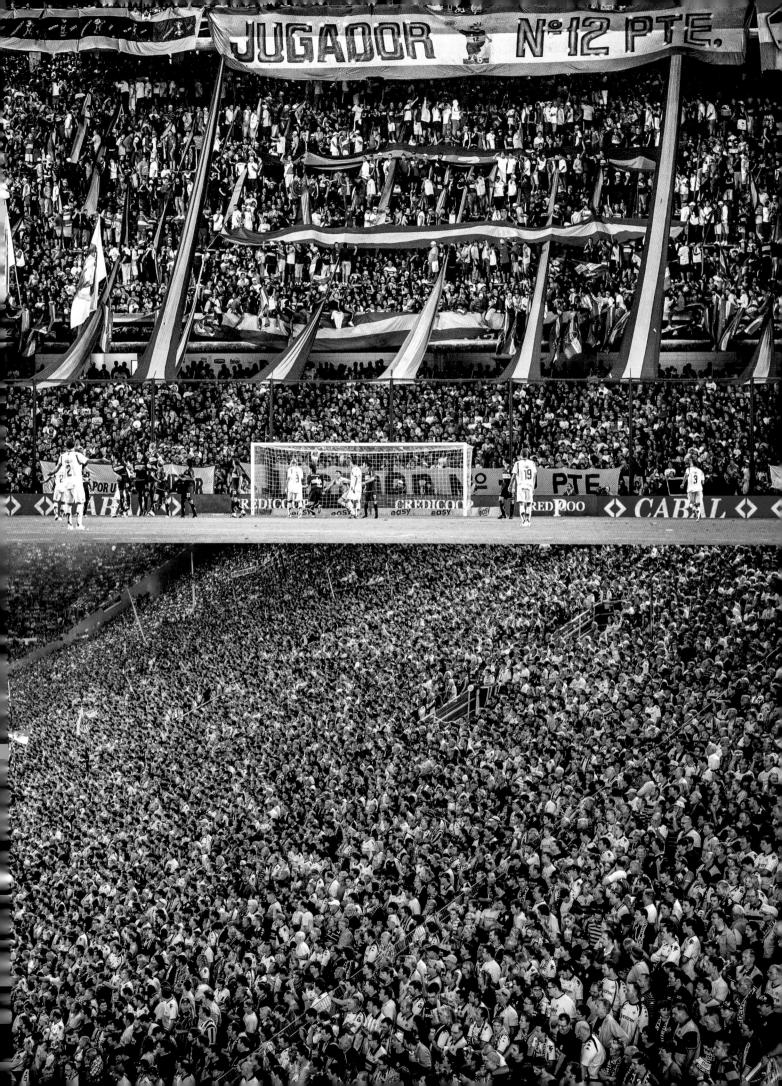

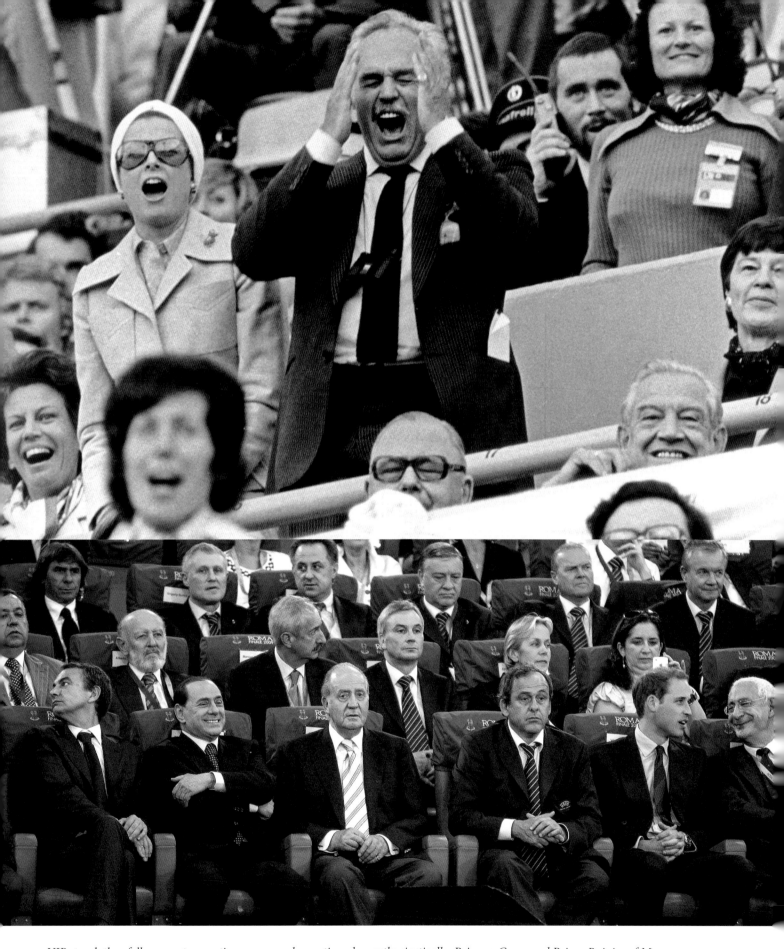

VIP stand: they follow events sometimes more and sometimes less enthusiastically: Princess Grace and Prince Rainier of Monaco (top left, 1974 World Cup Final), Mick Jagger (top right, 1998 World Cup Final), Prince Bernhard of the Netherlands (with glasses and pipe), Walter Scheel, ex-FIFA President Stanley Rous, Helmut Schmidt (bottom right, 1974 World Cup Final), José Zapatero, Silvio Berlusconi, King Juan Carlos of Spain, Michel Platini and Prince William (bottom left, 2009 Champions League Final).

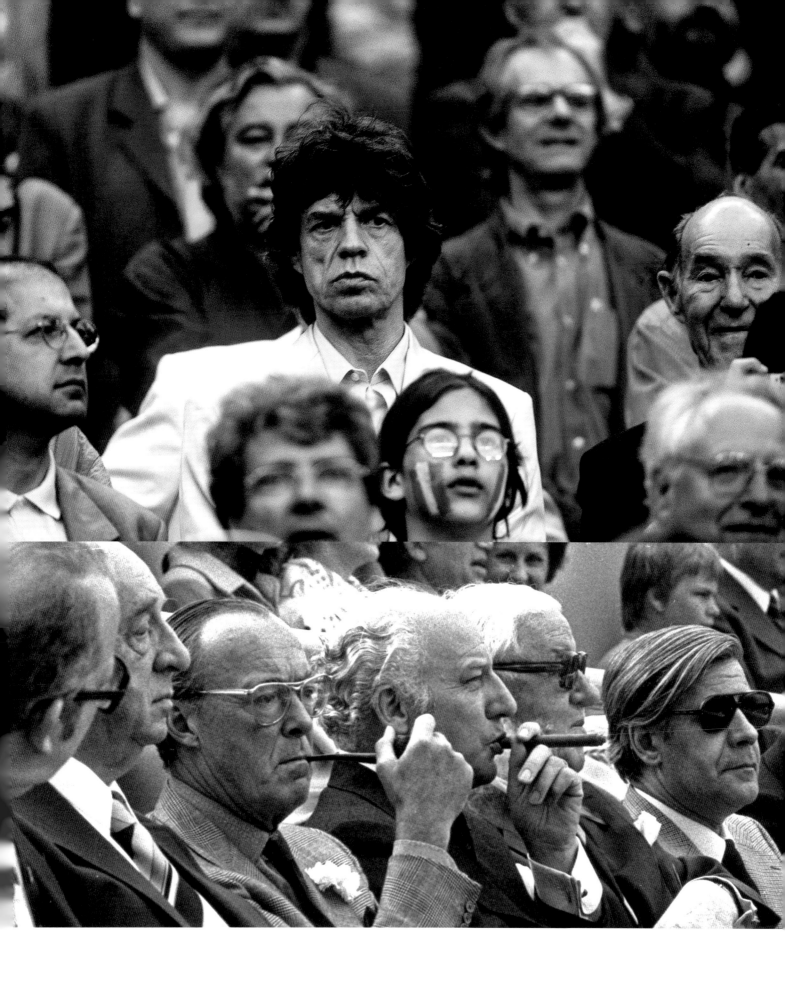

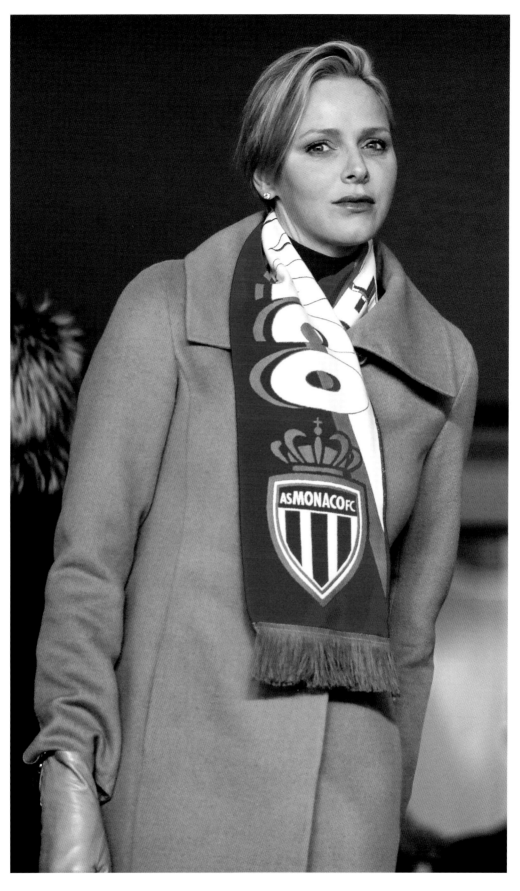

Hosting royal guests like Princess Charlène of Monaco (above) means creating elegant interiors: Giorgio Armani designed the Armani Lounge for Chelsea's Stamford Bridge (top right); the interiors of Juventus Stadium, opened in 2011, were created by renowned design company Pininfarina (bottom right).

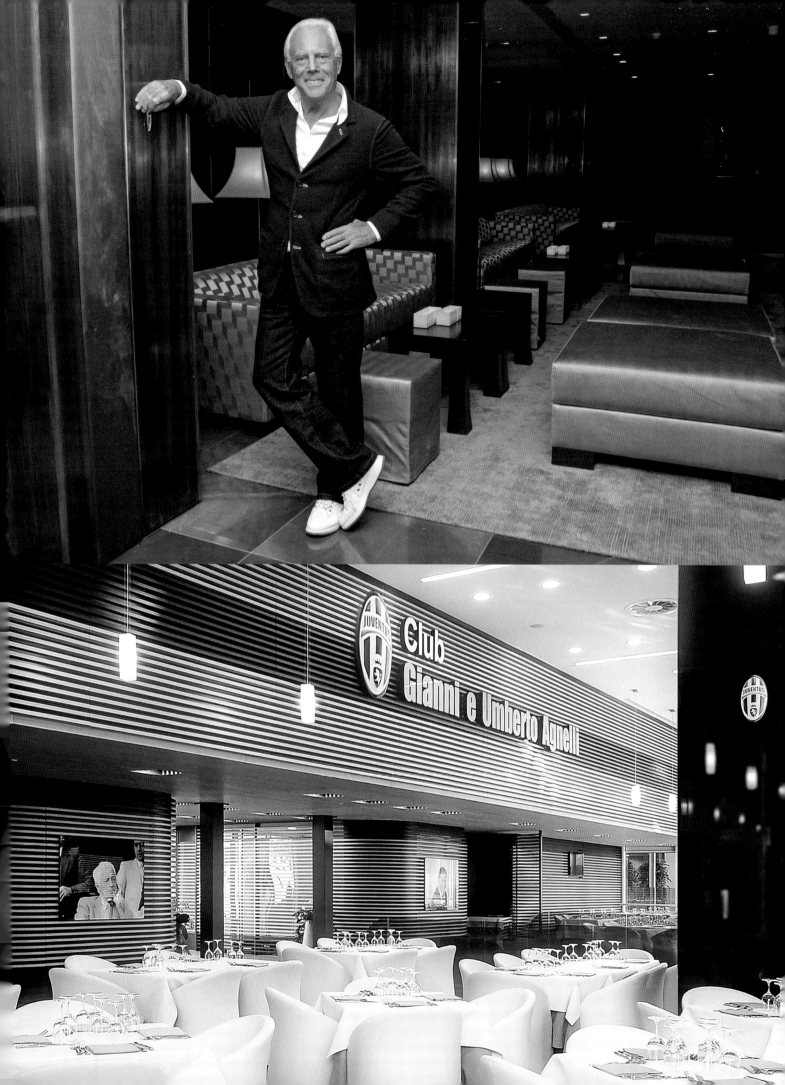

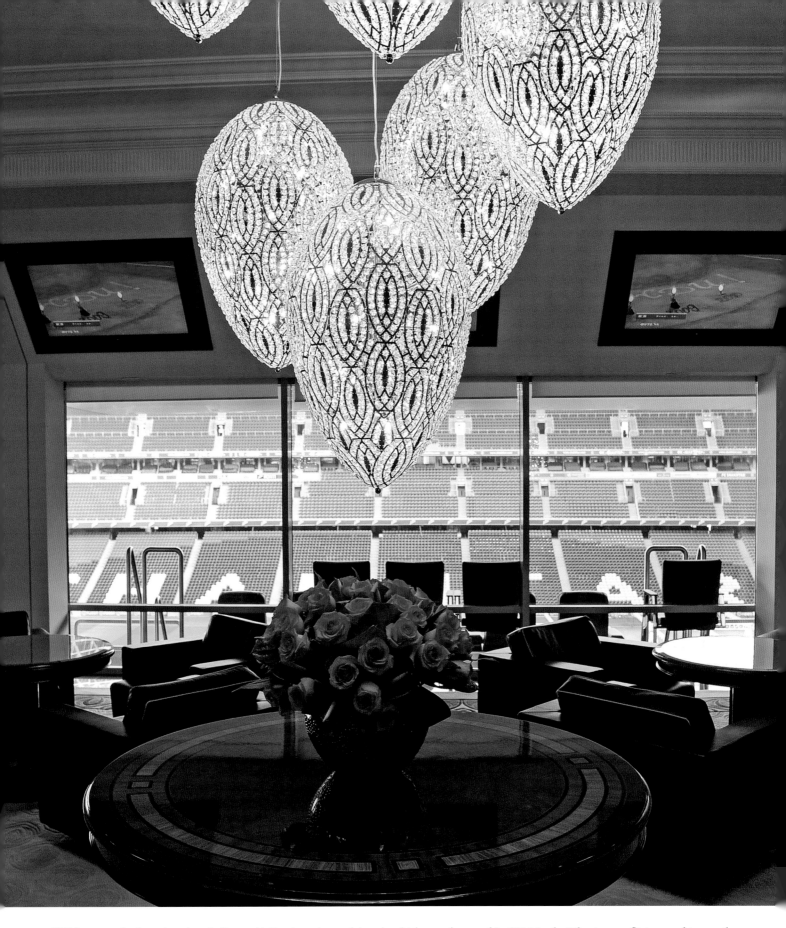

VIP lounges: the luxurious box in Donetsk's Donbass Arena (above), which was damaged in 2014 in the Ukraine conflict; more bizarre than fiction: you can watch football games reclining in the bath, like in the Ruhrstadion in Bochum (top right), or in one location inside St Pauli's Millerntor stadium where they take the term "substitute religion" for football literally (bottom right).

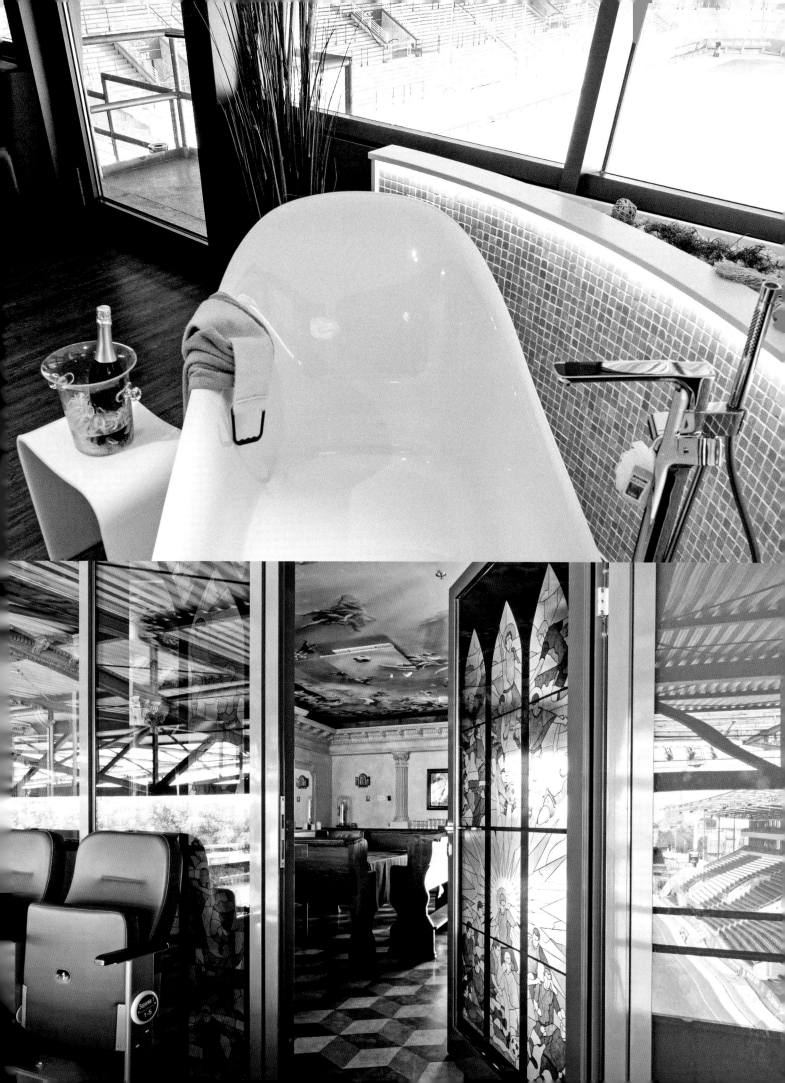

*Football's landmarks: the famous twin
towers of the old Wembley Stadium under
construction in 1923 and shortly before being
dismantled in 2003 (this page); the legendary
clock of Bern's Wankdorf Stadium (right):
in operation in 1954 during the World Cup
Final and in 2012; the clock is now situated
on a square in front of the Stade de Suisse
and displays the result of the last game in the
old Wankdorf stadium before its demolition
in 2001: Young Boys Bern 1 Lugano 1, in
front: Stéphane Chapuisat, Champions
League winner with Borussia Dortmund and
a YB player from 2002 to 2005.*

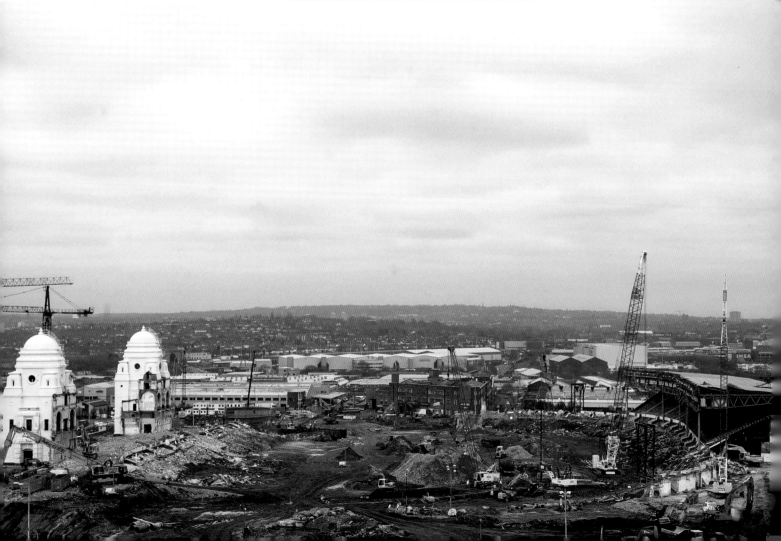

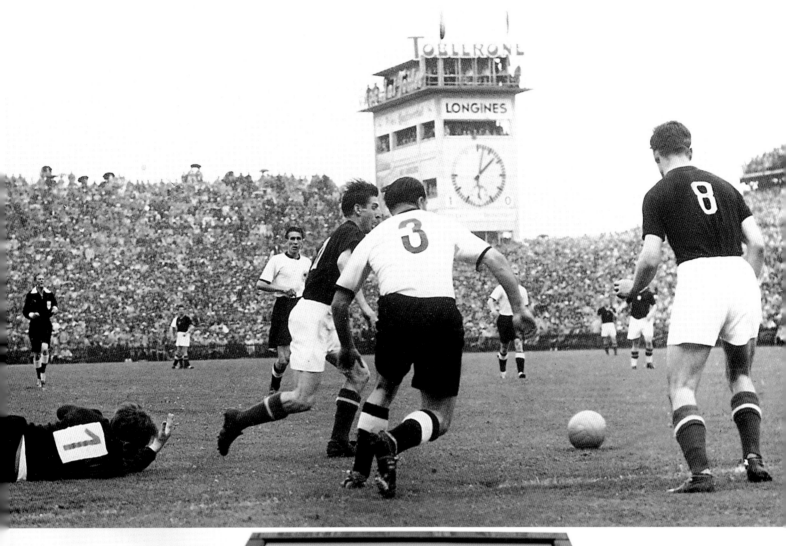

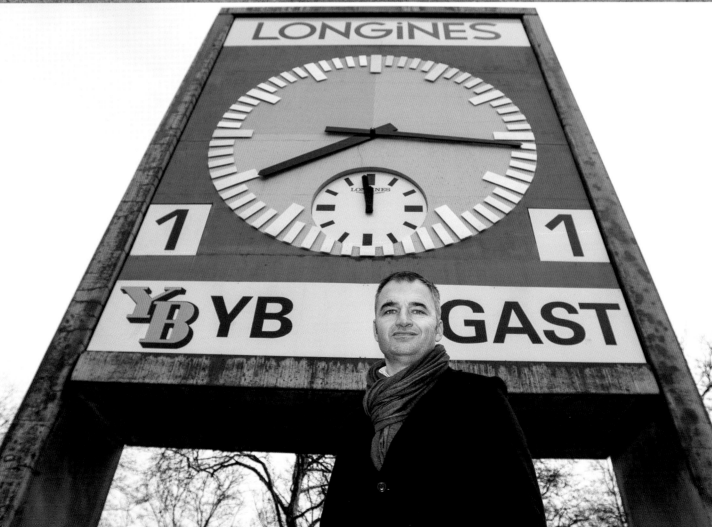

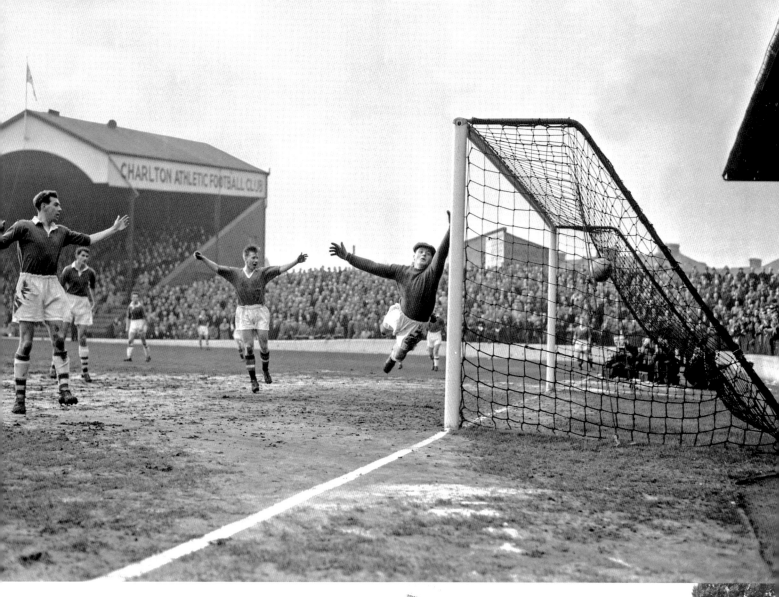

As time goes by: the famous home ground of Charlton Athletic, The Valley, has seen some turbulent times. "The Addicks" were in the First Division from 1936 to 1957 (top left, 1957), in the Second Division with a 70,000-capacity stadium until 1972 (top right, 1970), and temporarily forced to vacate their home in 1985 due to safety hazards, coupled with dwindling funds (bottom right, 1988), and finally returned to The Valley after its renovation in 1992. To leave the ground, fans filter through a residential area of south-east London (bottom left, 2006).

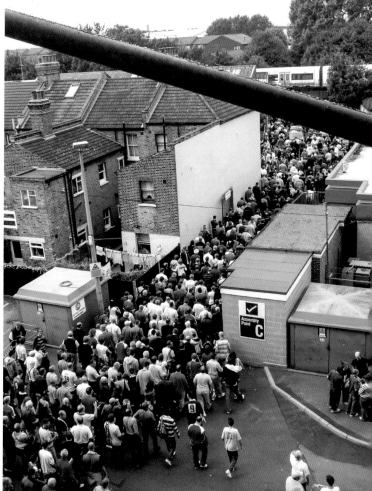

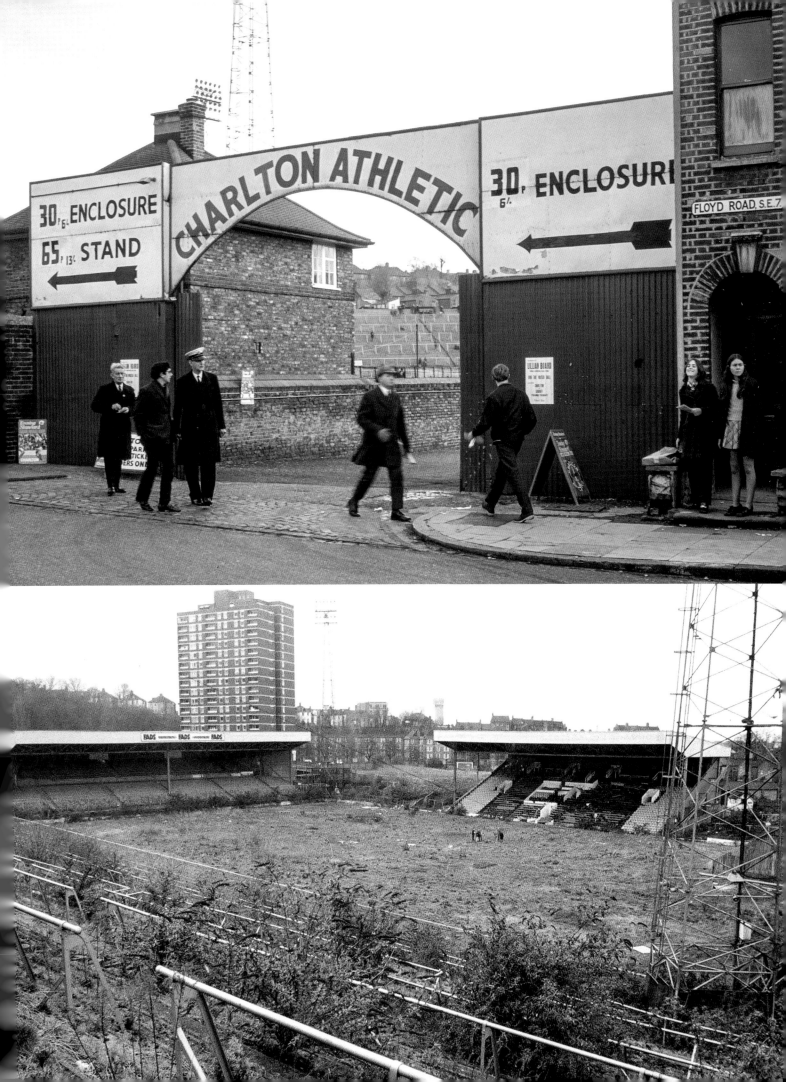

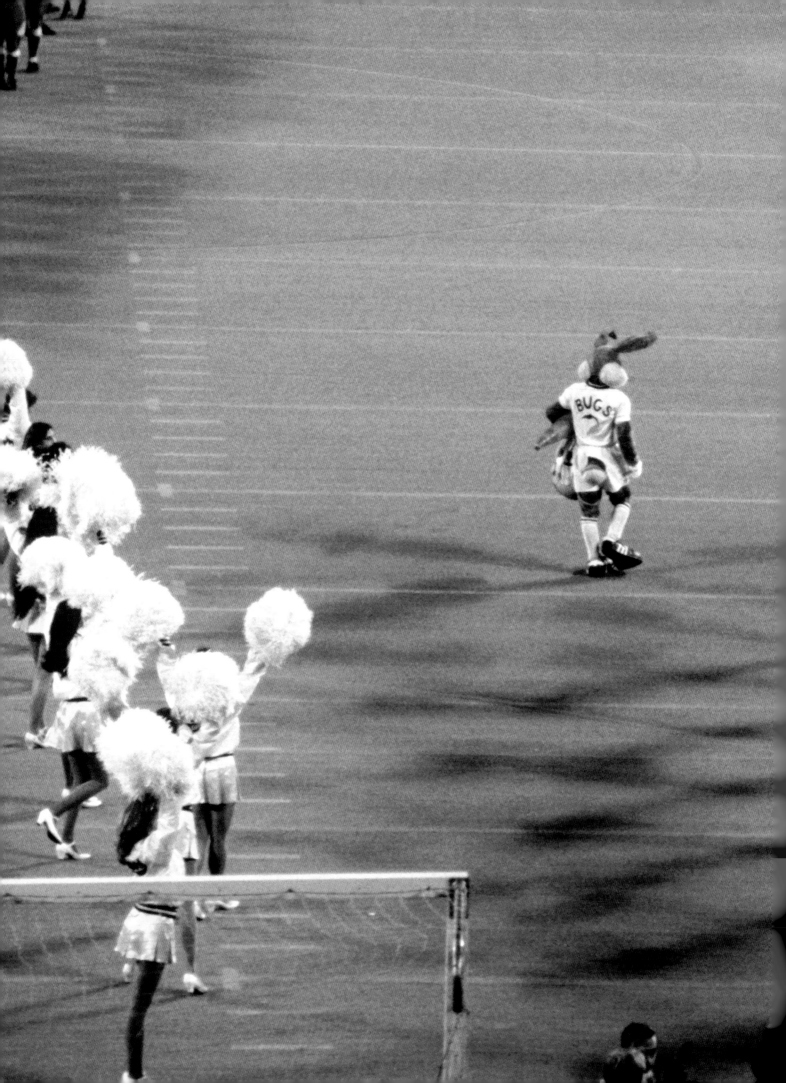

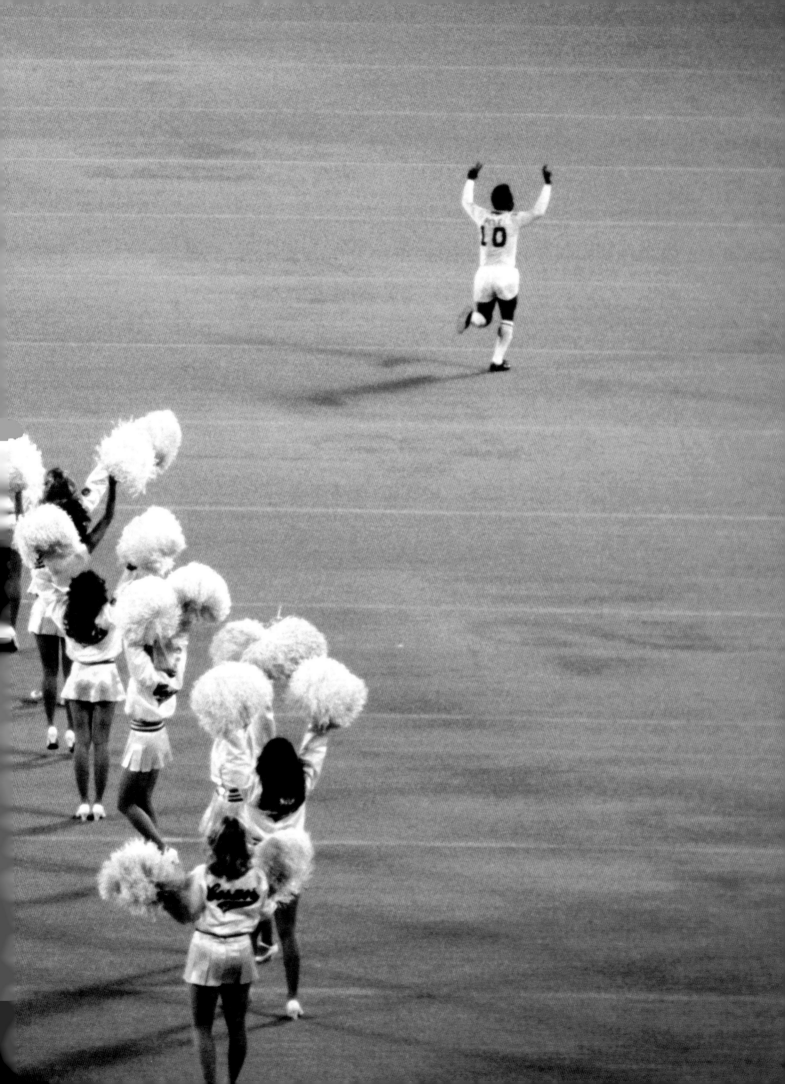

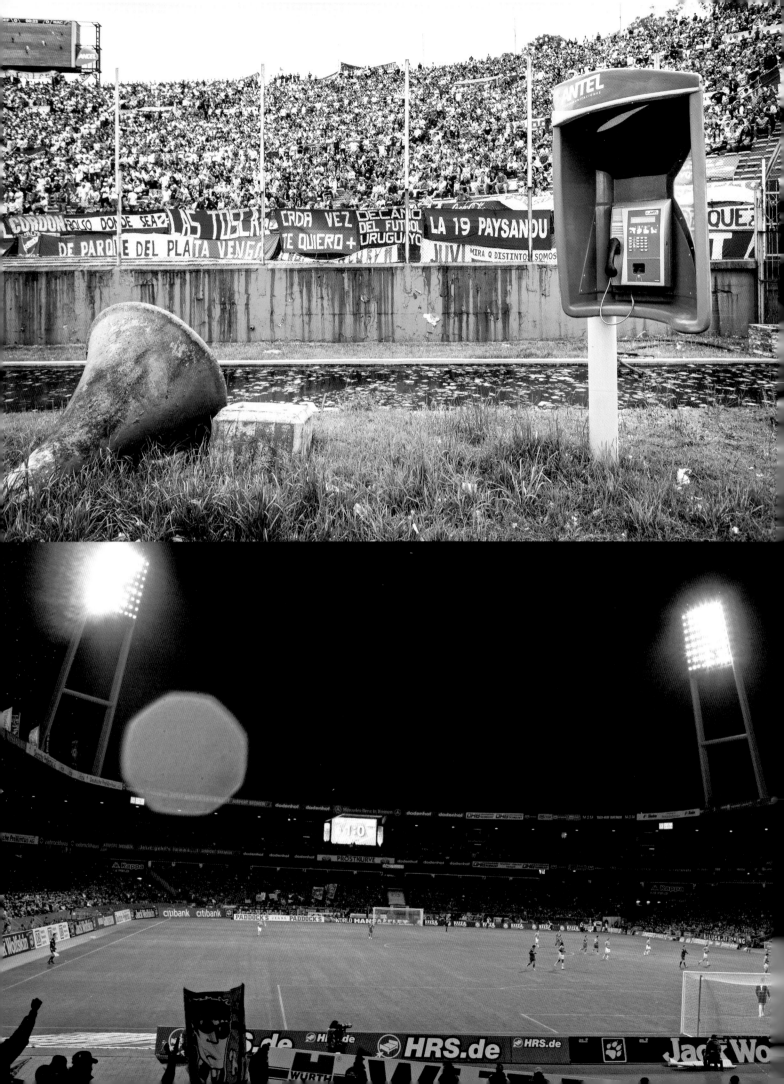

Anachronisms: at a football match in the US in the 1970s (pp. 44/45) the lines on the field show that football is just tolerated as a placeholder for the much more popular game of American Football; a telephone booth inside the Estadio Centenario in Montevideo (top left), the wooden stand at Craven Cottage in Fulham/London (above) or floodlight masts in Werder Bremen's Weserstadion (bottom left) seem caught in a time warp in the 21st century.

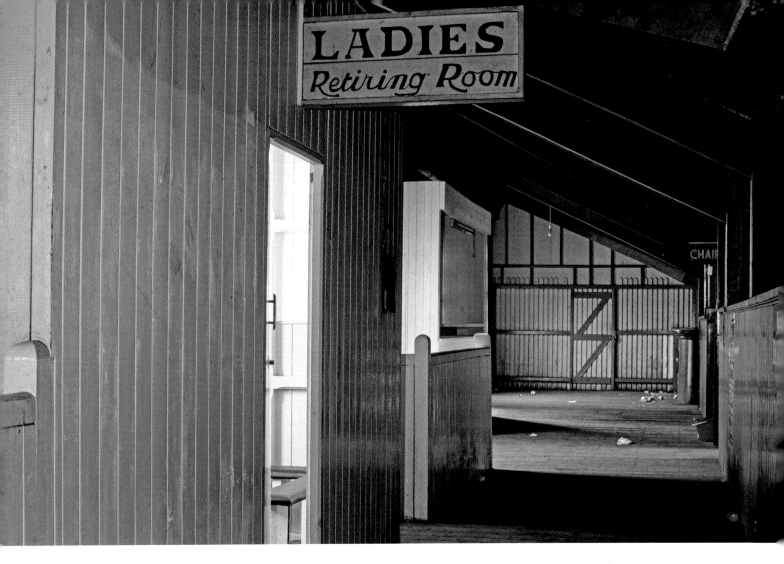

Football's quiet side: at Gigg Lane in Bury there used to be a quiet room where ladies had to retire to wait while their husbands watched the match (above). At Camp Nou in Barcelona, the stadium chapel offers space for silent prayer (top right), while at the club cemetery Schalke fans can rest in eternal peace (bottom right).

Following double-page spreads: Football is at home everywhere: in modern high glamour stadiums as well as among the favelas of Rio de Janeiro (pp. 50/51; photo: Olaf Heine). A legendary stadium in a bright ambiance: the Mestalla in Valencia (pp. 52/53).

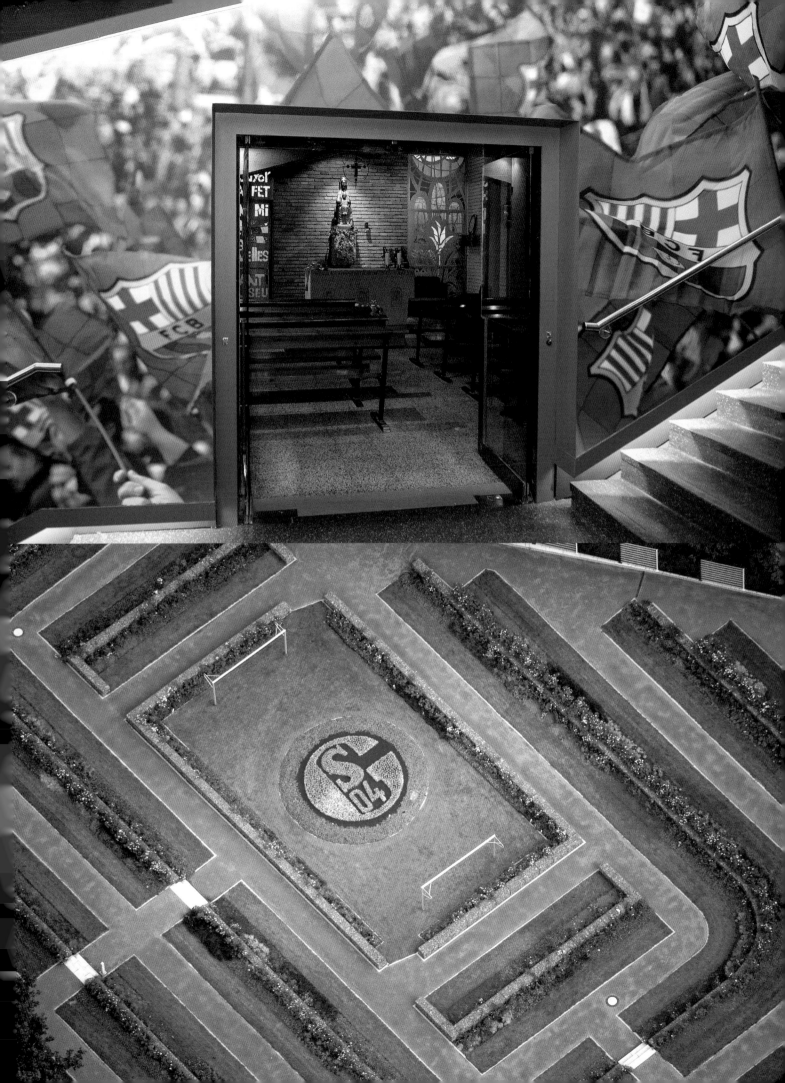

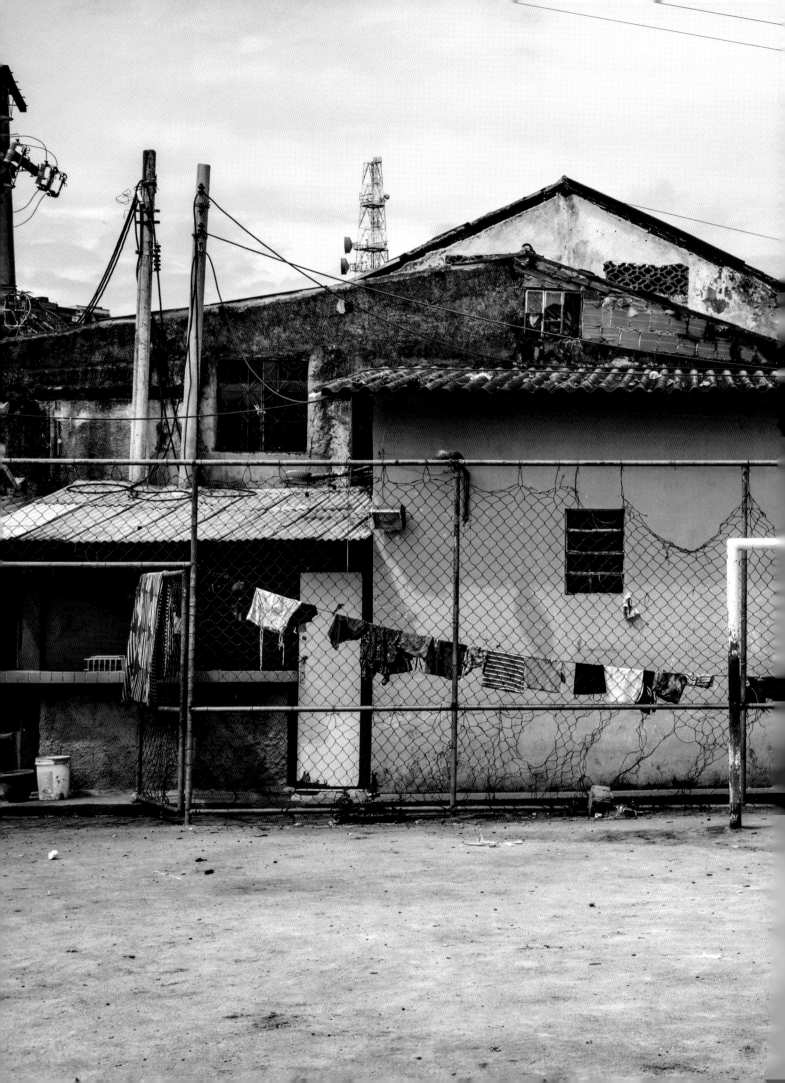

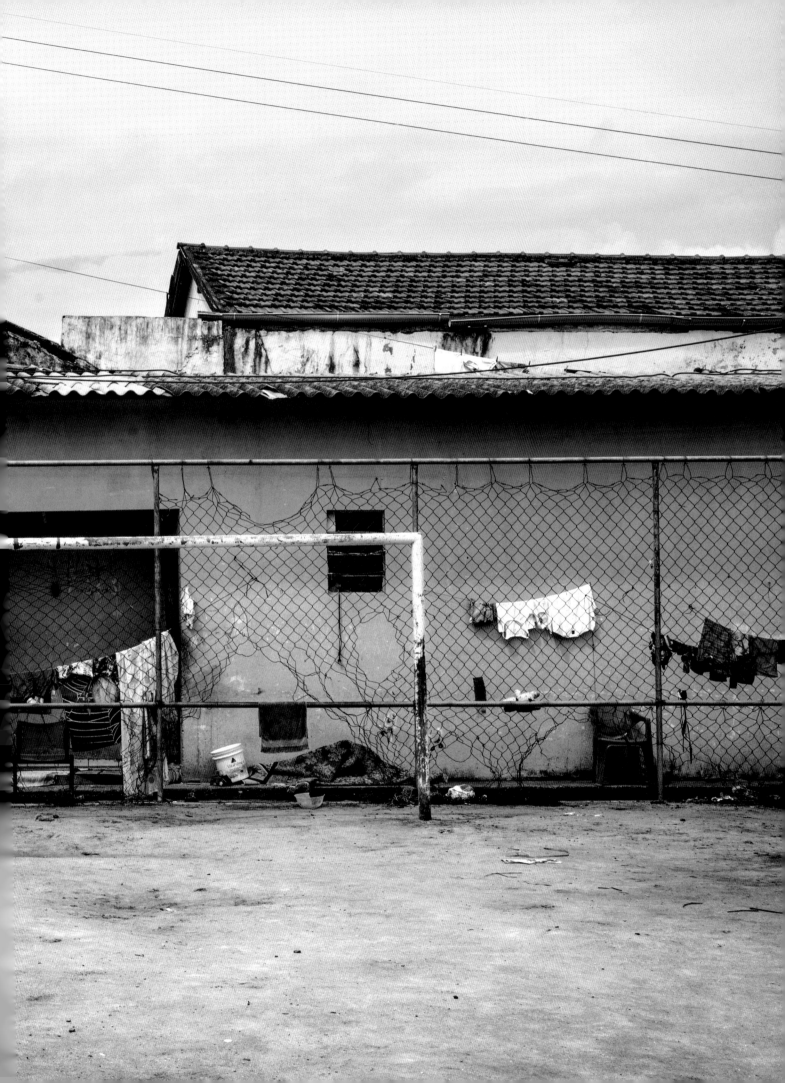

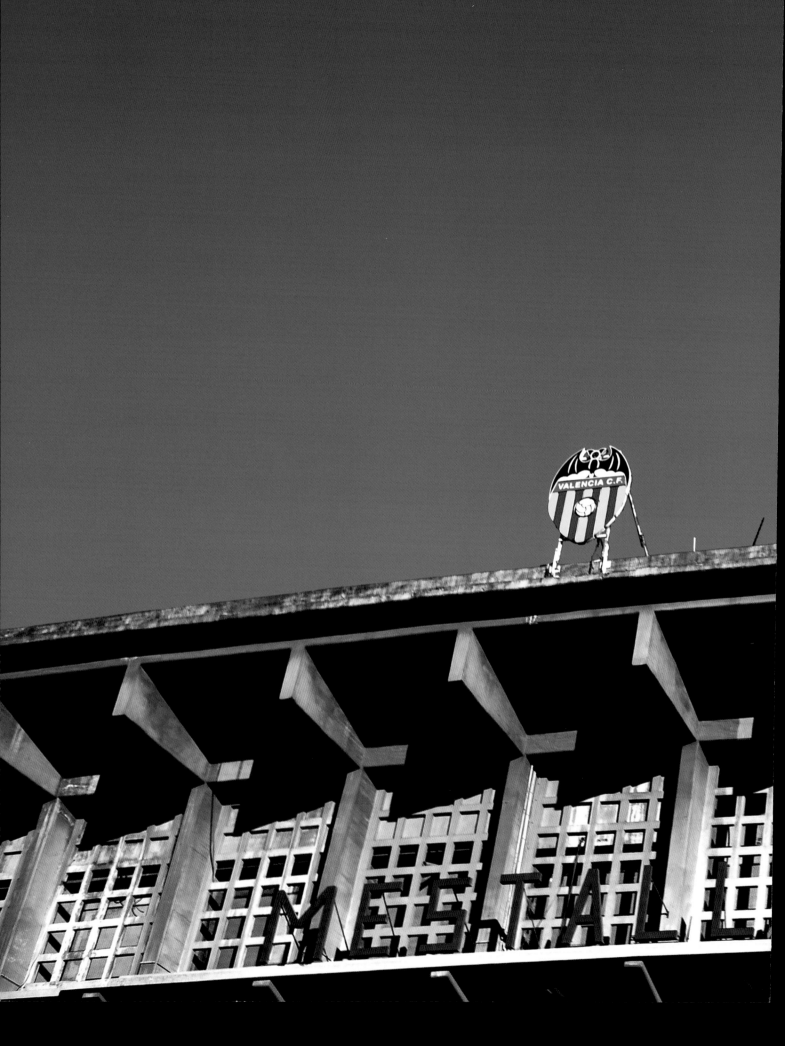

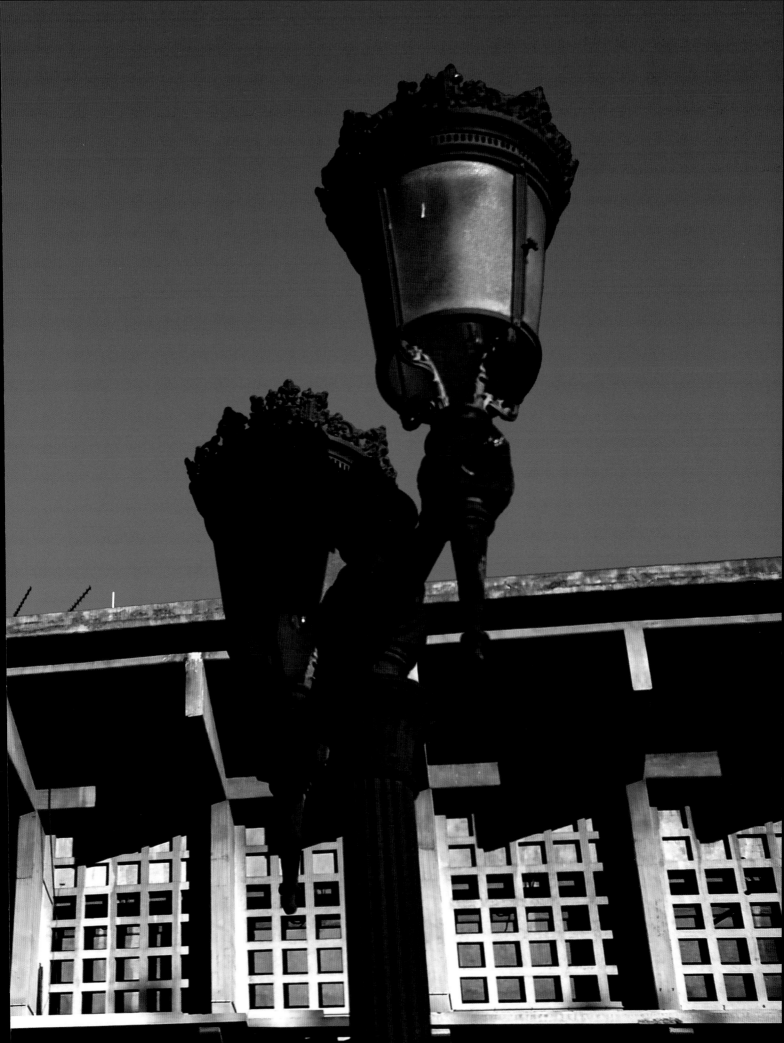

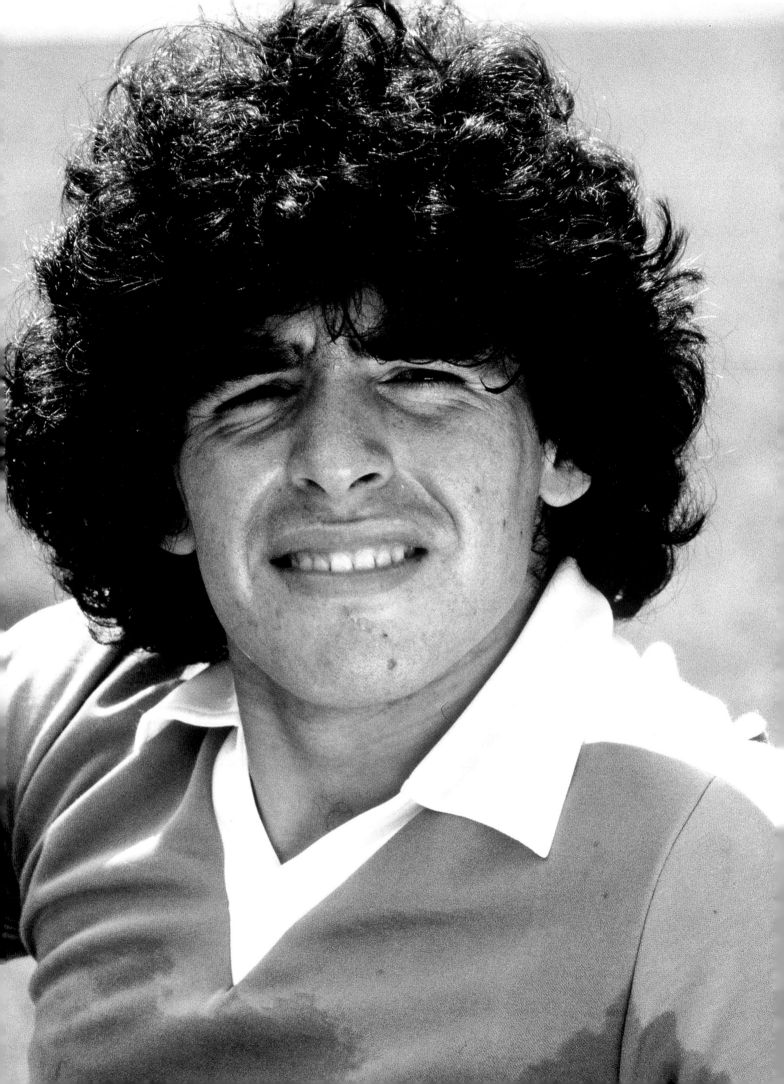

PEOPLE

The people are the invigorating force behind the game. The geniuses who perform on the hallowed turf are as important as the fans on the sidelines. Charismatic players were always more than just talented people who are marginally better soccer players than the rest. Pelé and Maradona were the great icons, while today it's Neymar and Ibrahimović. Our interest in their careers begins on the pitch and is sustained in real life, too. They are heroes to millions of fans. At least since the 1970s footballers are also pop stars; their images feature in teen magazines as collectable posters, or their homes appear in glossy lifestyle journals.

The US again plays a major role in the shift of focus from the sport to its glamorous side as entertainment. During the late 1970s and early 1980s, the North American Soccer League club, New York Cosmos, was *the* place to be for the game's more mature international stars. Carlos Alberto, Johan Neeskens, Pelé and Franz Beckenbauer all played for the club. In 1977, before Beckenbauer had left Bayern Munich and joined Cosmos for the then record transfer fee of two million US dollars, the Americans brought out the special VIP treatment for him, "The real deciding factor was a helicopter trip from the rooftop helipad of the Pan Am Building over downtown Manhattan. The flight took me to a different

"Our Diego": early on in his career Diego Armando Maradona was called "El Pelusa" ("Fluff") because of his mane of hair. Adulation for him knows no bounds; since 1998, a faith community – the "Iglesia Maradoniana" – has even made him the centre of their religion.

world – beyond the Hudson River in the direction of New Jersey to the Giants Stadium. As we were flying above the stadium, I yelled at them, "Okay, I give up, I'll come over!"

Beckenbauer wasn't enticed to the US because of the fantastic sporting opportunities, but instead for the generous fringe benefits. At the time, this was typical of the underlying change in football. The entertainment value was gradually taking over. It's hardly surprising that in 1976 the eccentric English pop star, Sir Elton John, became club chairman of suburban Watford FC. He invested heavily in the club and soon secured its promotion by three divisions to the English First Division. When Elton attended his first meeting as the club's new chairman, he arrived with died-pink hair and wearing shoes with twenty-centimetre high platforms! Seven years later, he looked on tearfully as his club finished runners up in the First Division. He was adept at combining his career as a musician with his role as a popular football club chairman. Watford FC players even joined in the backing vocals on Elton's 1978 album title track, "A Single Man".

David Beckham, the former England international, was unquestionably a great player, but his talent as a media star is possibly even greater. During the last twenty years, the top-selling magazines outside football made the husband of ex-Spice Girl, Victoria, the darling of their reports more times than any other player. This glamorous and successful couple leads a jet-set lifestyle. Yet the multi-million dollar advertising deals and frequent celebrity appearances also cast Beckham's career in another light, as football legend Pelé shrewdly observed, "Beckham's problem is that he married the most famous Spice Girl and now he's more a pop star than a soccer player." When Beckham left Manchester for Madrid in 2003, his new teammates saw his arrival as motivated not so much by sporting reasons than as part of a business deal. Fernando Hierro winked and said, "It will boost our ticket sales. But if David Beckham is going to bring along his seven Ferraris, space will be tight. Parking spaces at Real Madrid are at a premium."

Genuine people and strong characters have always been football's winners, regardless of any hype or intrigue. Famous coach, César Luis Menotti, sets a perfect example here. The organizers of the 1978 World Cup arranged for Menotti, a heavy smoker, to have an extra large ashtray on the touchline. Menotti and his Austrian counterpart, the Dutch team coach, Ernst Happel, spent the entire final match chain smoking. When Menotti and his team were finally crowned world champions and lifted the cup, he refused to shake hands with the then head of Argentina's military government, dictator Jorge Rafael Videla. "El Flaco" ("the slim one") is widely respected for his belief in tactical finesse. His view is that victory does not justify the means. Also, he would rather not regard any final result as a proper measure of his work, as he once said, "If our subjective views about artists only depended on the results, Julio Iglesias would be the best singer in the world. He produces best-selling records and CDs. But even if he were to sell twice as many – I still don't like his songs." That's not only a nice analogy. The idea that scoring goals and winning are not the only reasons why football's protagonists enter the hall of fame also helps to explain the allure of this sport.

Martial: coinciding with the start of Maradona's career, Argentina's national team won the 1978 World Cup without him. The enduring stigma: the heroic victory under Captain Daniel Passarella (double-page overleaf) was also a success for the military dictatorship under General Videla. Corresponding to this Passarella's nickname is "El Pistolero".

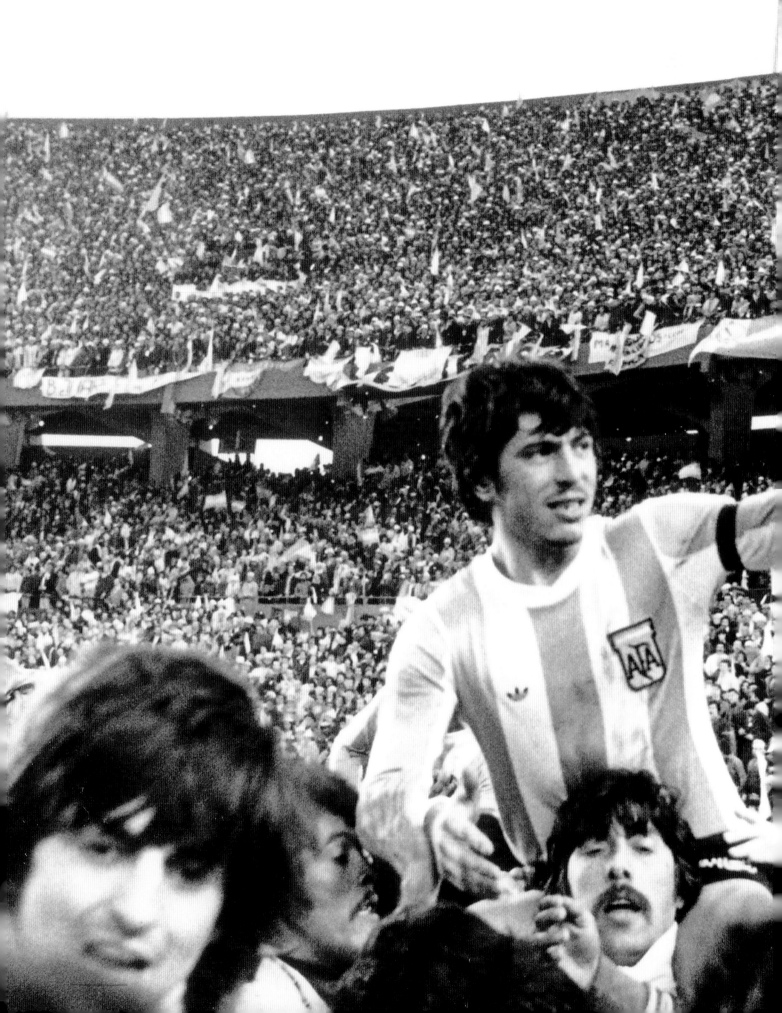

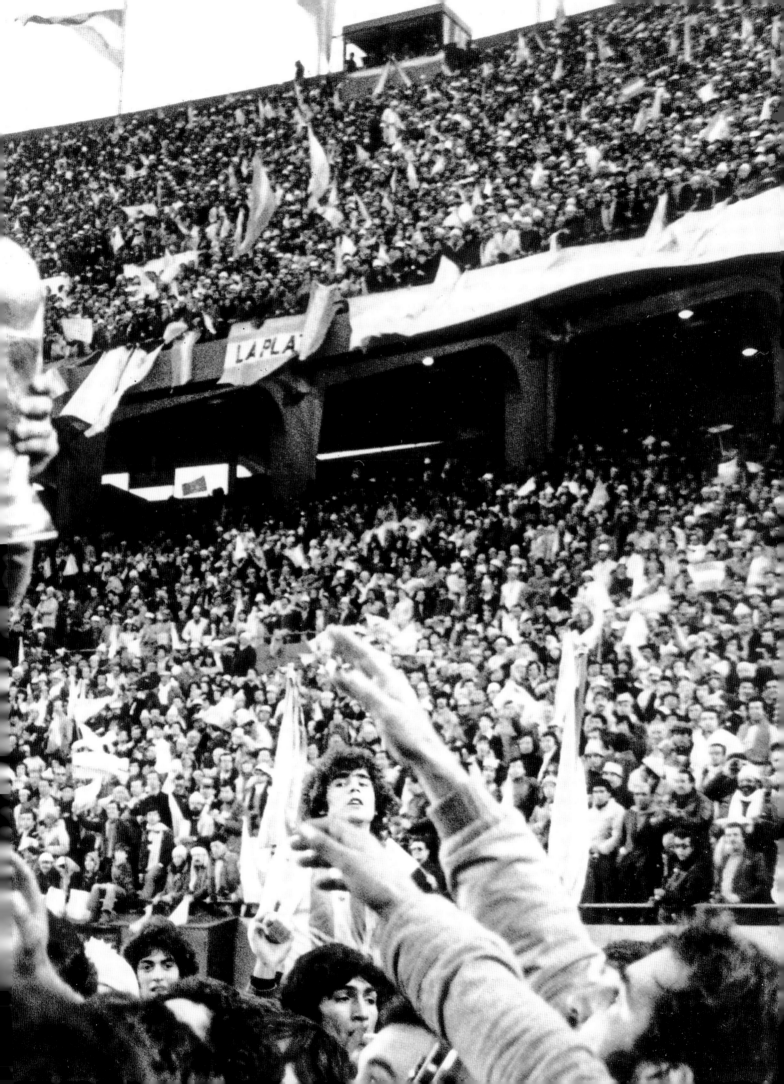

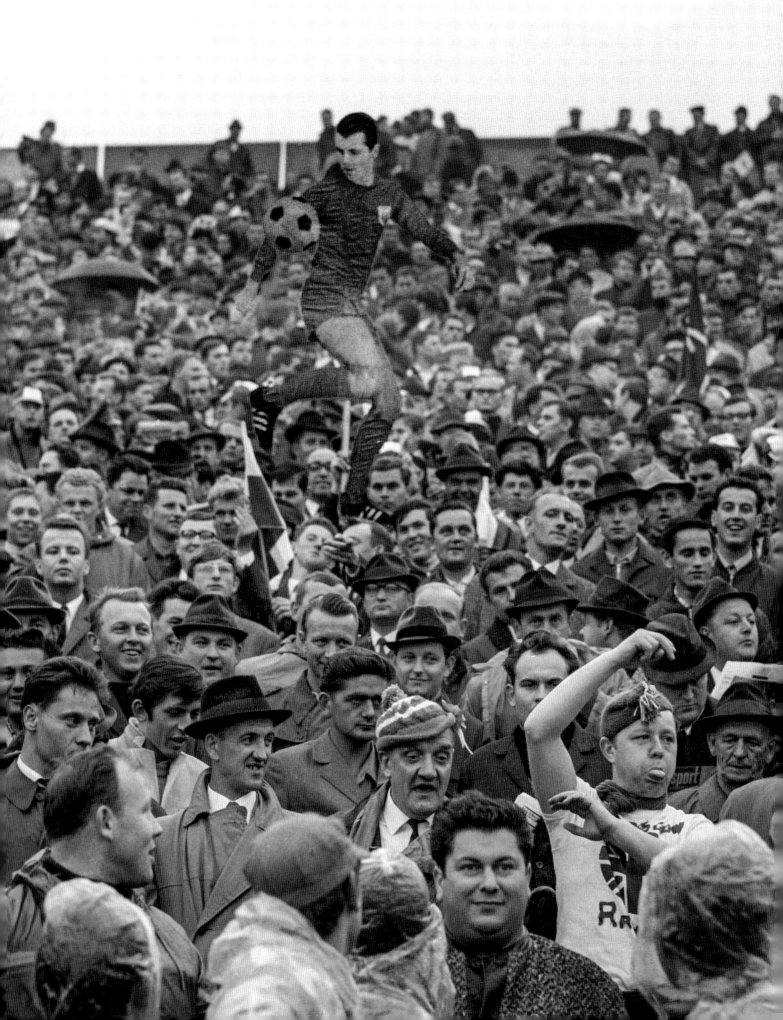

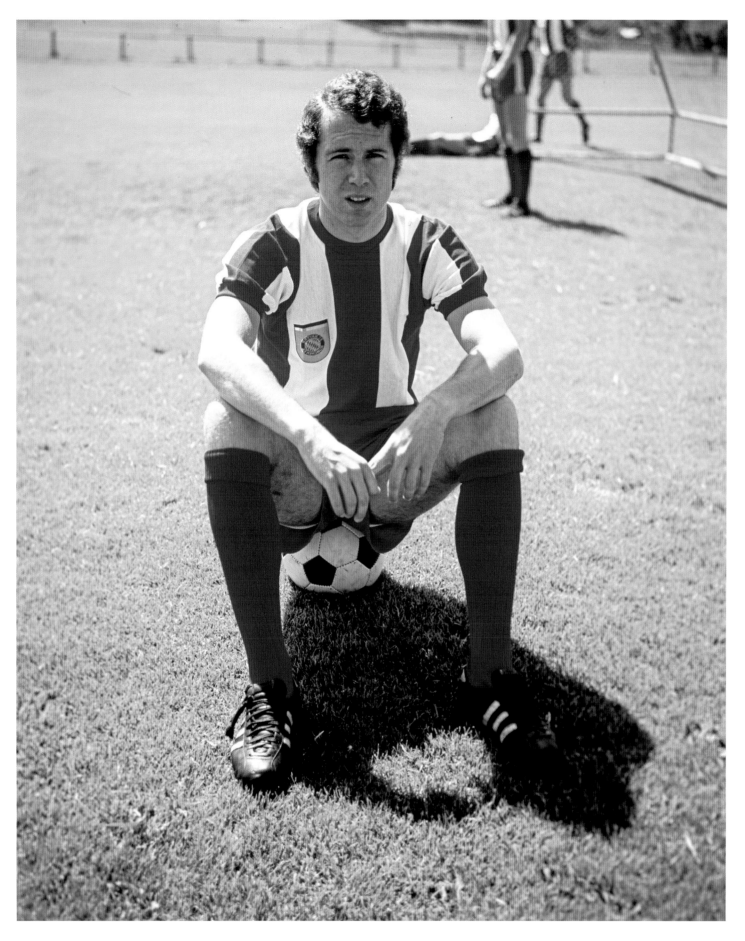

A towering figure: due to his many qualities and nicknames – from fortune-favoured "figure of light" to the tireless pundit known as the "Kaiser" ("The Emperor") – at least Germans easily forget that Franz Beckenbauer really is one of the all-time greatest footballers.

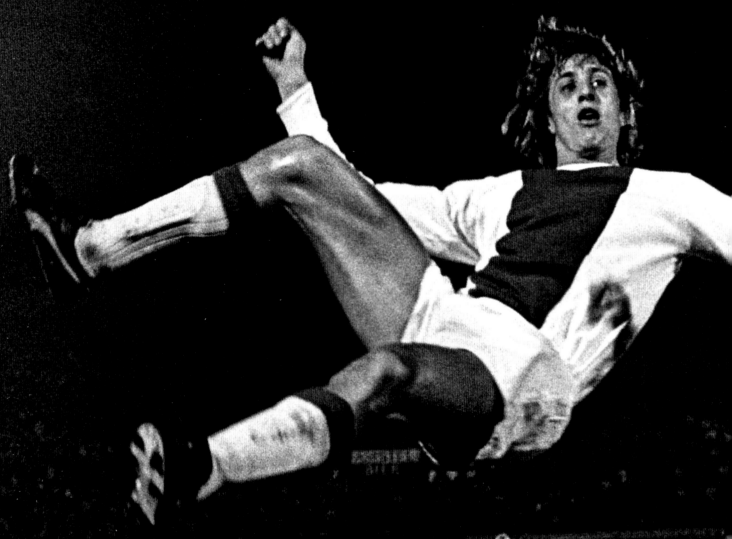

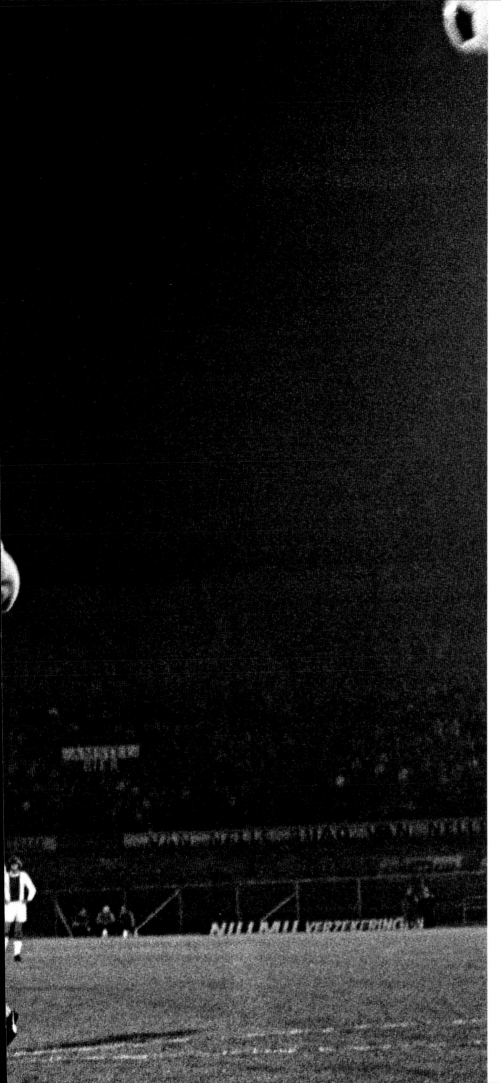

Saviour of the Catalans: Johan Cruyff won the European Cup (now UEFA Champions League) three times in an Ajax shirt (left). After his transfer to Barcelona in 1973, he immediately won the Spanish league for them, and more crucially for the Catalans, won 5:0 with Barça at Real Madrid. In his honour, the fans named him "El Salvador" ("The Saviour").

Double-page overleaf: Only the King: in the nickname stakes, "The Emperor" Beckenbauer took his place ahead of Pelé whom they call "O Rei" ("The King"). Pelé is otherwise omnipresent: on a Brazilian TV production (top left, 1969), with Johnny Carson filming the Tonight Show *(right, 1973) and as a football ambassador at New York Cosmos with Muhammad Ali (bottom left, 1975).*

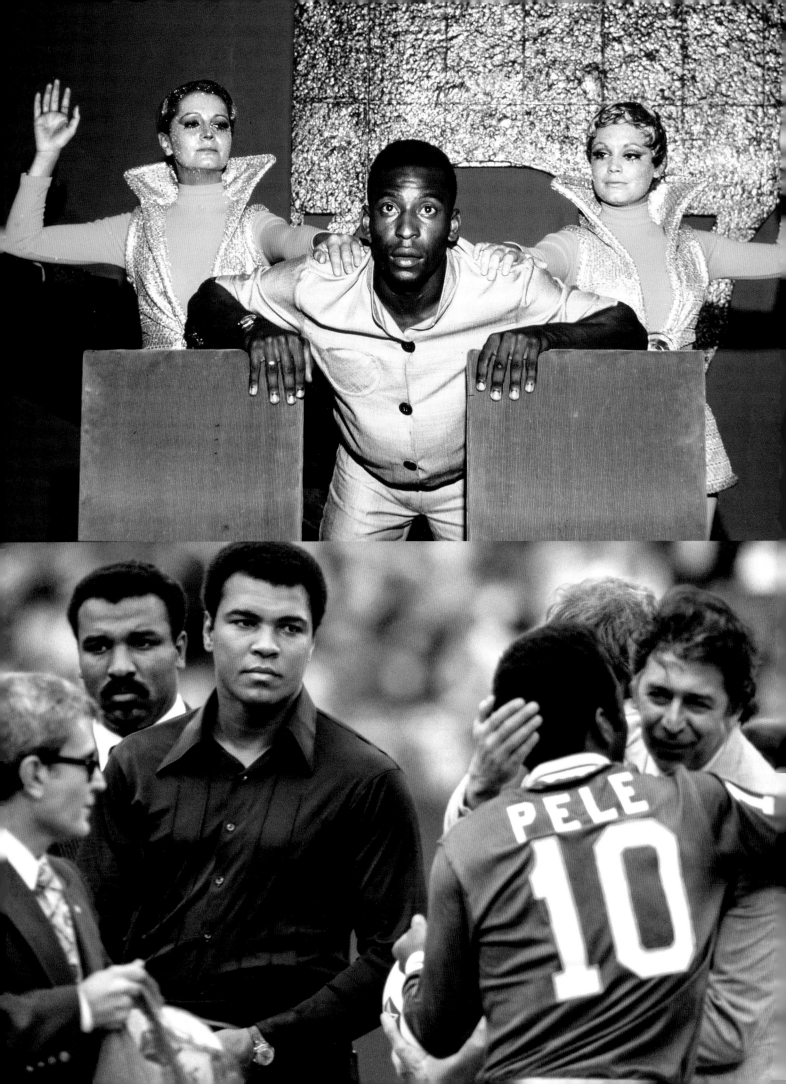

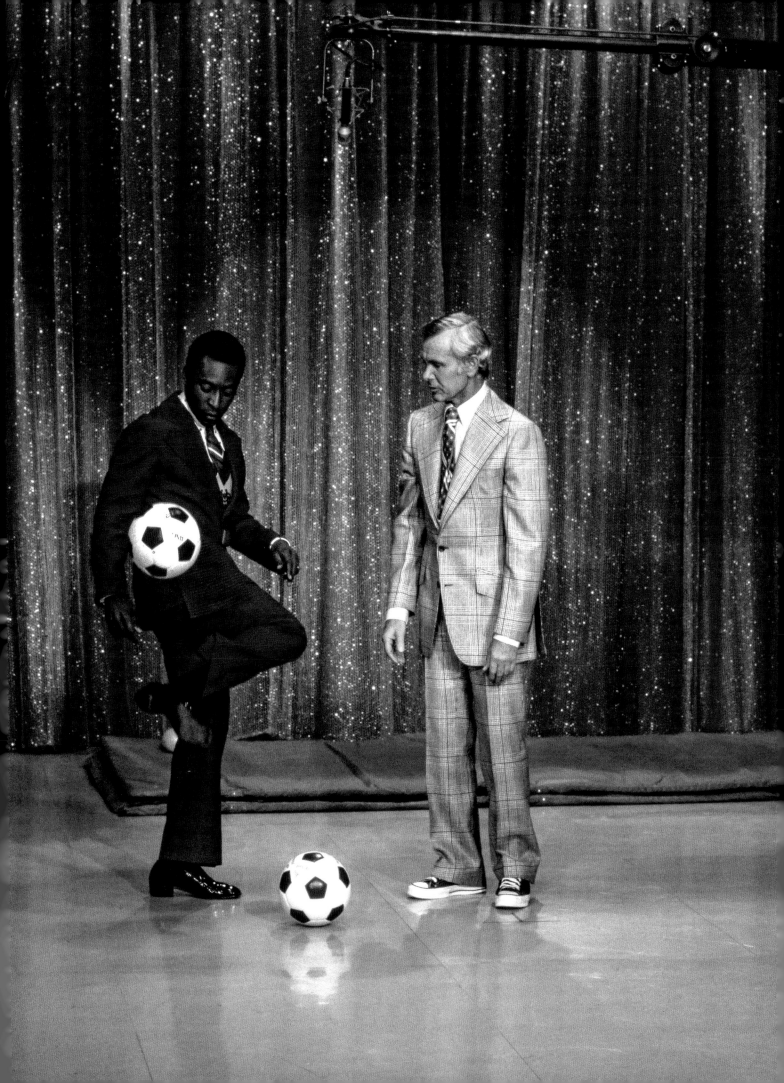

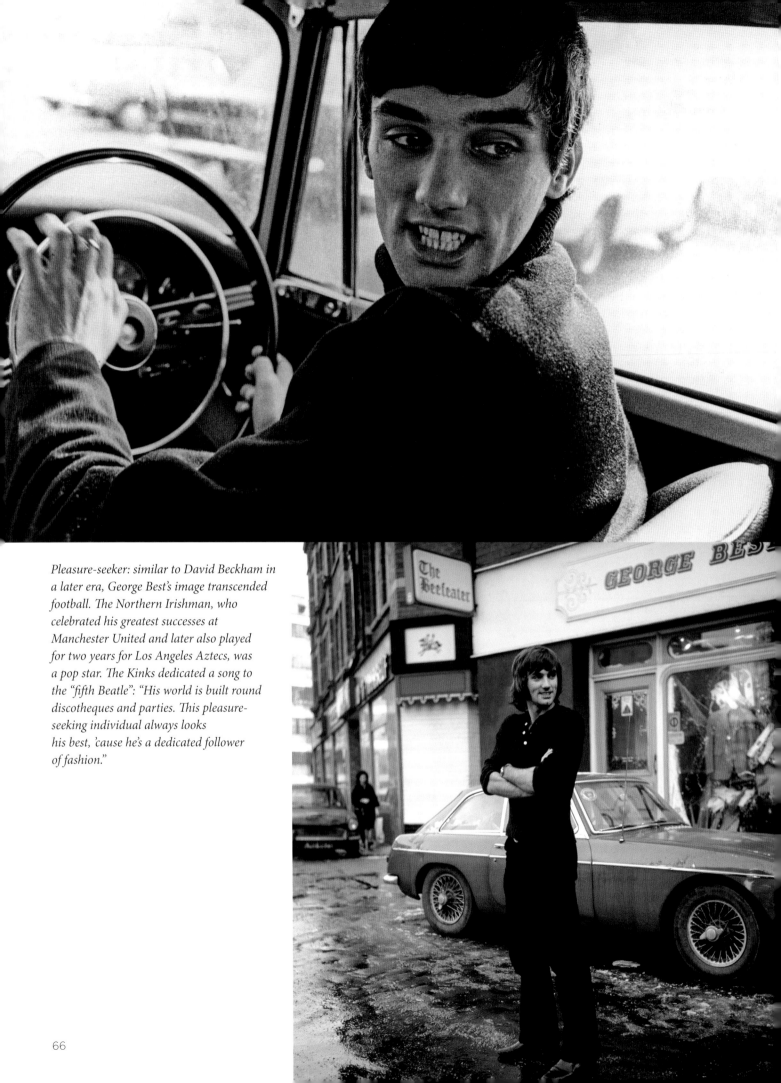

Pleasure-seeker: similar to David Beckham in a later era, George Best's image transcended football. The Northern Irishman, who celebrated his greatest successes at Manchester United and later also played for two years for Los Angeles Aztecs, was a pop star. The Kinks dedicated a song to the "fifth Beatle": "His world is built round discotheques and parties. This pleasure-seeking individual always looks his best, 'cause he's a dedicated follower of fashion."

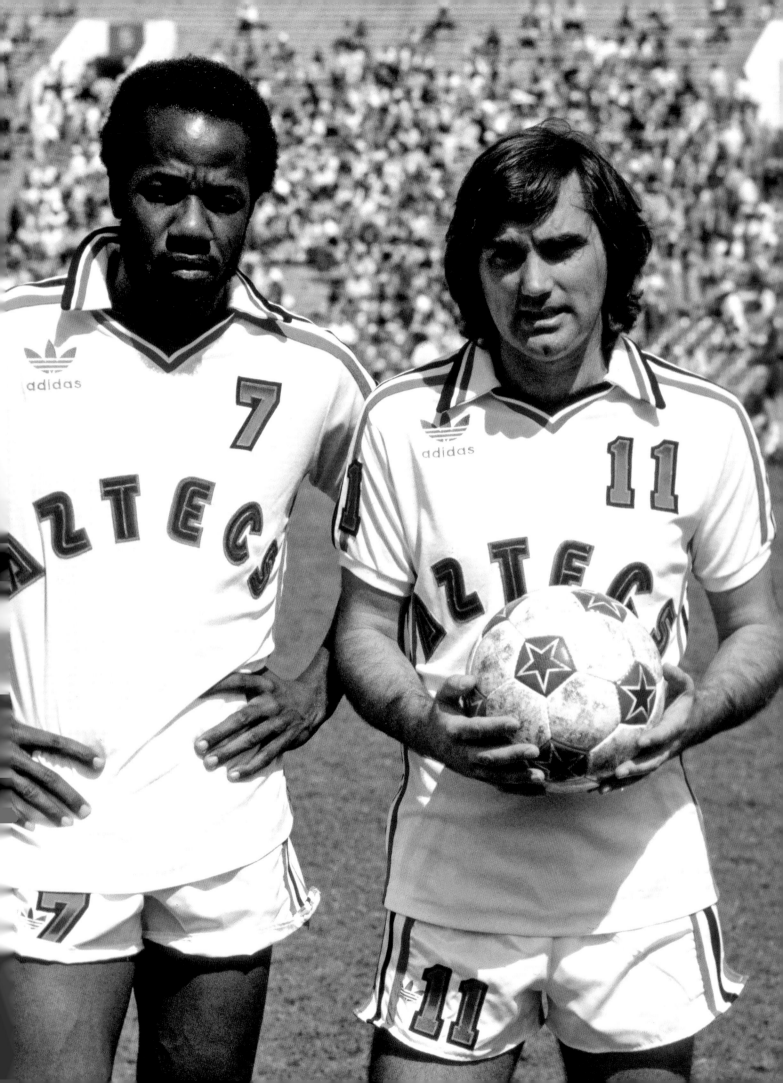

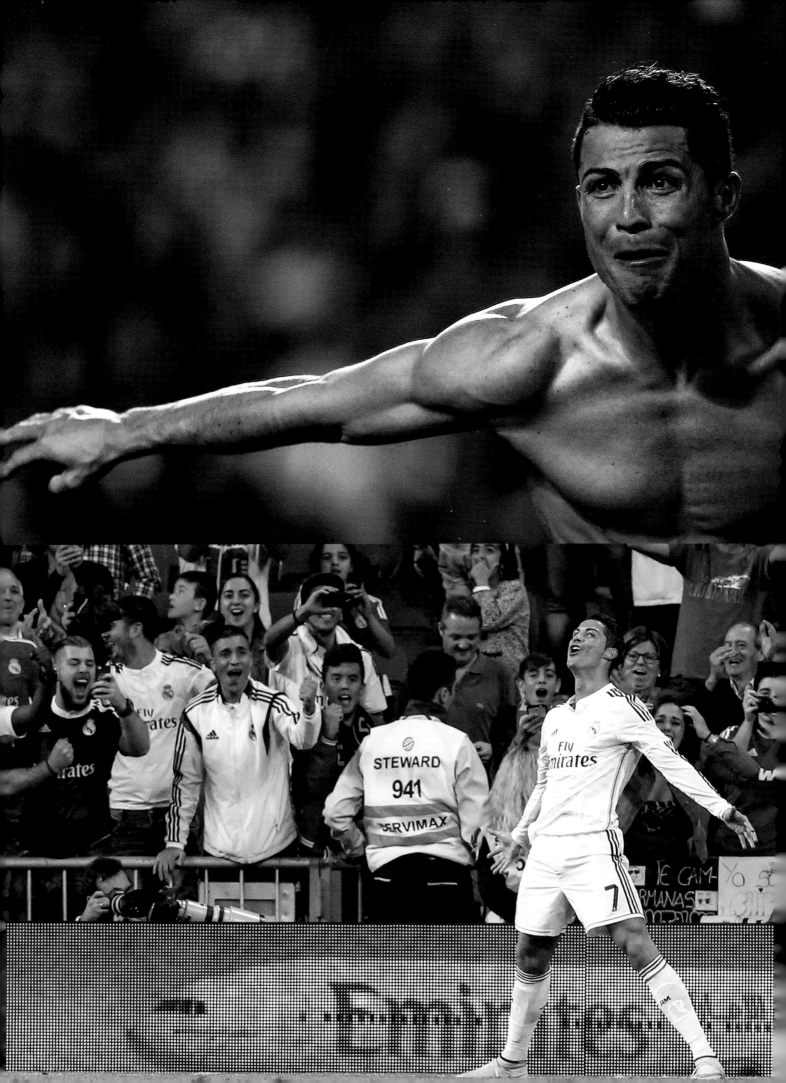

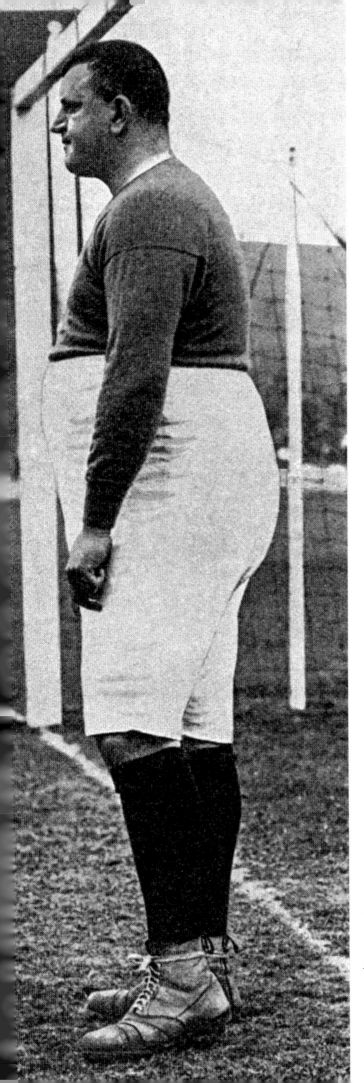

100 years and nearly 50 kilos: in vital statistics, that's how much there is between Cristiano Ronaldo and William "Fatty" Foulke (this page). They were never in direct competition – and that should be a relief for "CR7" who is so keen on striking poses. In a match in October 1898, Liverpool forward George Allan challenged Sheffield United's goalkeeper Foulke in the six-yard box. The Liverpool Post *described Fatty's reaction back then, "he seized him by the leg and turned him upside down."*

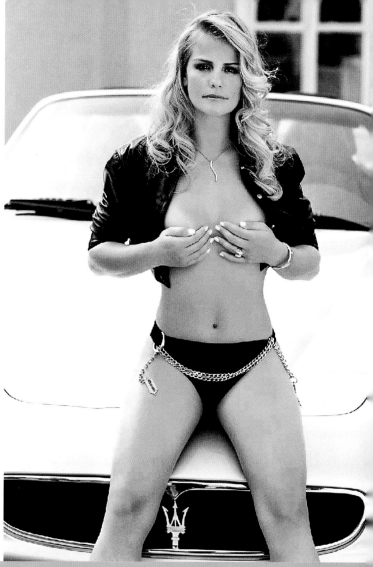

WAGs: "wives and girlfriends" are not just arm candy for their soccer-playing husbands. Milene Domingues, ex-wife of Ronaldo (British tabloids always call him "the fat one" to tell him apart from Cristiano Ronaldo), is a model and played for Brazil in the 2003 women's World Cup (this page). Right: Gerard Piqué can hardly match Shakira's popularity.

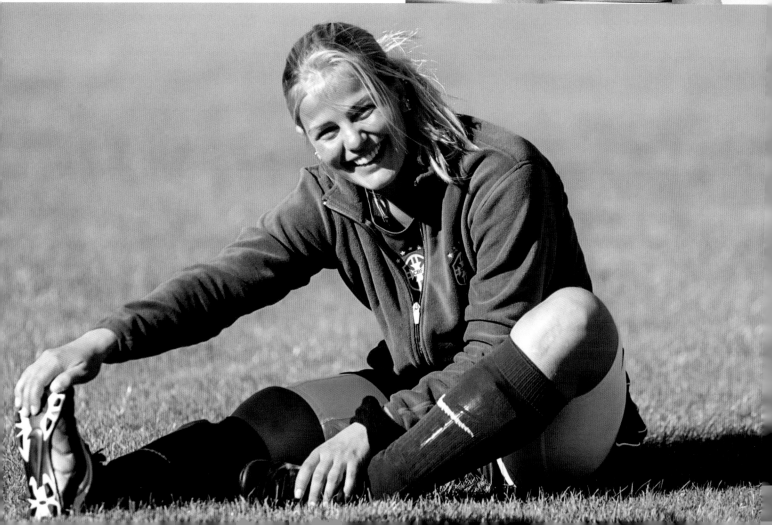

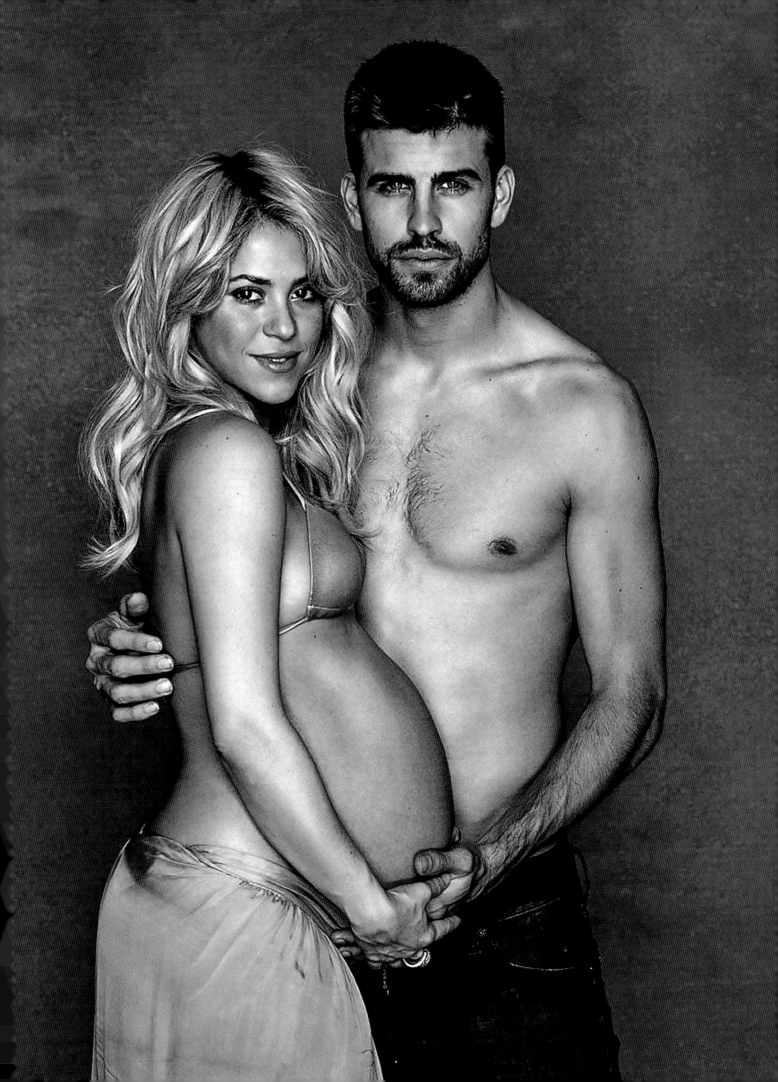

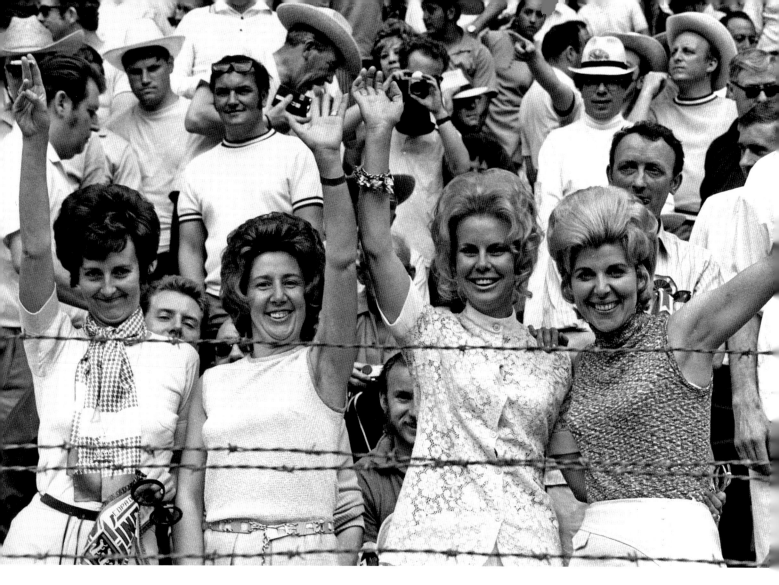

More WAGs: Kathy Peters, Judith Hurst, Tina Moore and Frances Bonetti cheer on their husbands – Martin, Geoff, Bobby and Peter – at the 1970 World Cup (above). Adriana and Christian Karembeu (top right) were married for 12 years. The 1998 world champion and "Miss Wonderbra" make just as attractive a couple as Ferenc and Erzsébet Puskás in the 1950s (bottom right).

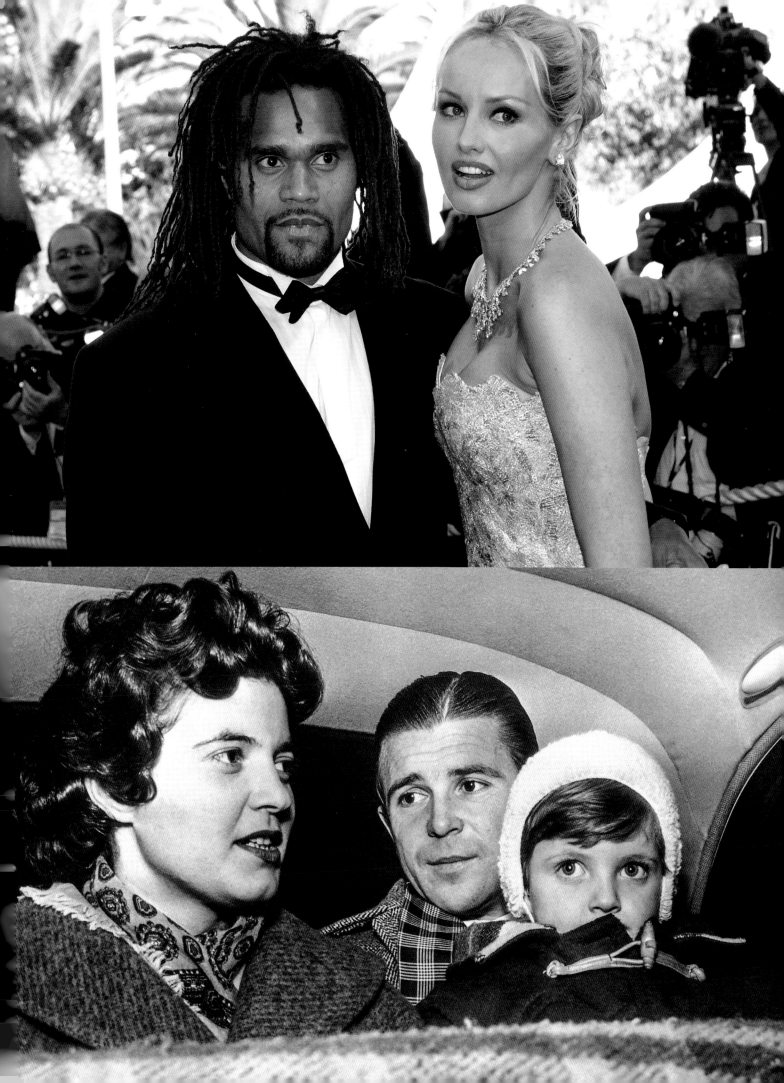

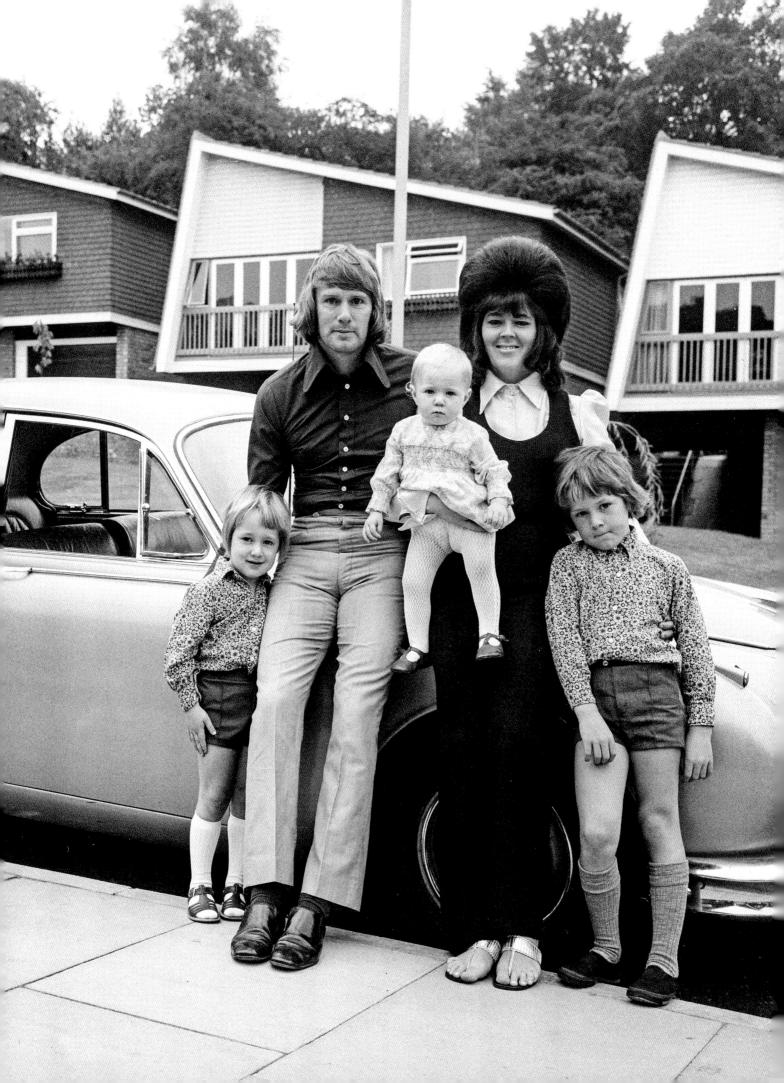

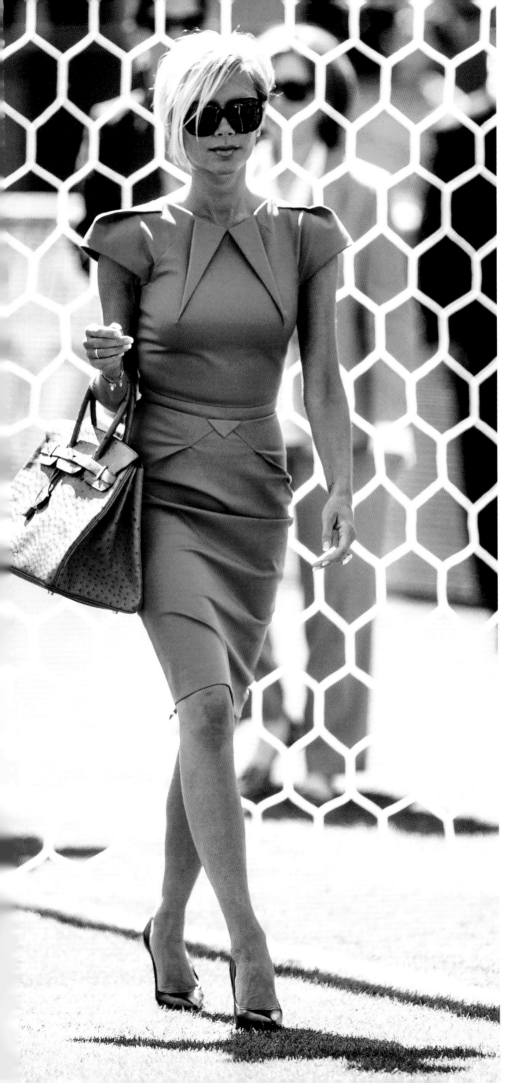

Even more WAGs: why three double-page spreads of players' wives? Because by the 1970s the public was already interested in home feature stories about the players, their cars and their wives' hairstyles (left: David Wagstaffe of Wolverhampton Wanderers with his family) and because there's "Posh Spice" aka Victoria Beckham (this page).

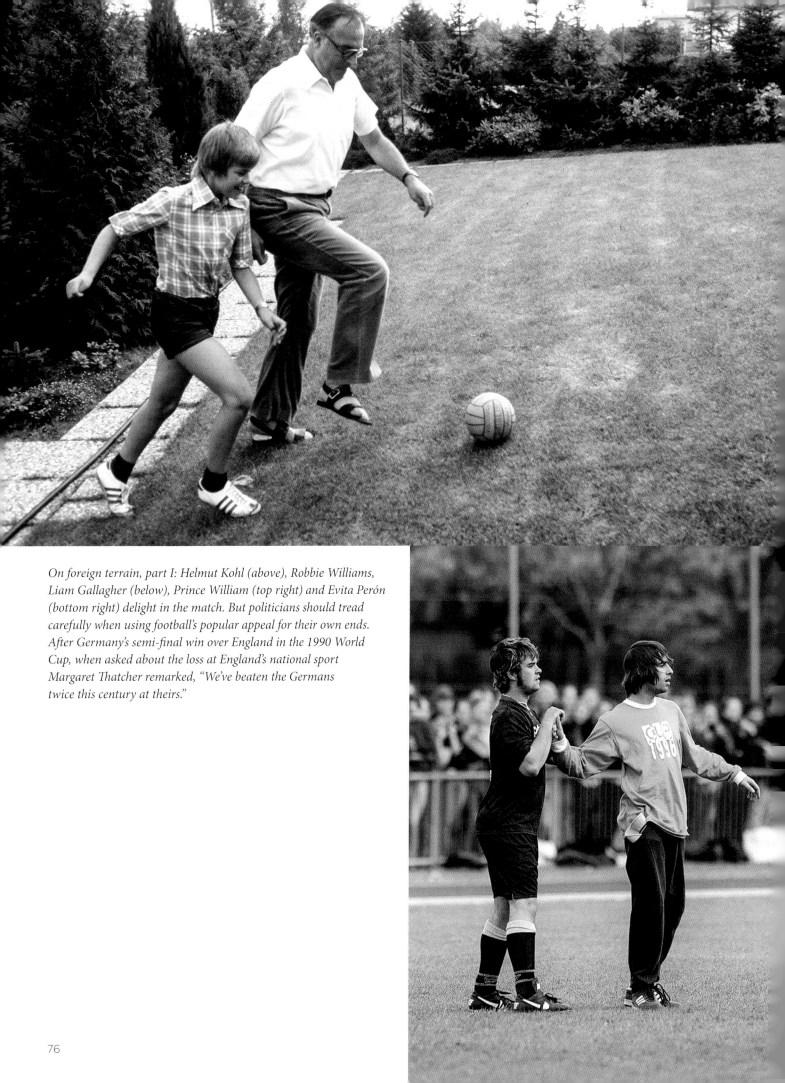

On foreign terrain, part I: Helmut Kohl (above), Robbie Williams, Liam Gallagher (below), Prince William (top right) and Evita Perón (bottom right) delight in the match. But politicians should tread carefully when using football's popular appeal for their own ends. After Germany's semi-final win over England in the 1990 World Cup, when asked about the loss at England's national sport Margaret Thatcher remarked, "We've beaten the Germans twice this century at theirs."

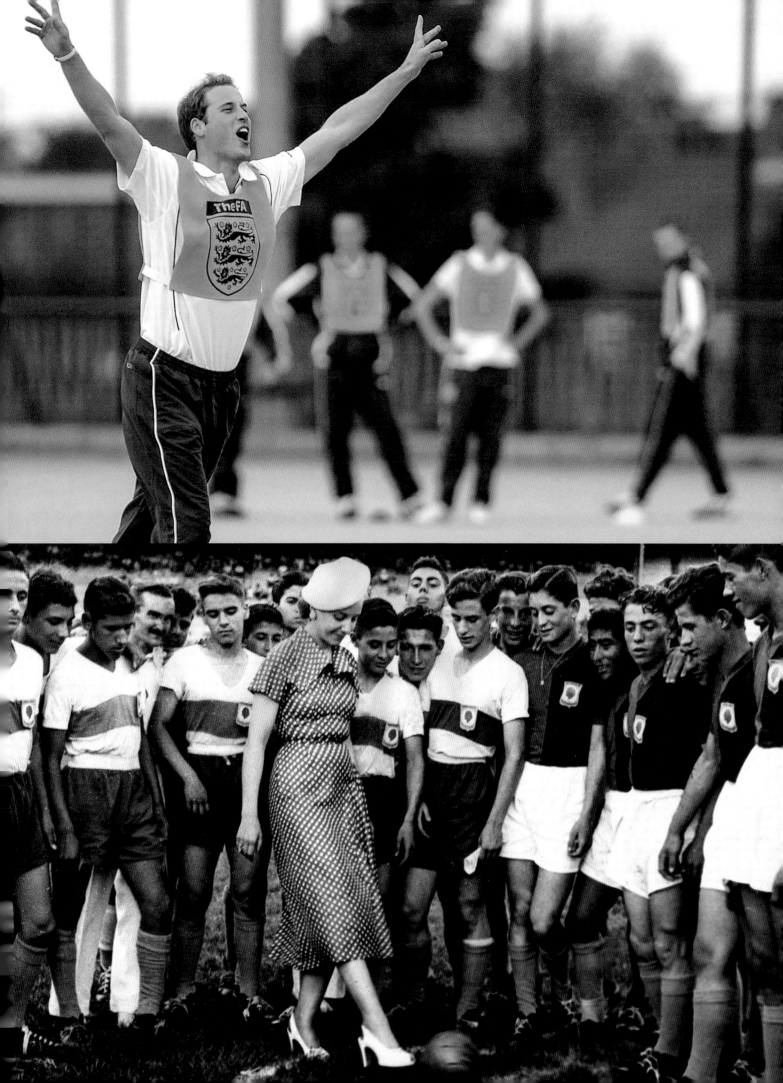

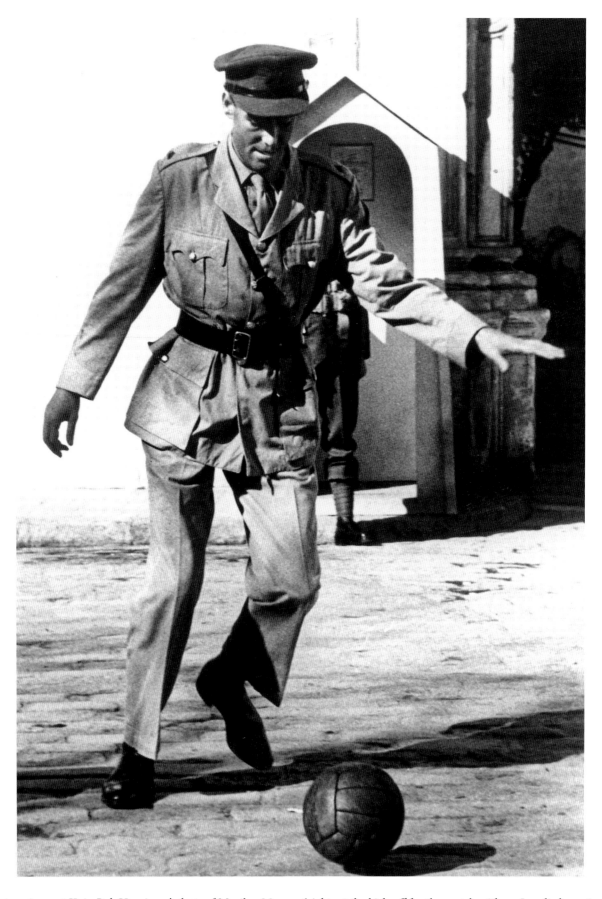

On foreign terrain, part II: in Bob Henriques' photo of Marilyn Monroe (right, at the kick-off for the match with an Israeli eleven in 1957 at Ebbets Field, Brooklyn) she cuts a similarly attractive figure as fellow actor Peter O'Toole (above, during a break while filming Lawrence of Arabia *in March 1962), although in the actual footage Marilyn's shooting technique looks less graceful.*

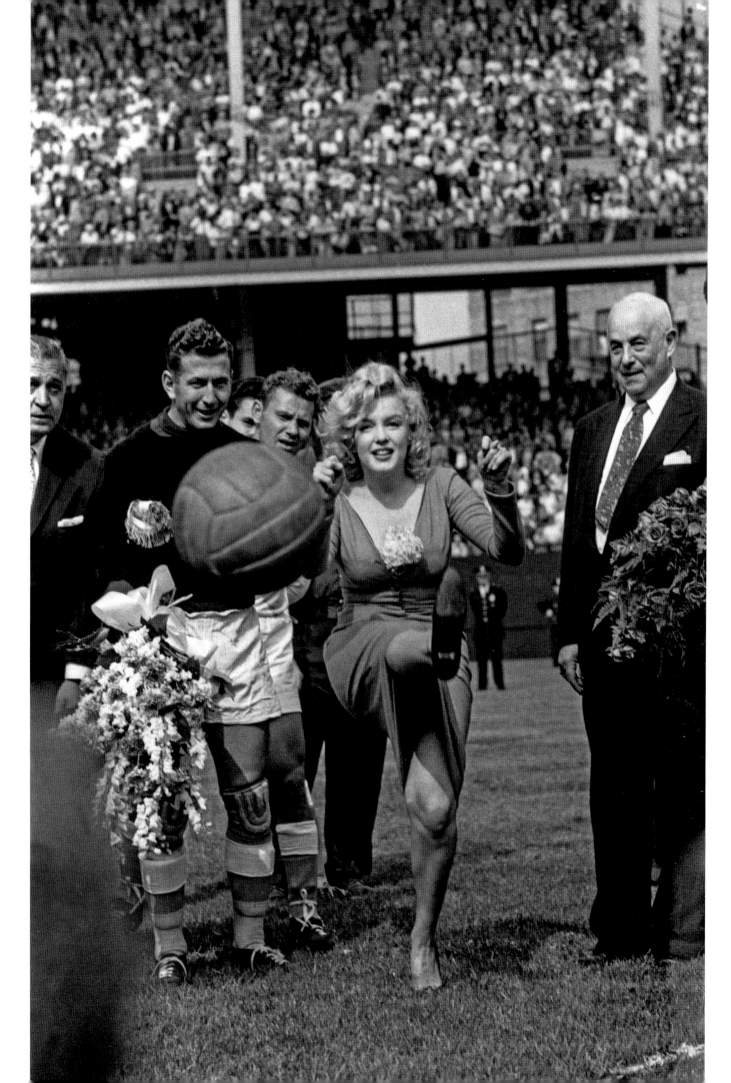

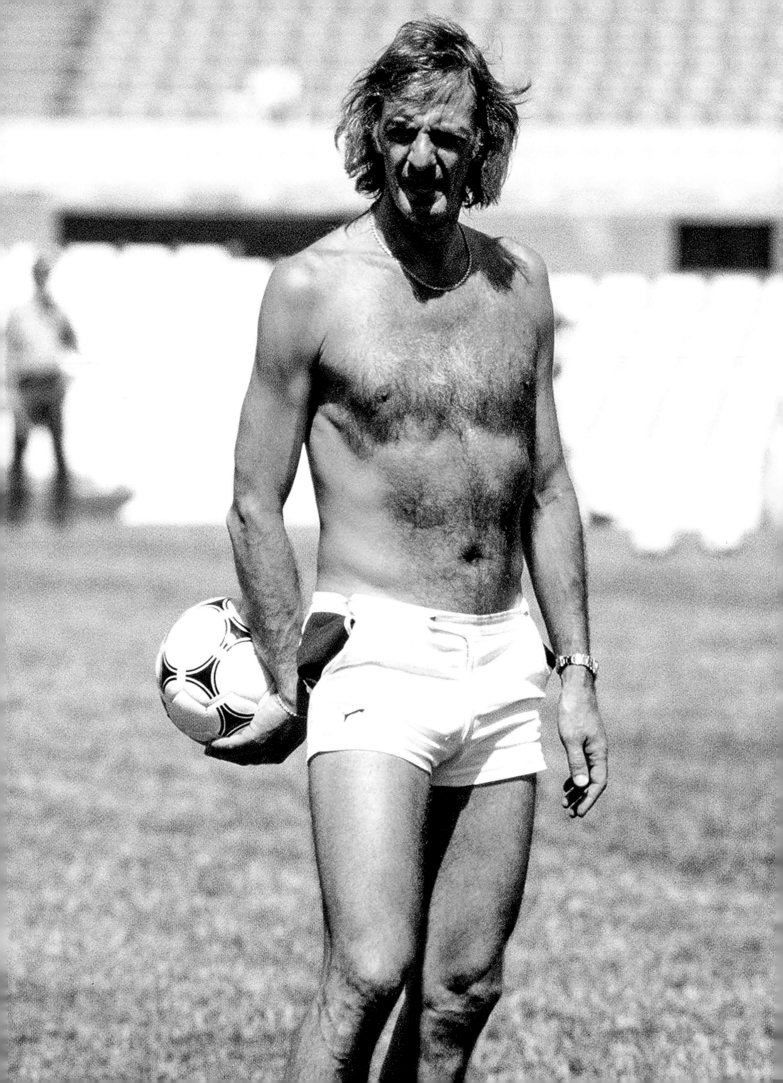

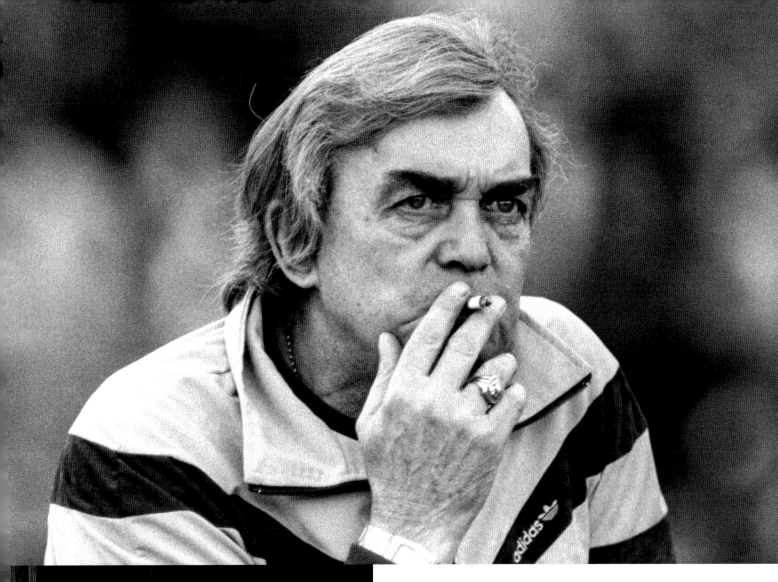

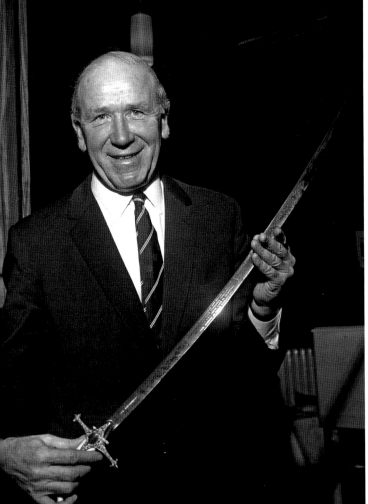

Movers and Shakers... and Stylists: they were genuine movers, not only influencing football as managers in their time, but also setting trends: César Luis Menotti (left), Ernst Happel (above) and Matt Busby (below). While Menotti was regarded as a creative mind, "Wödmasta" ("World Champion") Happel was more of a hard taskmaster and voiced his scepticism about too much psychology in football, "Whenever I hear the word motivation, I feel ill."

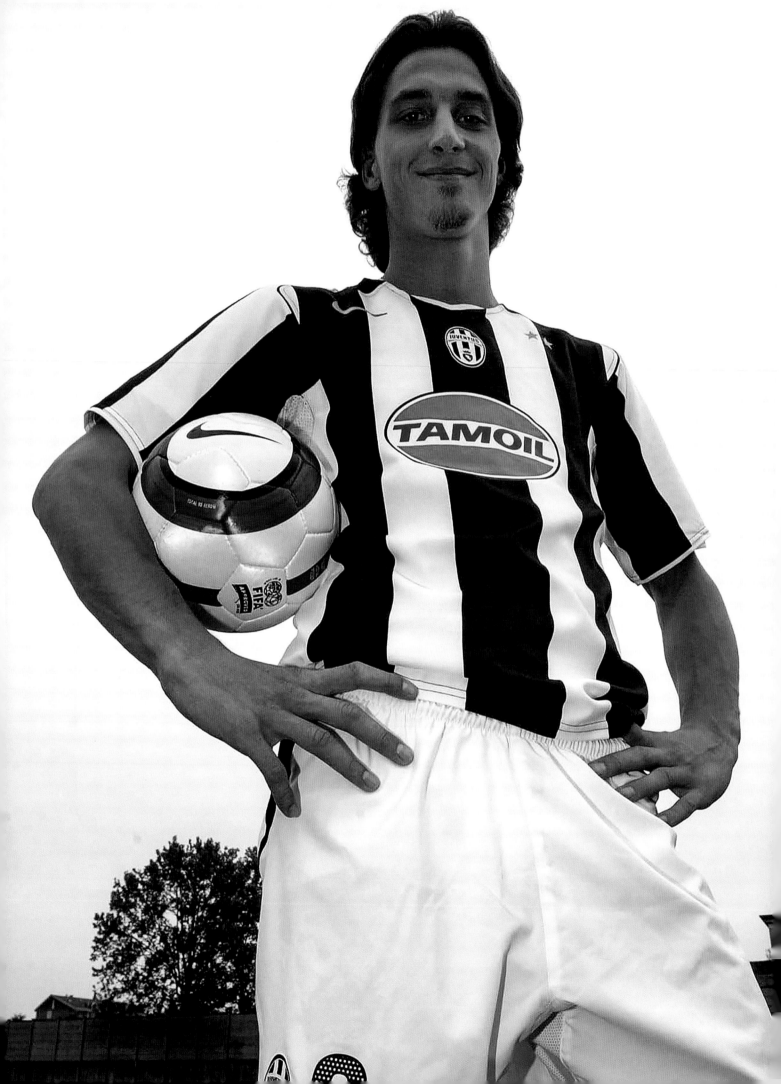

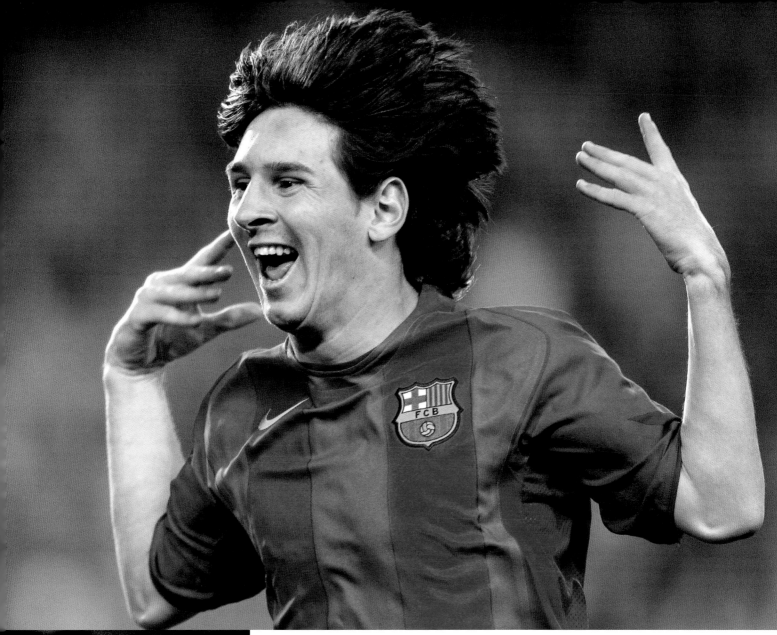

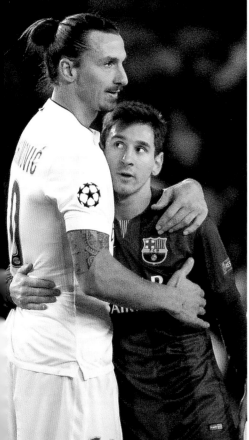

Ibra-kadabra and the flea: early in this millennium they started out their professional careers at top European clubs with stunning talent and accompanying high expectations. Zlatan Ibrahimović at Ajax and Juventus (left), "La Pulga" Lionel Messi (above) at Barcelona. When they meet, like in the Champions League in 2014 (below), it's as footballing equals. And it's fair to say: they delivered on their promise.

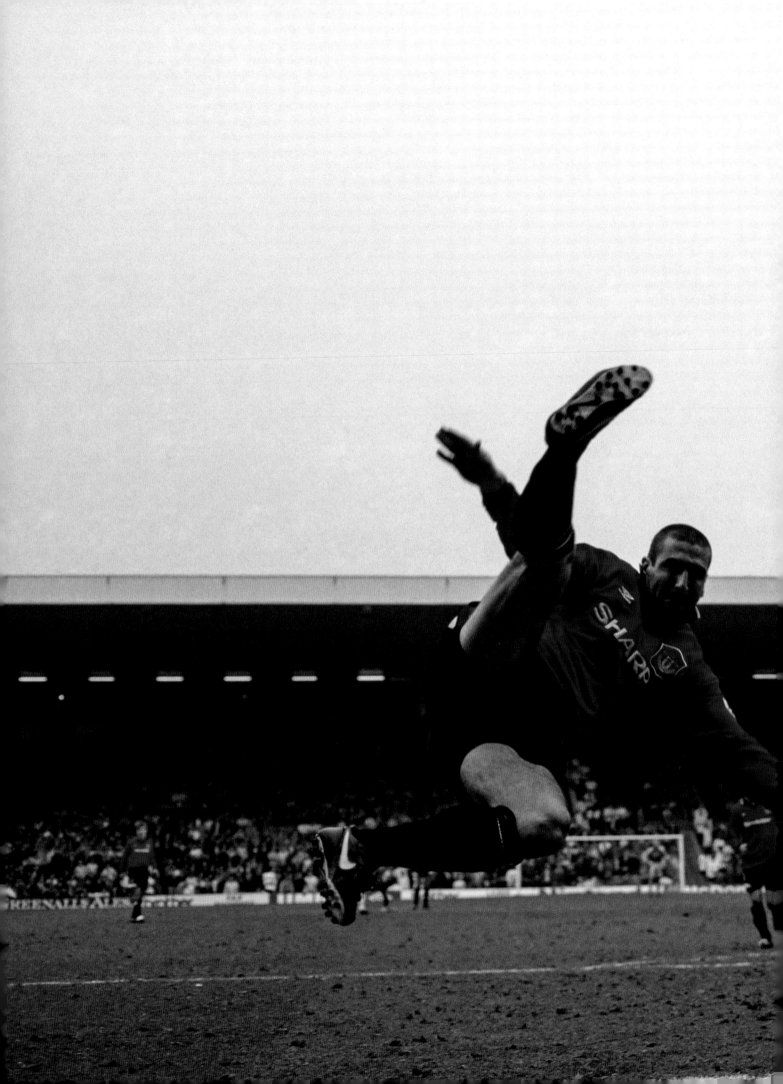

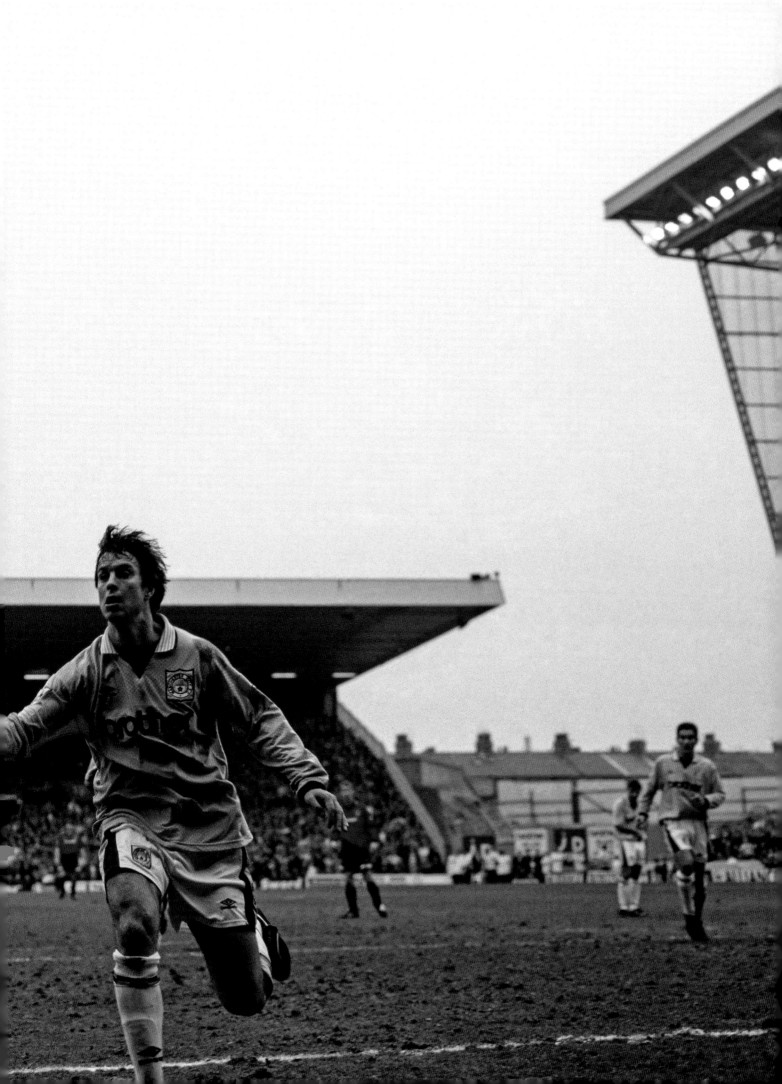

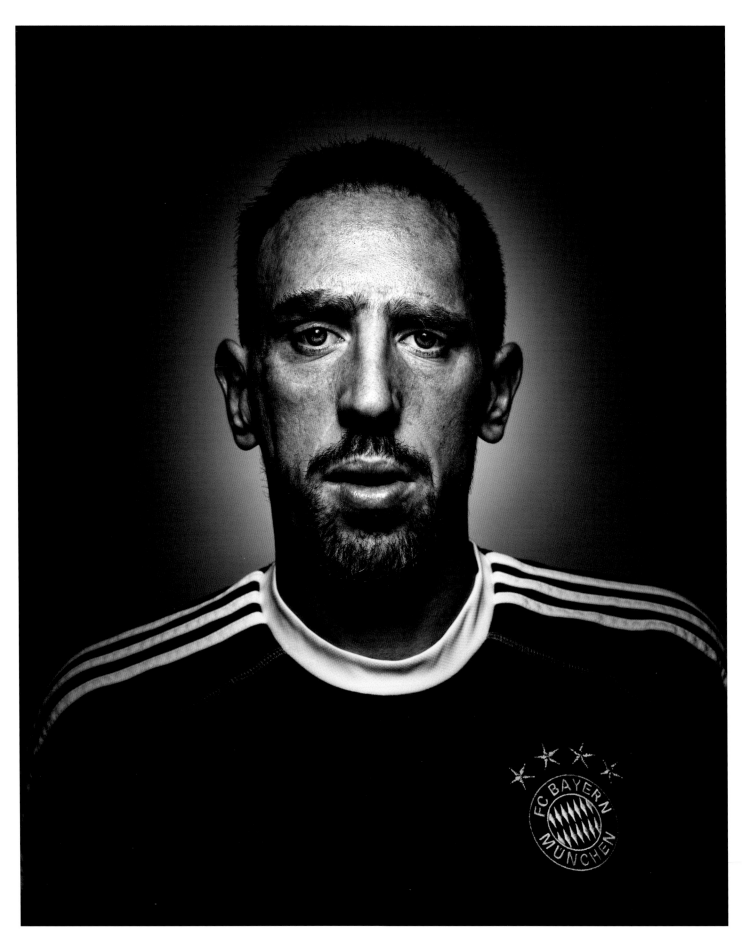

"Les Enfants Terribles": that's football's name for eccentrics like Frenchman Éric Cantona (previous double-page), Franck Ribéry (above) and Michel Platini (right). In Jean Cocteau's novel, Les Enfants Terribles, the protagonists only hang "onto the world by a thread" – occasionally, the same goes for footballing high-flyers.

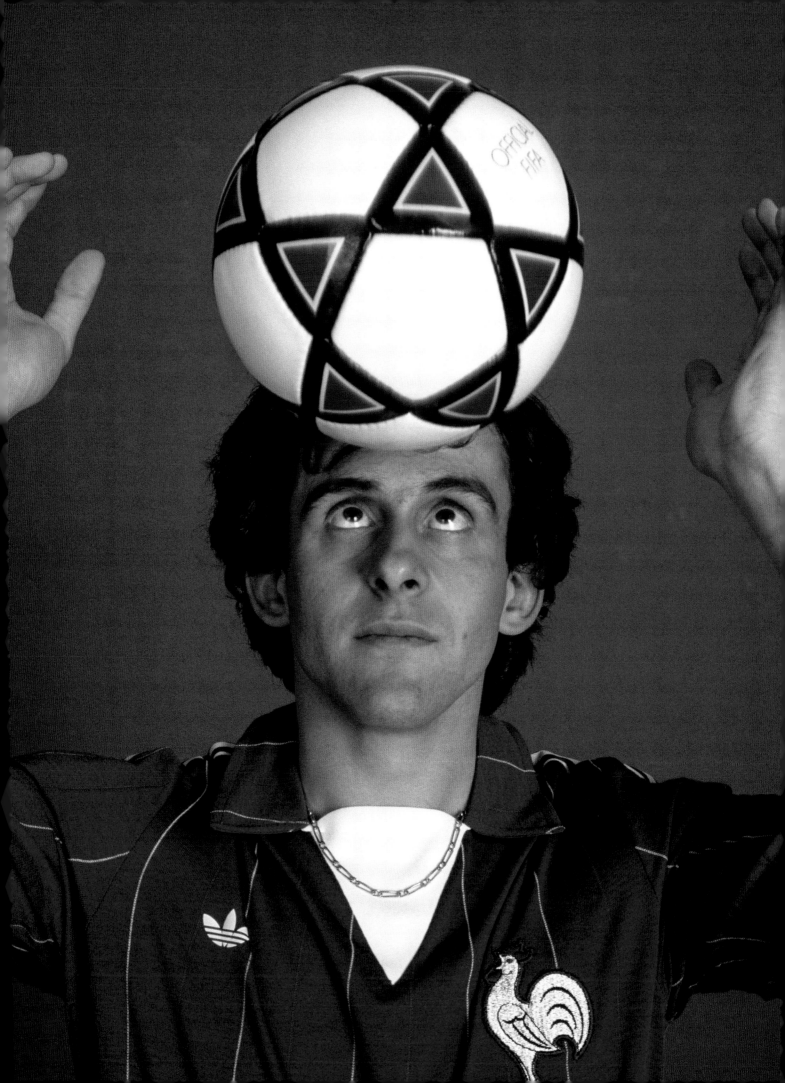

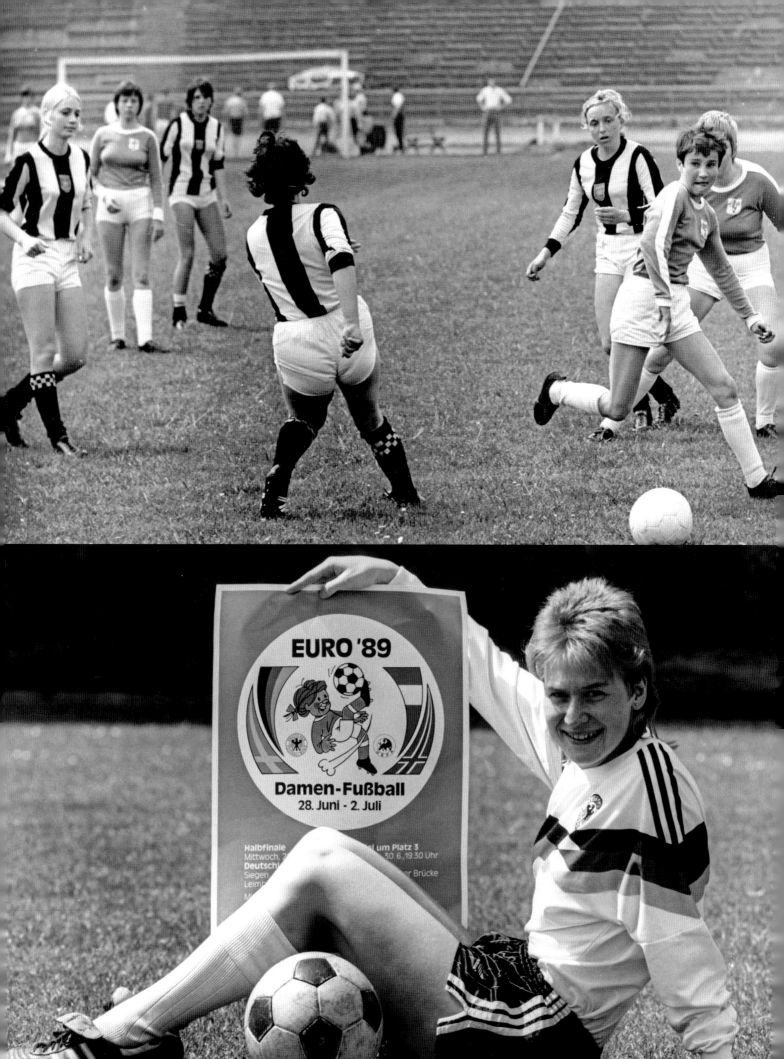

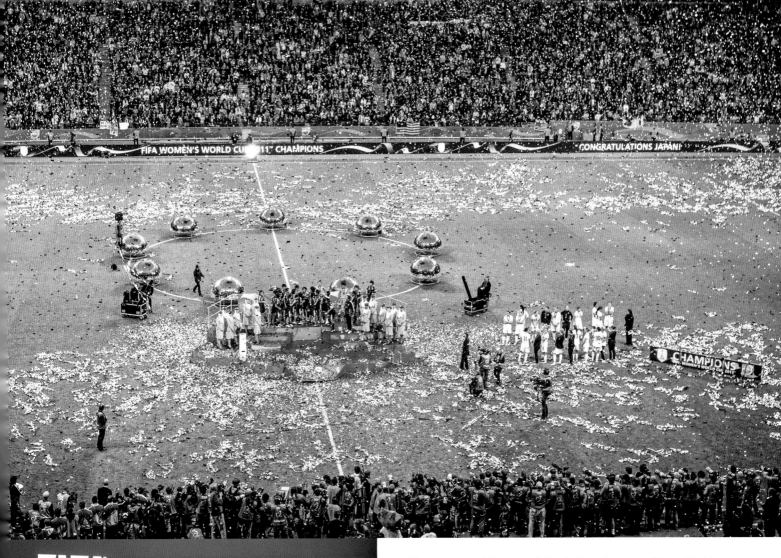

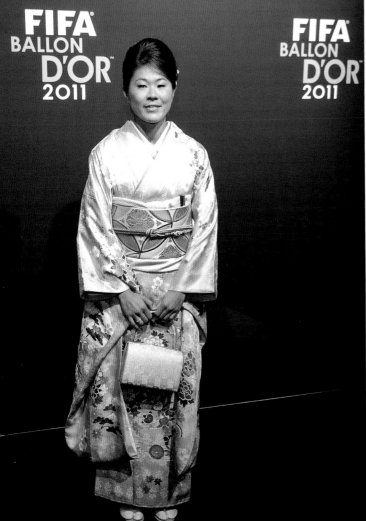

Publicity surge: while women's football in the 1970s, like at Turbine Potsdam (top left), was mainly played away from the public eye and even Britta Unsleber's promotion for the 1989 European Cup in "ladies' football" looked amateurish (bottom left), the 2011 World Cup in Germany with its Japan vs. US final in Frankfurt (above) and stars like Marta, Hope Solo and Homare Sawa (below), attracted worldwide interest.

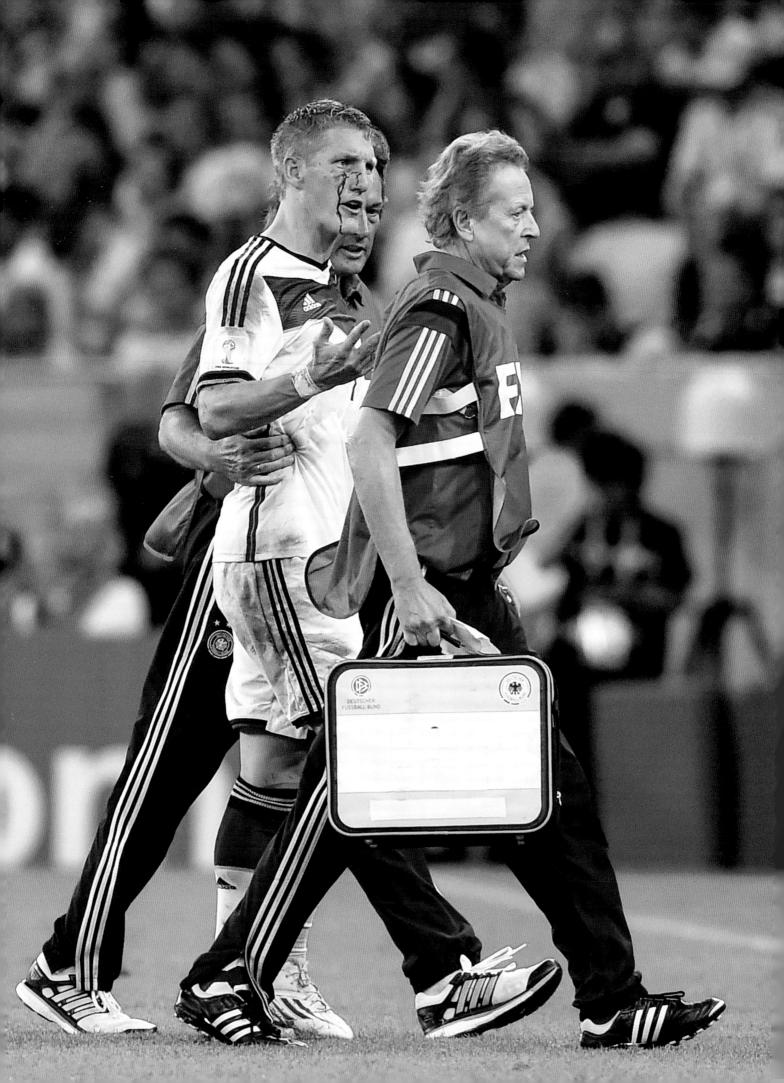

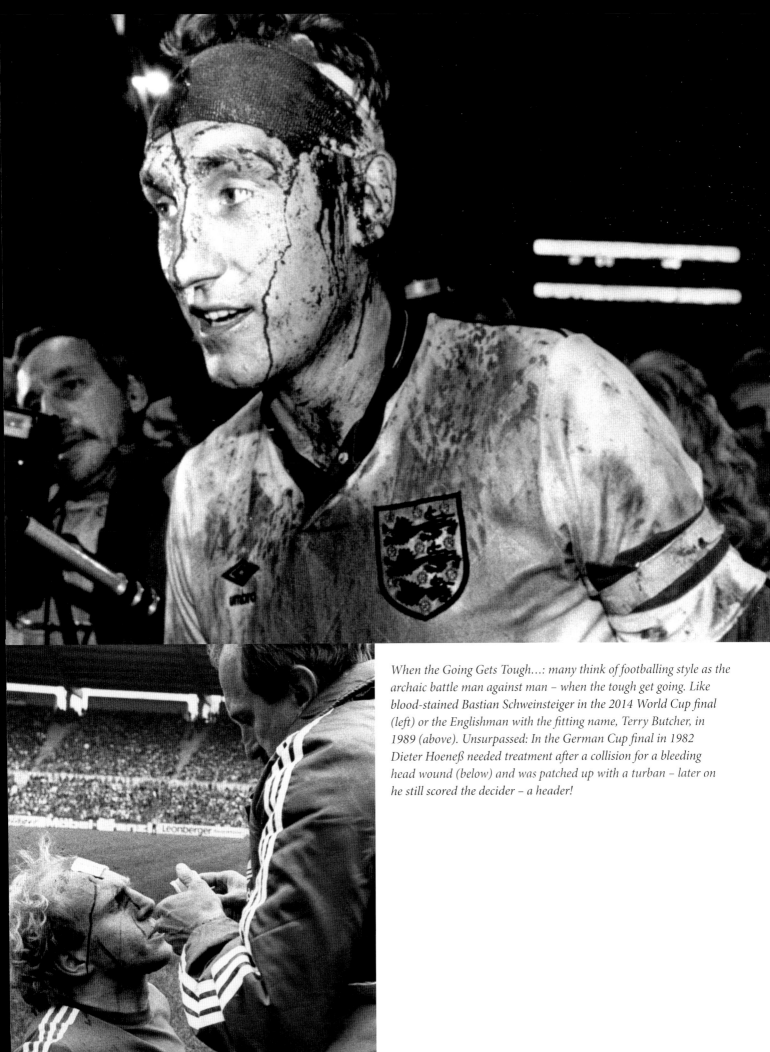

When the Going Gets Tough…: many think of footballing style as the archaic battle man against man – when the tough get going. Like blood-stained Bastian Schweinsteiger in the 2014 World Cup final (left) or the Englishman with the fitting name, Terry Butcher, in 1989 (above). Unsurpassed: In the German Cup final in 1982 Dieter Hoeneß needed treatment after a collision for a bleeding head wound (below) and was patched up with a turban – later on he still scored the decider – a header!

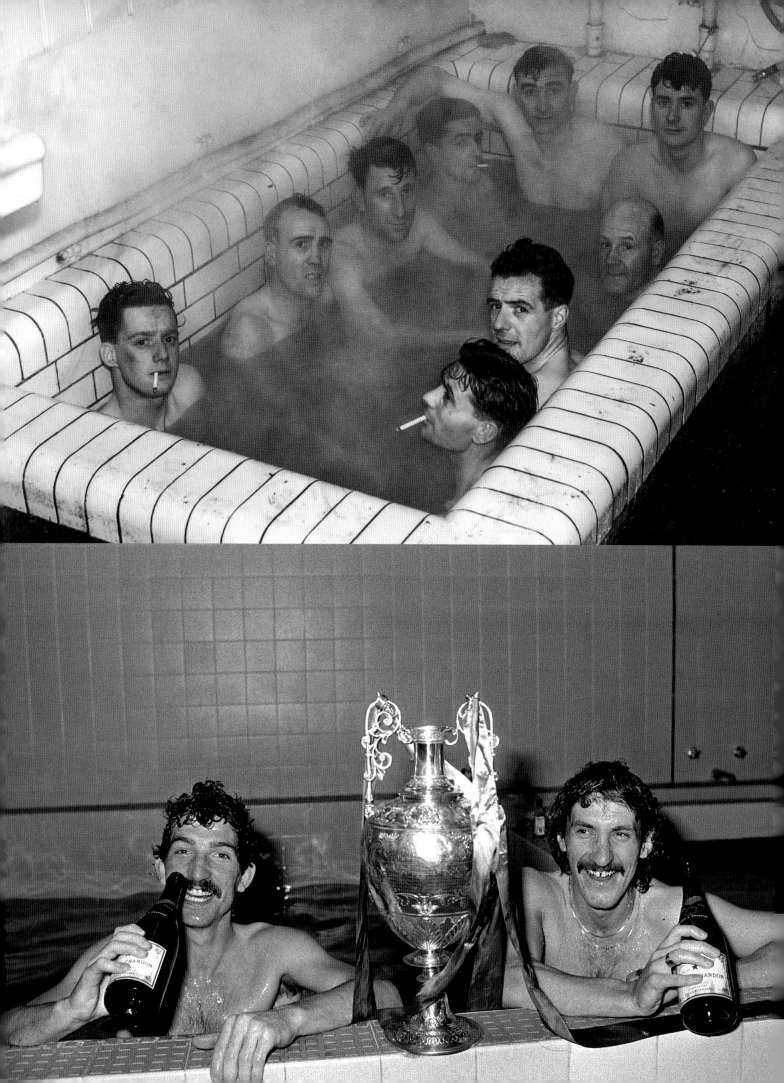

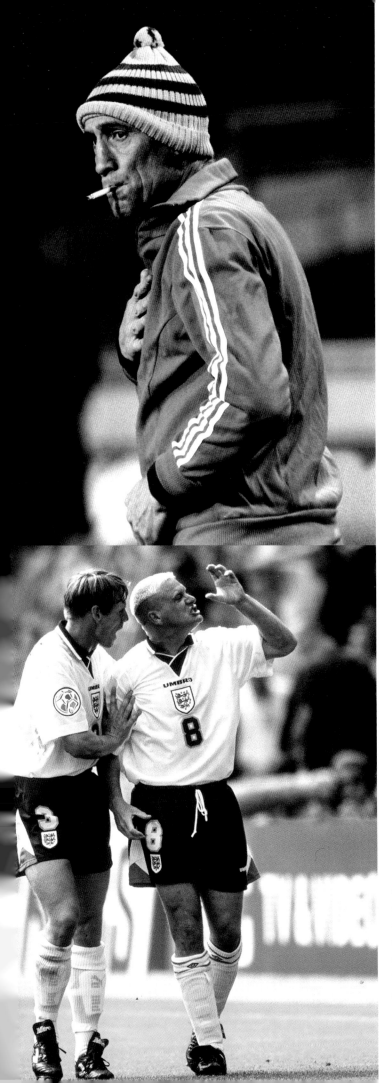

Frowned upon in our health-conscious age: footballers (top left: Ipswich Town players recovering in a hot tub in 1939) or managers (above: Italy's team manager Enzo Bearzot in 1980) who smoke. By contrast, alcohol is perfectly acceptable as a reward (like Graeme Souness and Terry McDermott enjoying a drink after Liverpool won the league in 1980, bottom left). Some can hardly wait, while they're still on the pitch (below: Stuart "Psycho" Pearce and Paul "Gazza" Gascoigne, 1996).

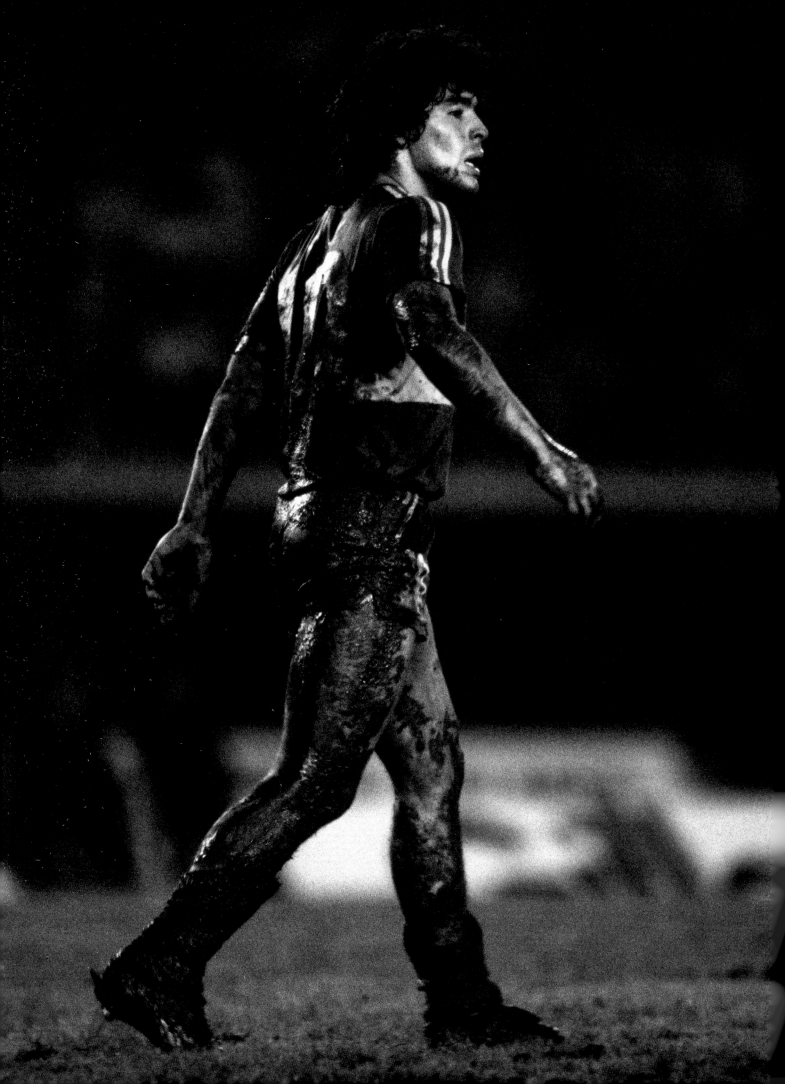

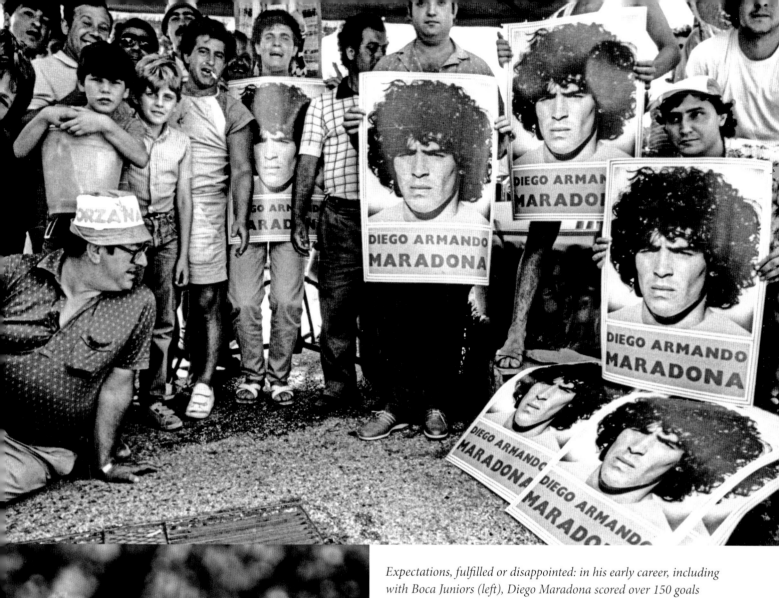

Expectations, fulfilled or disappointed: in his early career, including with Boca Juniors (left), Diego Maradona scored over 150 goals between 1976 and 1984. For Napoli supporters, his arrival in 1984 caused a wave of enthusiasm (above). And they weren't let down. Diego gifted the Southern Italians two championships in the unequal battle against rich clubs from the North. In the words of a Napoli fan, "Maradona has given the downtrodden people of the South a little of their dignity back."

At the 2014 World Cup in Brazil, the Germans and an injury prevented Neymar, whom they call "Joia" ("Gem"), from fulfilling his country's title hopes. After their 1-7 semi-final defeat, only dejection reigned among the Brazilians.

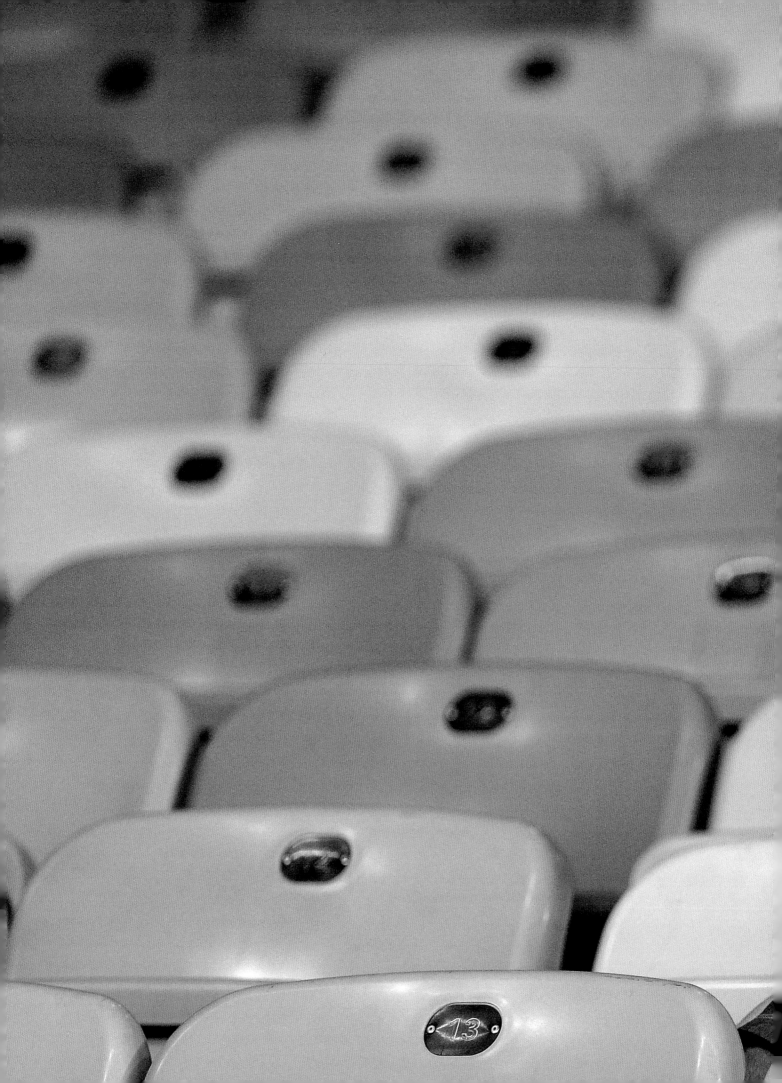

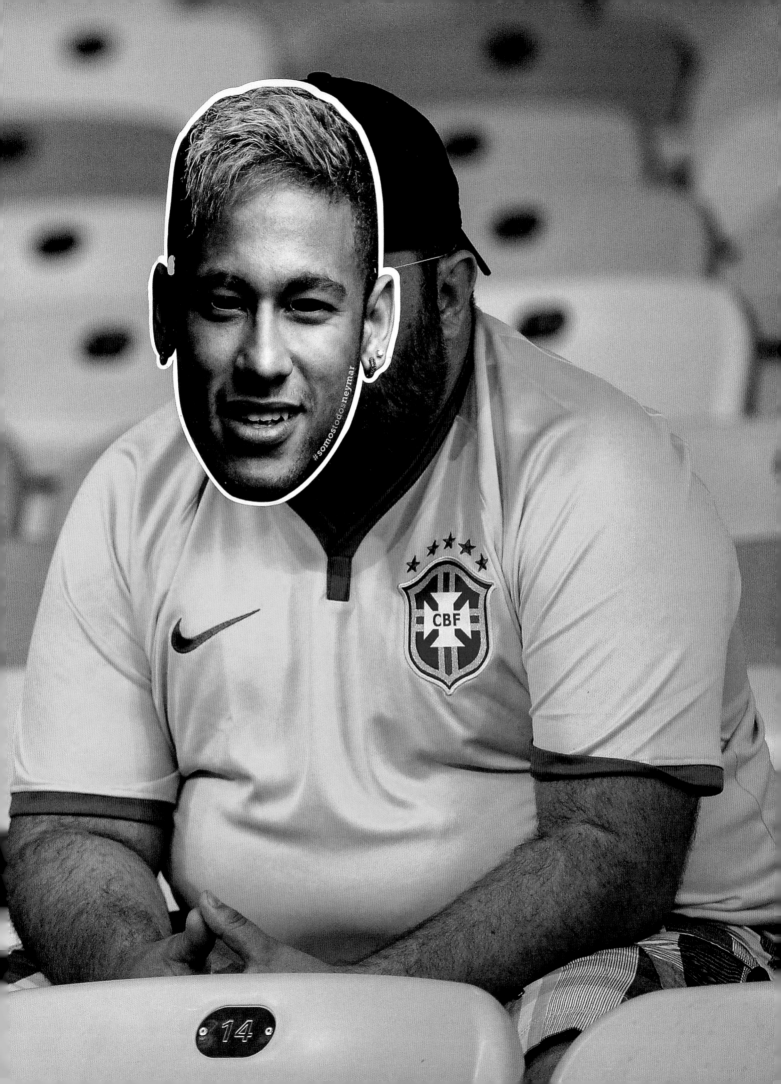

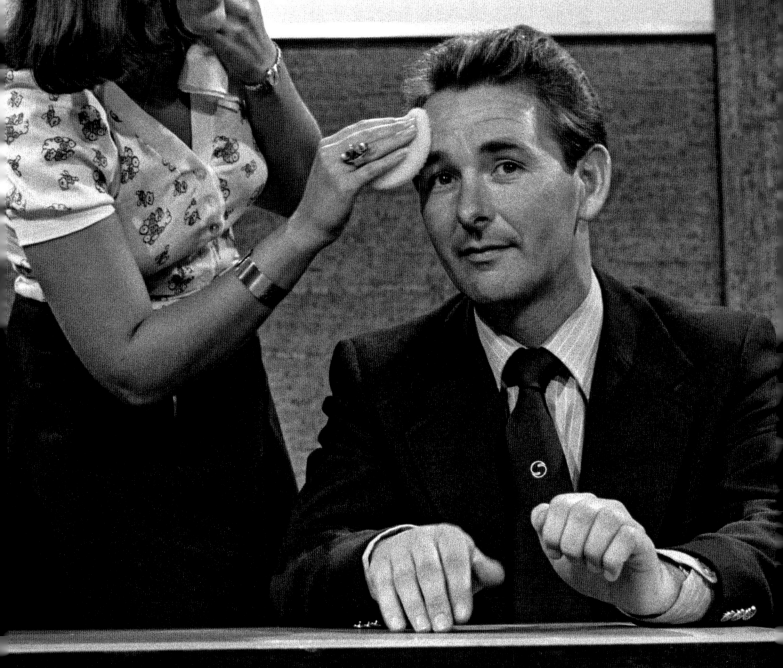

FASHION

Football matches used to be real festival occasions when the fans celebrated with their fashion parade. Until the late 1960s, however, the supporters were not adorned in team paraphernalia. Instead, they usually wore their Sunday bests. Games were commonly played at weekends, mainly on Sundays after church. Supporters generally arrived at the ground wearing a smart suit, complete with tie and hat.

The varying array of fashions in the stands went in tandem with the players' changing sportswear on the pitch. In the early days, the team kit traditionally comprised cotton shirts with vertical or diagonal stripes, preferably with a collar and long sleeves. At the start of the 1970s when mass textile production was introduced, synthetic materials like polyamide or polyester became popular. Football jerseys reflected contemporary trends, while at least club colours and crests largely stayed the same. The growing opportunity for football clubs to embark on the cost-effective production of articles emblazoned with their signature designs soon gave rise to a brand-new market of official club merchandise. Nowadays, almost any household gadget is available with a club's logo – from toasters to ballpoint pens, hand towels, screwdrivers, cuddly toys and bed linen. The top-selling items are still exclusive club clothing.

Appearances: Brian Clough with a make-up artist in the studio of football TV show The Big Match. *Renowned for his outspoken views, the manager once said of one of his players, "John Robertson was a very unattractive young man. If one day, I felt a bit off-colour, I would sit next to him. I was bloody Errol Flynn in comparison."*

Team shirts now generate big business for professional football clubs. Major clubs like Bayern Munich earn a fifth of their annual revenue from official merchandise sales. Real Madrid even refinances a substantial share of its superstar transfer deals with the income from international sales of its team jerseys. When top star Cristiano Ronaldo transferred from Manchester United to Real Madrid in 2009, in the first year Madrid sold 1.5 million shirts bearing Ronaldo's name. After the 2014 World Cup, Real Madrid sealed an eighty-million-euro deal to sign Columbian talent, James Rodríguez, from AS Monaco. In the first two days after news of the transfer was released, 345,000 "James" shirts changed hands across the shop's counter. Total sales reached a massive 33.6 million euros!

Another major revenue stream for clubs is to cultivate an air of nostalgia among the fans. Football strips are unmistakeable, not just for their distinctive colours and styles, but also because of the sponsor's logo on the front. The Uruguayan club CA Peñarol was the first international club to launch corporate sponsorship on its shirts, as early as in the mid-1950s. By the 1970s the European clubs had caught up. Only a single club adhered to its 100-year-plus tradition of leaving the front of its team jerseys completely blank. Barcelona FC only decided in 2006 to put the Unicef logo on its shirts. Four years on and the first sponsorship deal in the club's history was eventually signed – it instantly broke all records. Advertising on the front of the Barcelona jersey is currently worth 30 million euros to a corporate sponsor.

Given these figures for sponsorship deals and merchandise, it is not surprising that the clubs bring out a new strip every year. Unveiling the team's latest kit is usually nothing special. But during the 2013/14 season when the iconic Italian football club Napoli launched a new shirt with army camouflage pattern, even high-ranking military personnel voiced their protest. General Mauro Del Vecchio, the former head of Italy's Nato forces in Afghanistan, said, "The colours of a military uniform belong in a world that has nothing to do with football. I think these two worlds should be kept separate." Unfortunately, the club's President,

Aurelio De Laurentiis, had praised the shirt's green and brown camouflage colours as a "war jersey". Napoli supporters were not deterred: the first batch sold out within a few hours.

Besides team colours, other looks in the fashion stakes have consistently met with adulation from the media and supporters. Lavish sportswear, extravagant tattoos and designer hairstyles are a good way to be noticed. Since the 2002 World Cup, supporters also appreciate how the appearance of their favourite stars can become a national talking point. After Victoria Beckham saw her husband, David's mohican hairstyle on TV, in embarrassment she quickly dispatched his hairdresser Aidan Phelan from Britain to Japan "in the interest of the England team". Phelan shared Victoria's view, commenting on the hairstyle, "David has obviously been putting his football first... It seems that it needs a bit of care." Unfortunately, there was no happy ending to this episode. Sporting a fresh haircut, Beckham, along with the England players, was knocked out of the World Cup in the next match against Brazil.

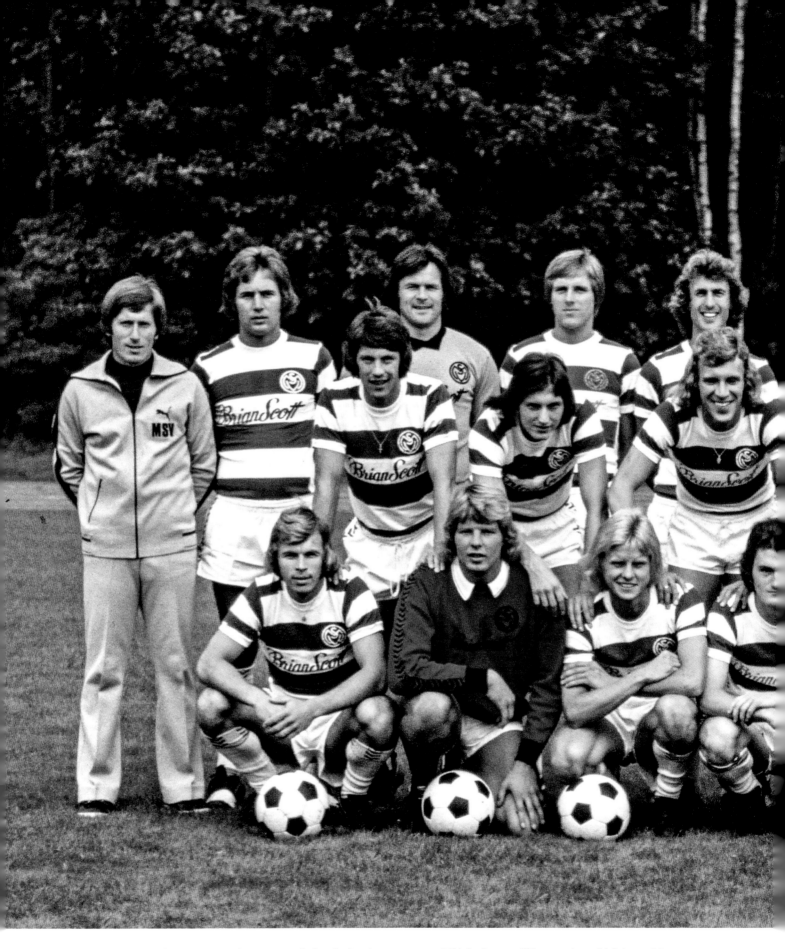

Studies in style: team photos are eagerly anticipated ahead of each new season. Which player will be wearing which jersey? In retrospect they give a glimpse of the prevailing Zeitgeist: the boys of MSV Duisburg (above, 1974/75 Season) epitomize the 1970s with their flares and hairstyles.

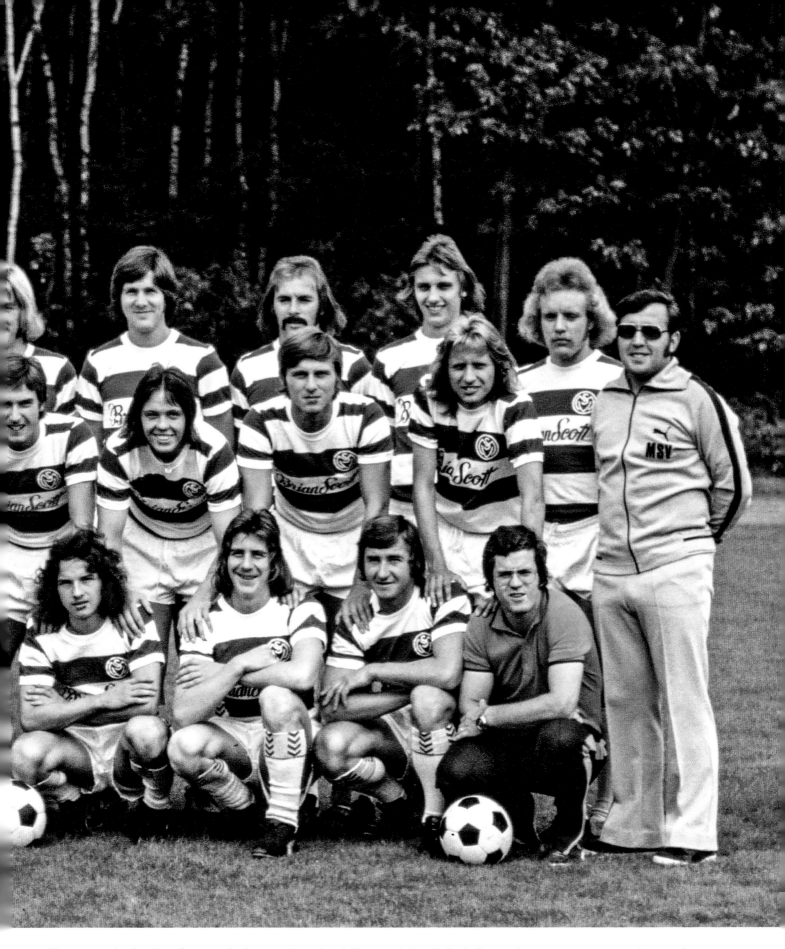

Double-page overleaf: early 20th century high-waist shorts (top left), Spanish female footballers in the 1950s wearing court shoes to play soccer (top right), braces and white socks are en vogue at Bayern Munich in 1988 (bottom left) and Napoli players line up in 2013, sporting a camouflage look (bottom right).

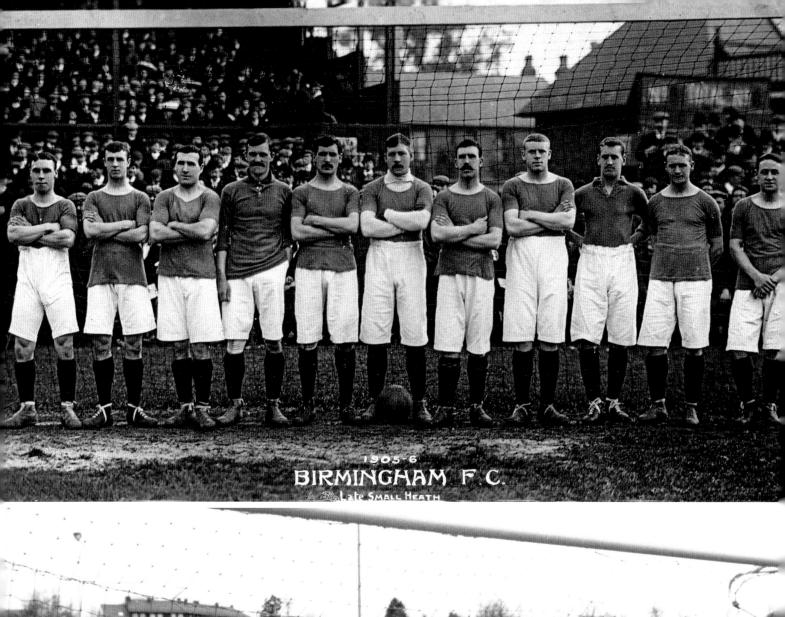

1905-6
BIRMINGHAM F.C.
Late Small Heath

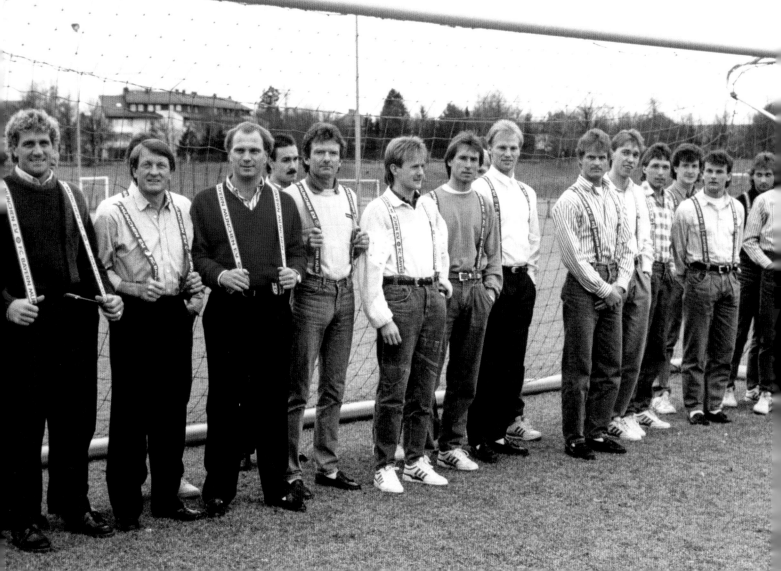

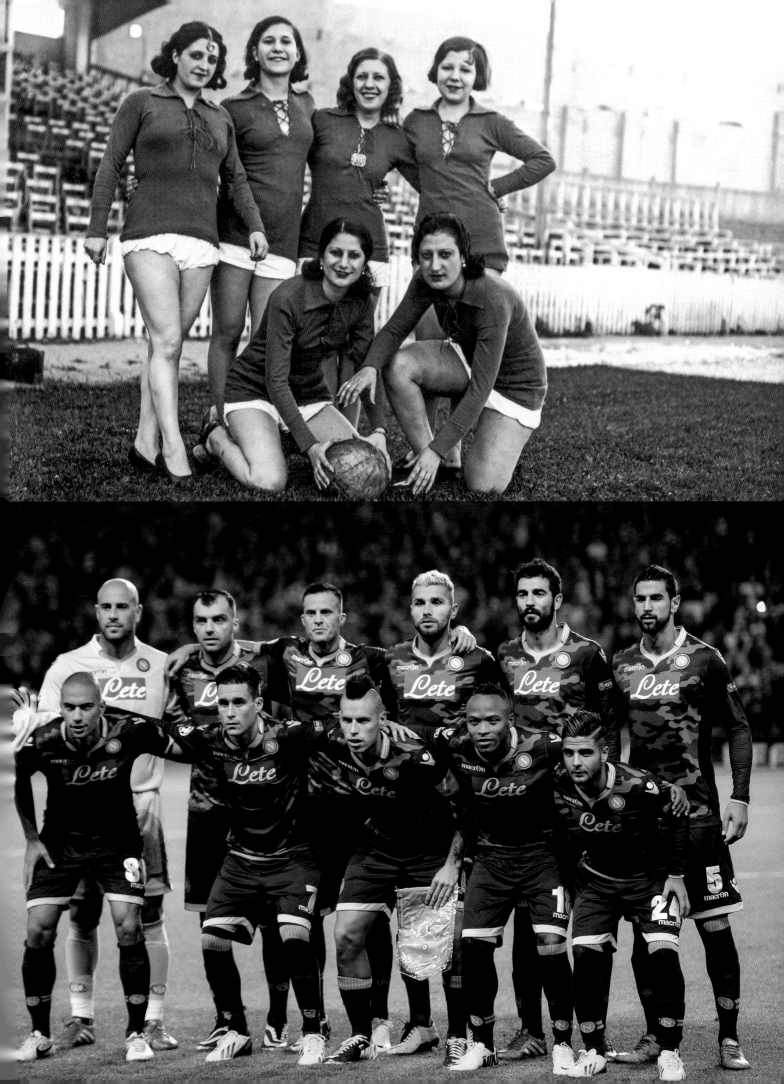

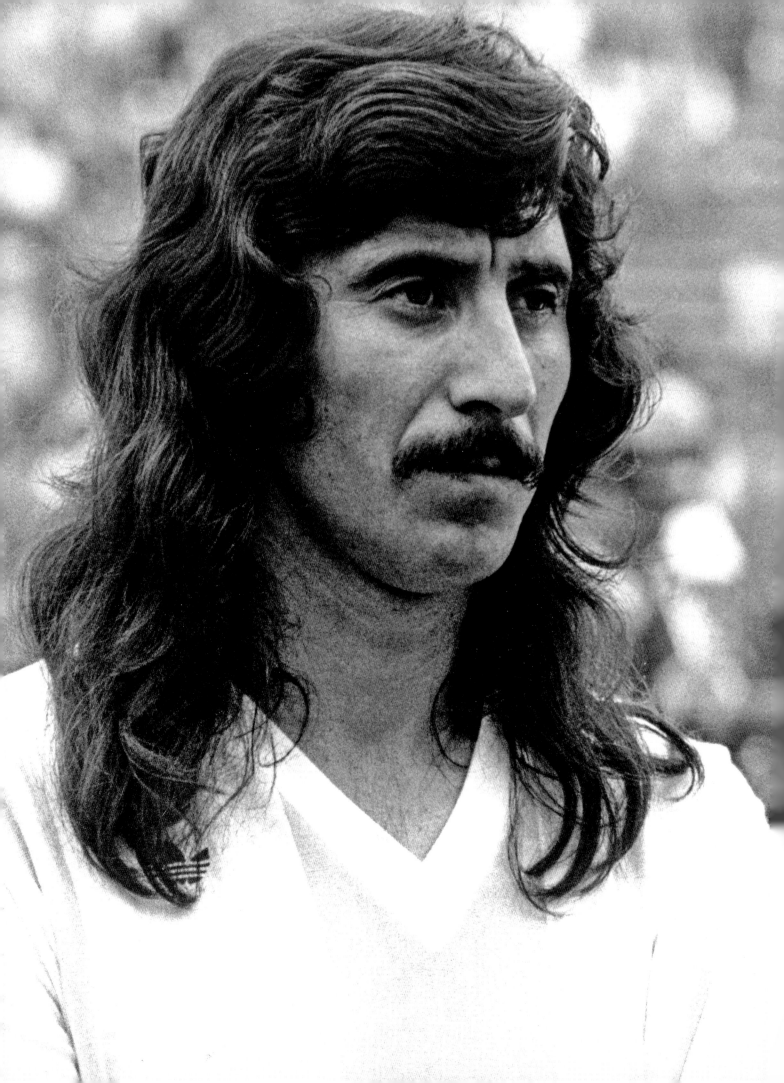

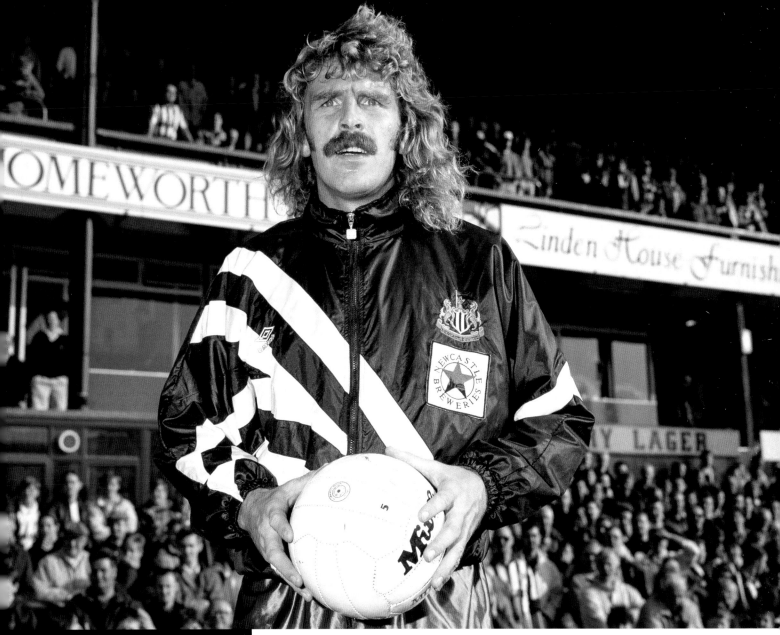

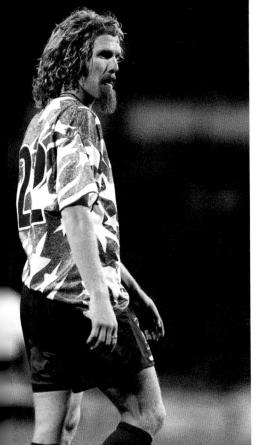

Hairstyle I: Rubén Hugo Ayala (left), Brian Kilcline (above) and Alexi Lalas (below) embrace the motto "The more the better". In this case – the more hair, the more irresistible the look. They would have had no chance with Daniel Passarella, Argentina's manager from 1994 to 1998: he dropped players from the team, if he thought their hair wasn't short enough. He tolerated, in his words, "no homosexuals" and "no women" in the team. Quoting John McEnroe, "You can't be serious, man!"

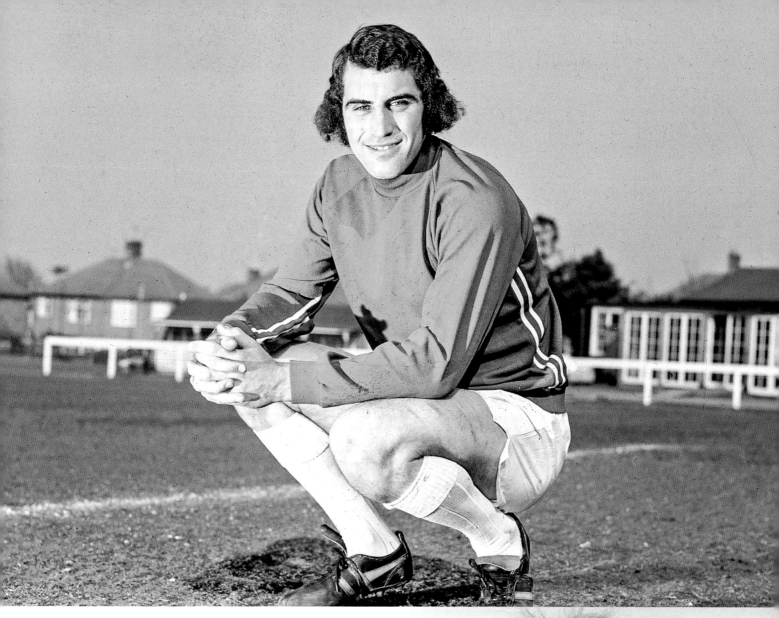

Hairstyle II: In a friendly match against England in 1995, Colombia's keeper René Higuita saved a shot not with his hands, but with his heels – a "scorpion kick". The flabbergasted British sports commentator Des Lynam remarked, "Goalkeepers are crazy!" They're also incredibly style-conscious, as proven by Peter Shilton (above, 1969), Norbert Nigbur (below, 1973) and Uwe Kamps (right, 1984).

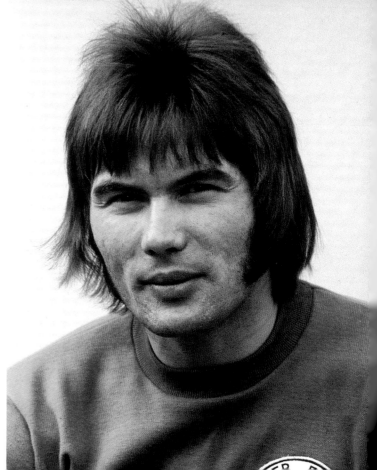

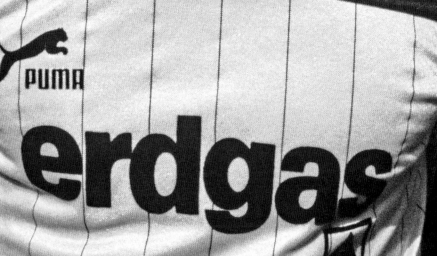

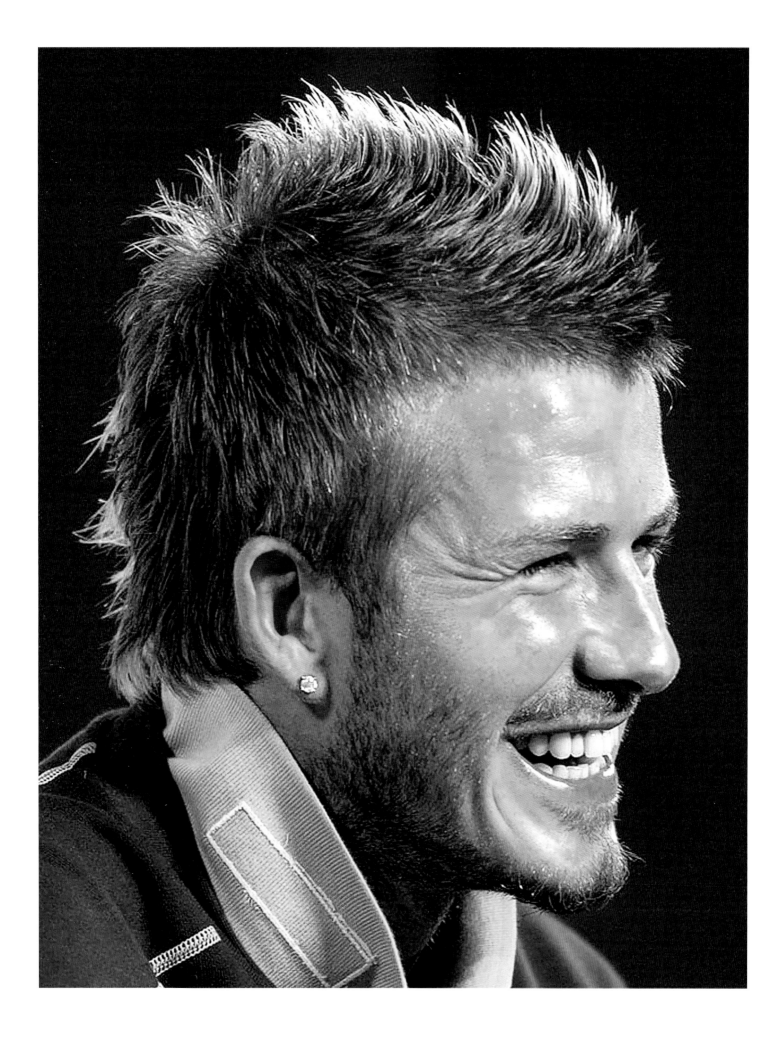

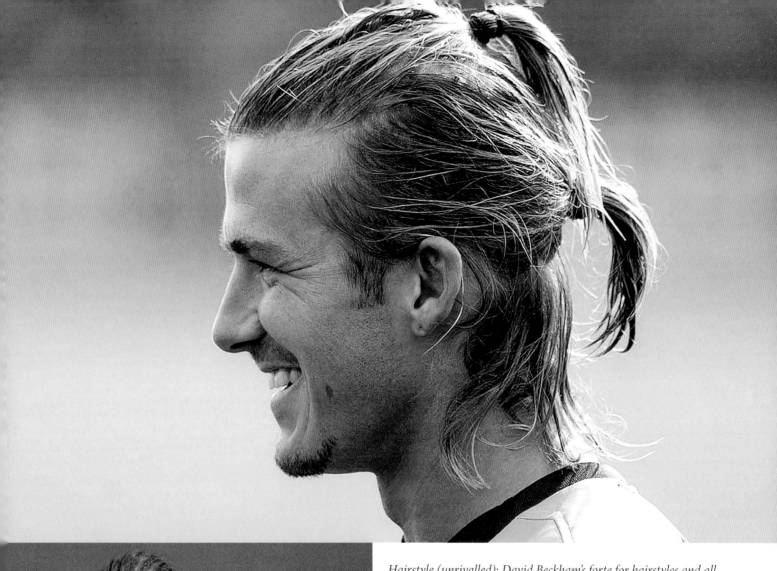

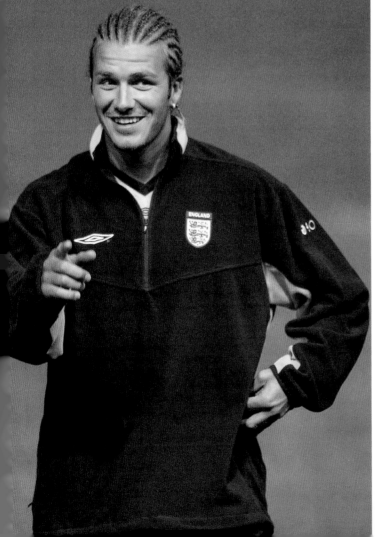

Hairstyle (unrivalled): David Beckham's forte for hairstyles and all other fashion matters (left: May 2002, above: August 2003, below: May 2003) puts him in a league of his own. Only his daughter Harper questions his reputation as a style-icon with model physique. In a US talk show, David revealed his little girl had said to him, "Daddy, I love you so much but I don't like that you're so chubby!"

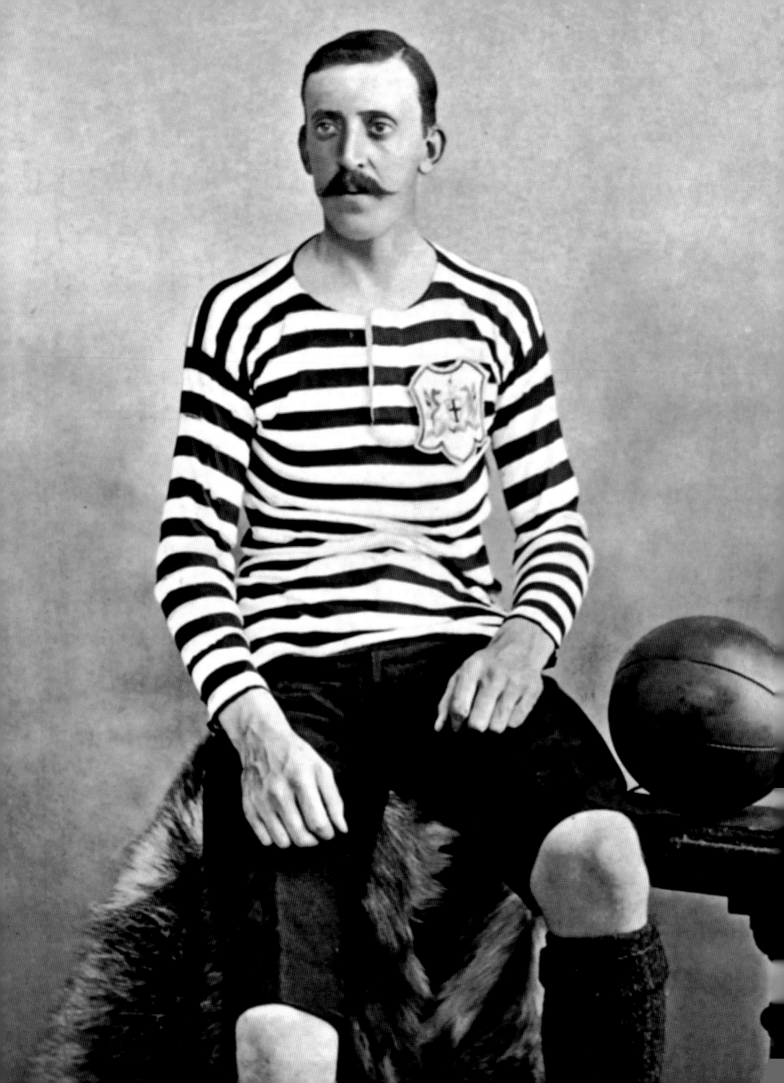

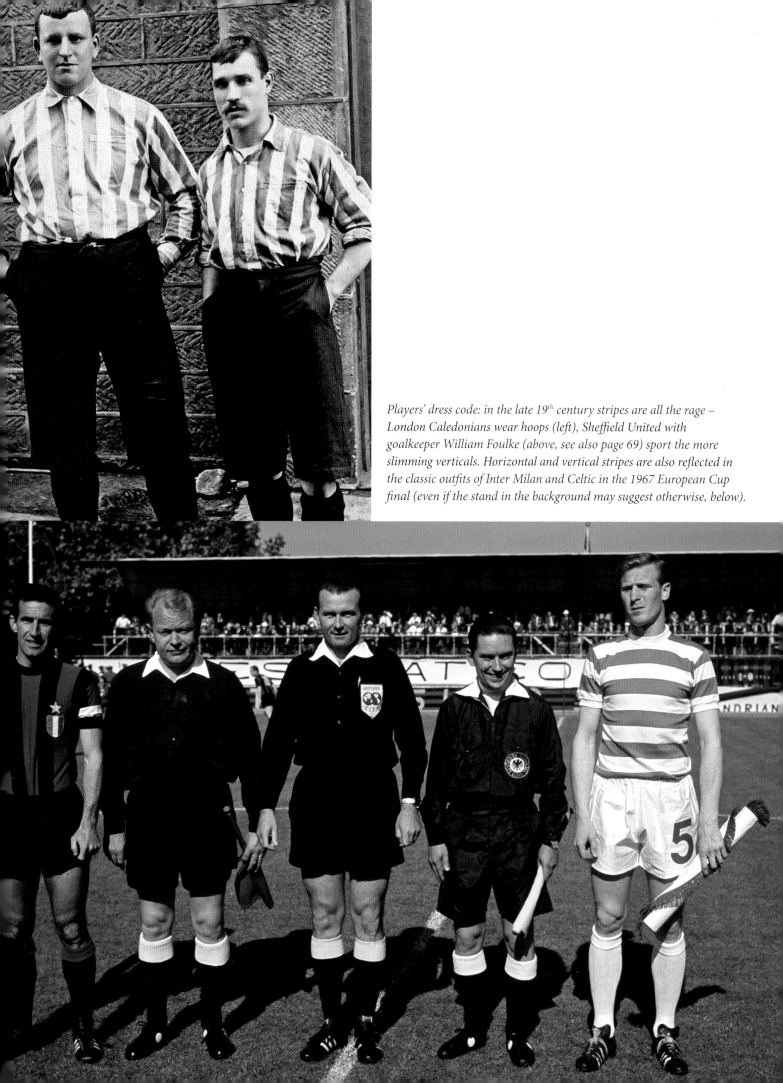

Players' dress code: in the late 19th century stripes are all the rage – London Caledonians wear hoops (left), Sheffield United with goalkeeper William Foulke (above, see also page 69) sport the more slimming verticals. Horizontal and vertical stripes are also reflected in the classic outfits of Inter Milan and Celtic in the 1967 European Cup final (even if the stand in the background may suggest otherwise, below).

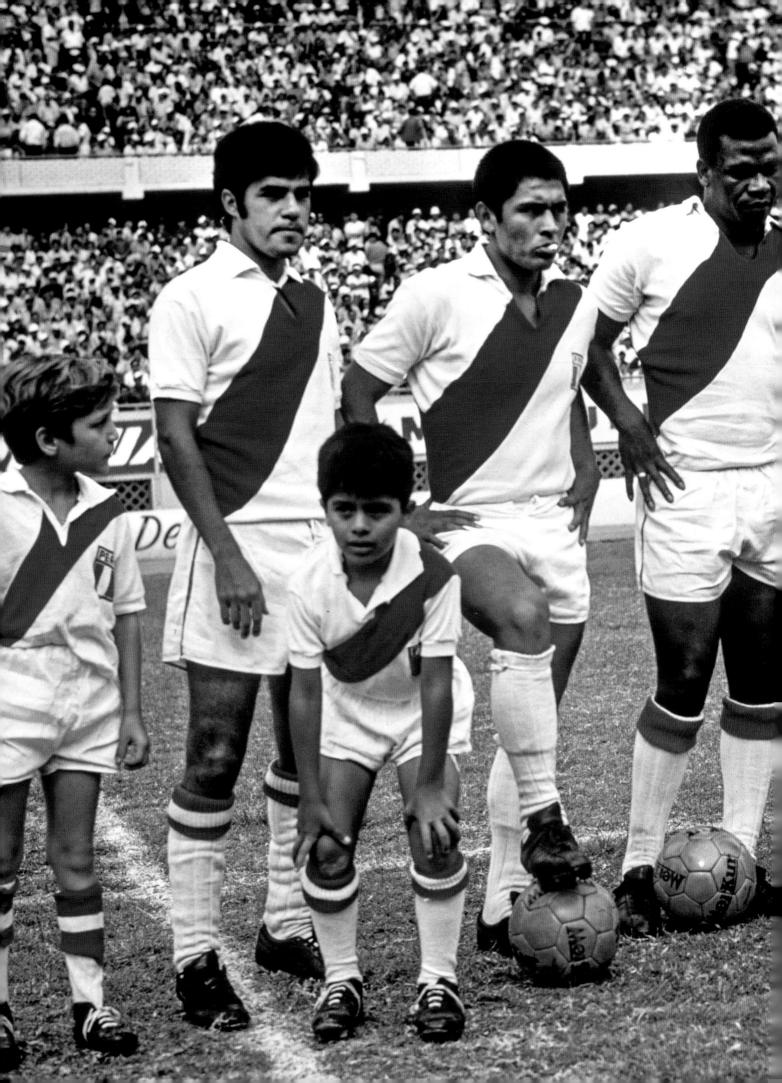

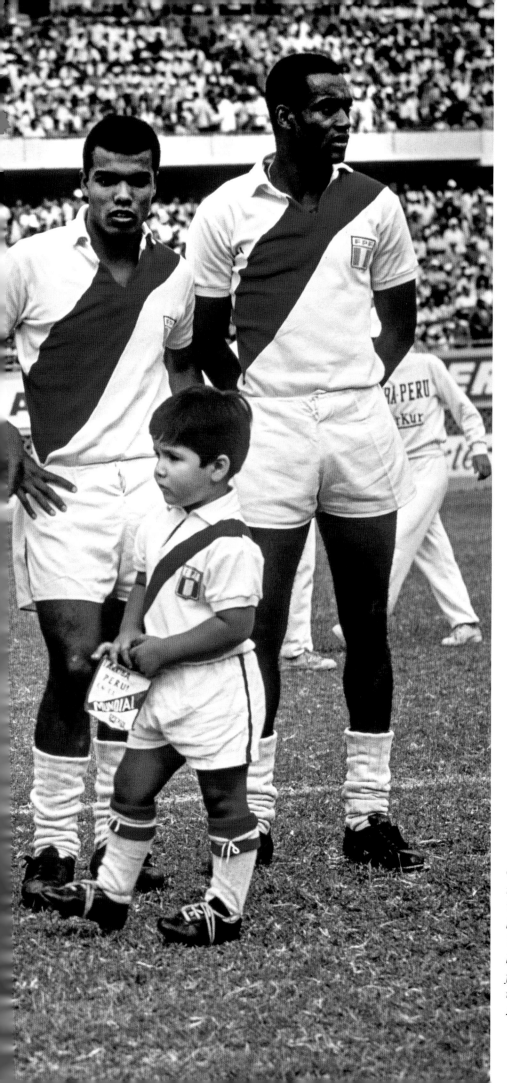

Classic: like royalty, Peru's players appear in their legendary white jerseys with red sashes. The team and their young escorts not only looked fabulous in this kit in 1970: at the World Cup in Mexico the Peruvian team, led by free-scoring Teófilo Cubillas (second from right), achieved its biggest success in reaching the quarter-final, where they lost 2-4 to Brazil.

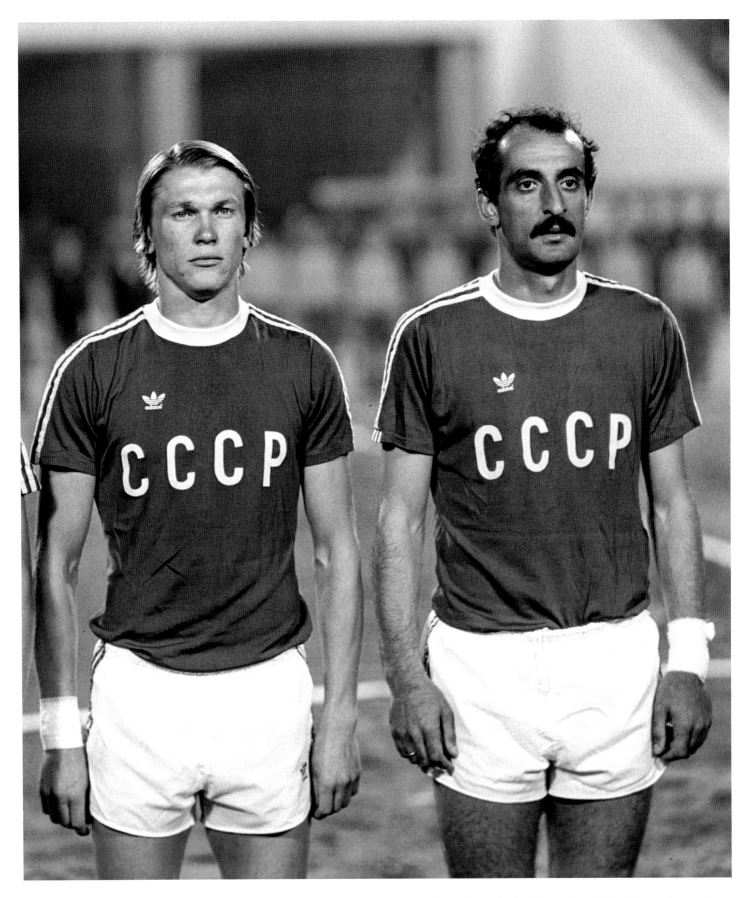

No frills: in the 1970s, the USSR team (above: Oleg Blochin and David Kipiani) and Schalke 04 (right: Klaus Fischer) also favour shirts with plain designs. Only the collar on Fischer's shirt revealed a trace of the typical love of extravagance back then.

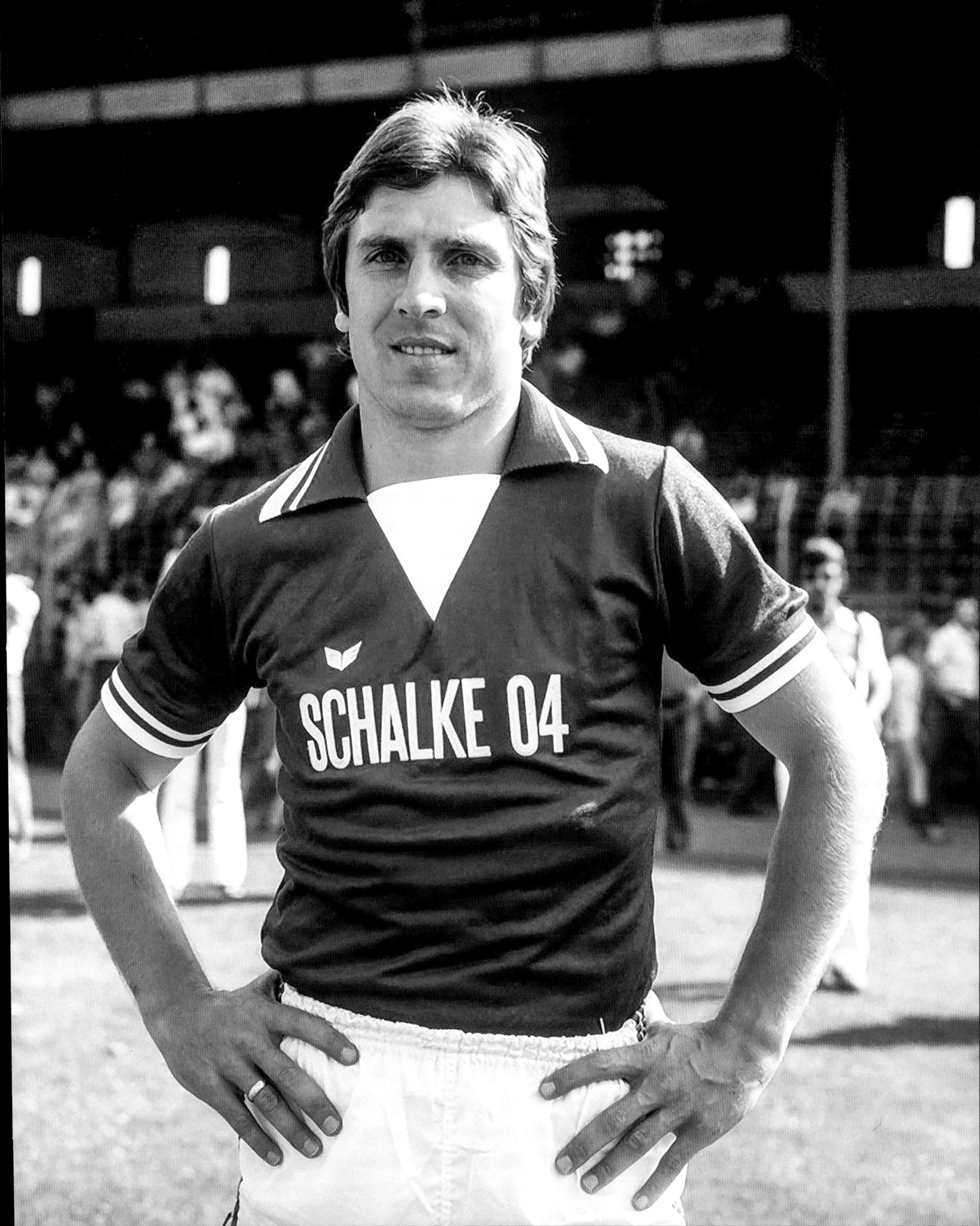
SCHALKE 04

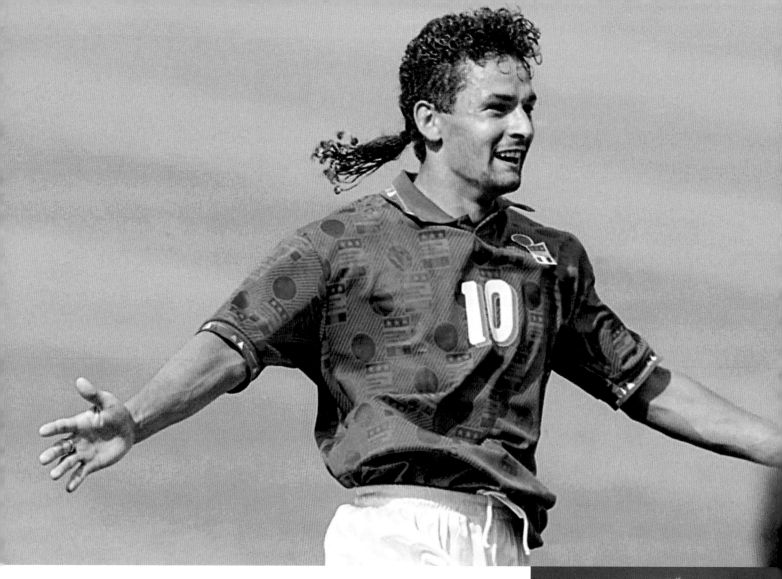

Fashion faux pas: the 1990s were a tricky time for fashion trends – lots of luminous colours, the grunge look and drainpipes. Roberto Baggio's hairstyle (above), Jorge Campos's look (right) and the rainbow strip of Bochum (bottom) – you've seen enough. Baggio, one of the best players in an otherwise colourless 1994 World Cup, has a sensible motto: "You shouldn't take life too seriously and certainly not football."

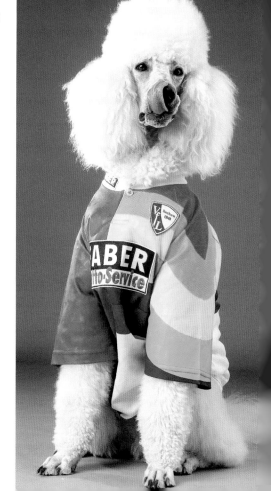

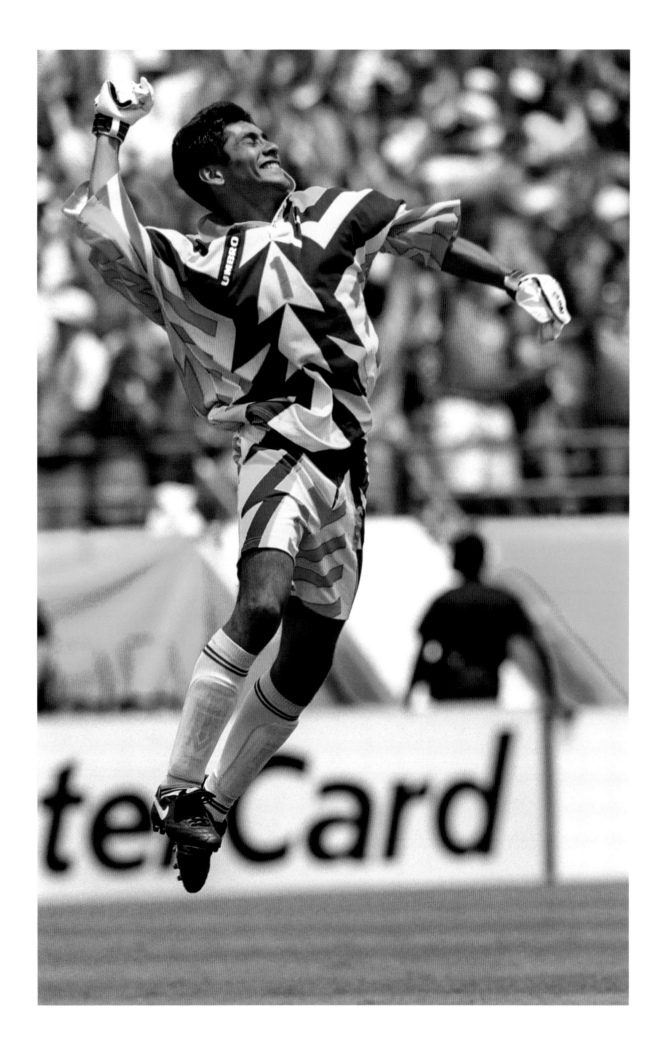

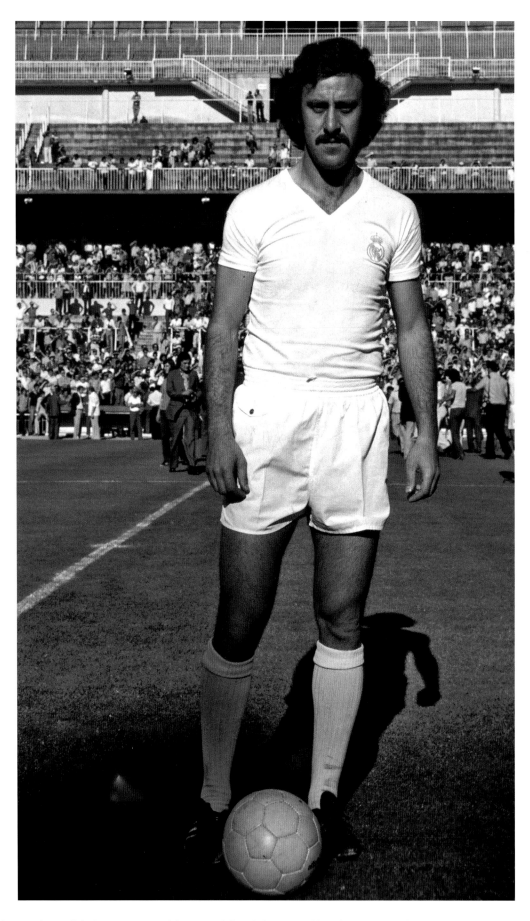

Timeless: Real's white outlasts all fashions. Vicente del Bosque (above), later World and European Champion as Spain's manager, as well as style icon Günter Netzer (right) cut dashing figures in white. The myth of Real is explained by the numerous stars who played for "Los Blancos" from Di Stéfano to Zidane – as well as by the writer, Javier Marías, in his anthology Salvajes y sentimentales *(Savageness and Sentiments: Football Letters).*

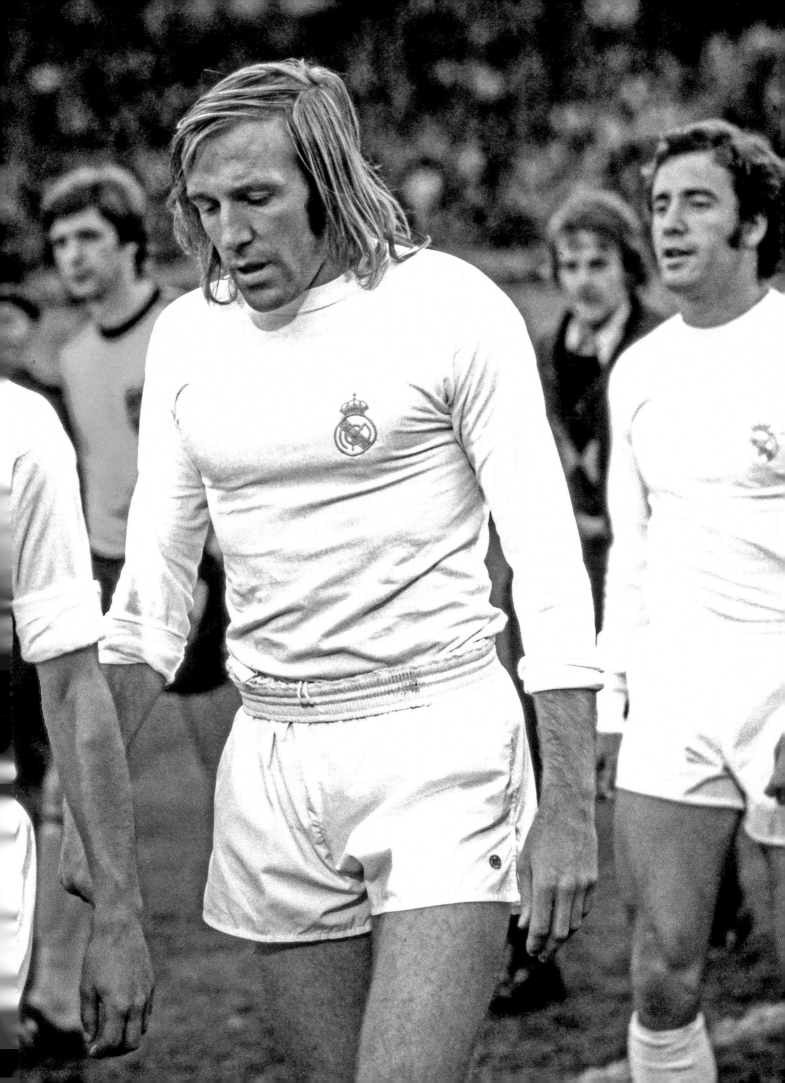

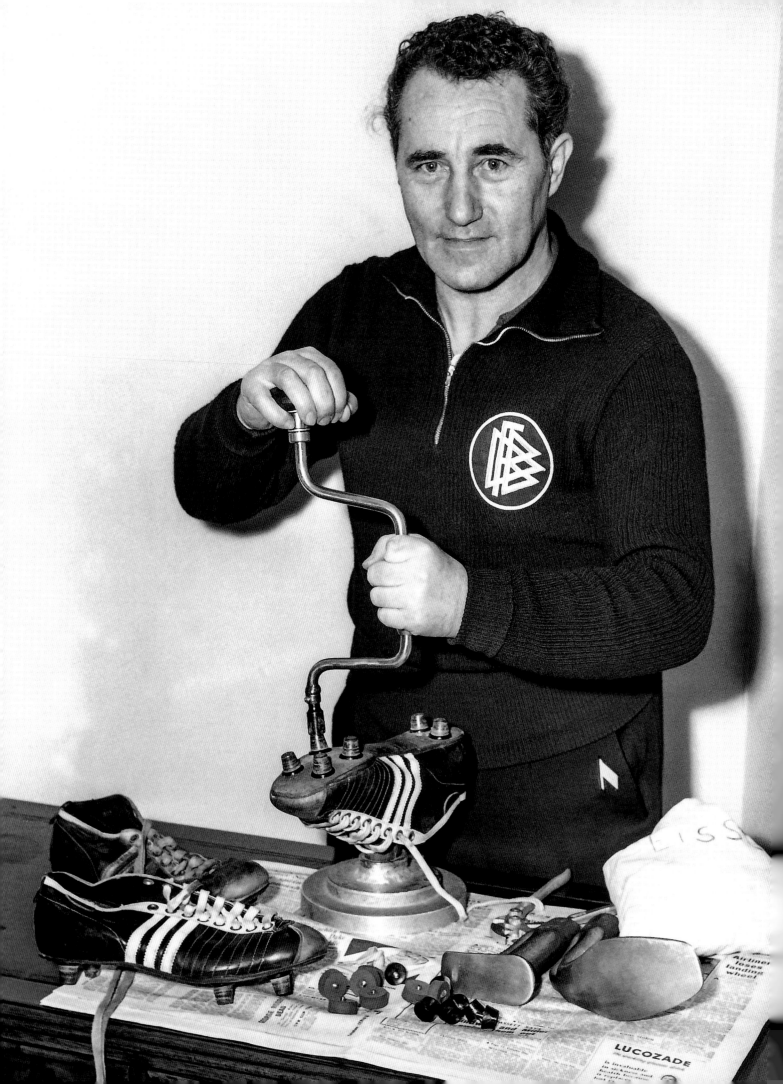

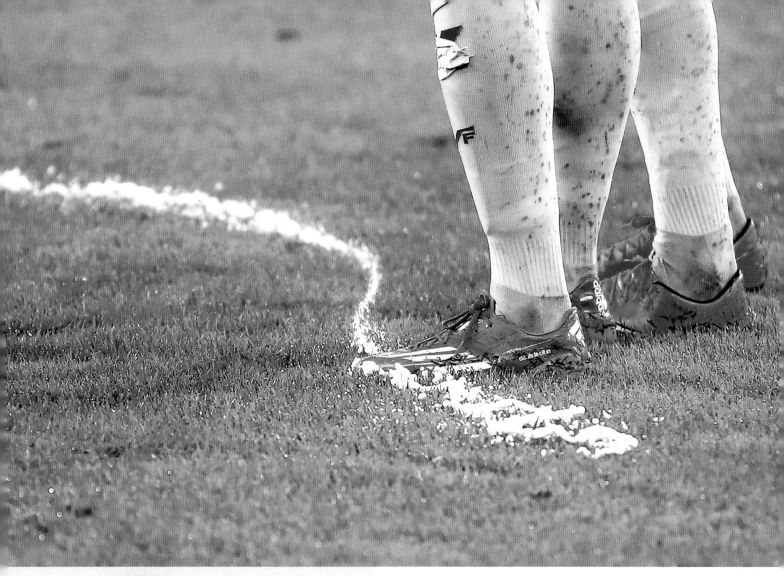

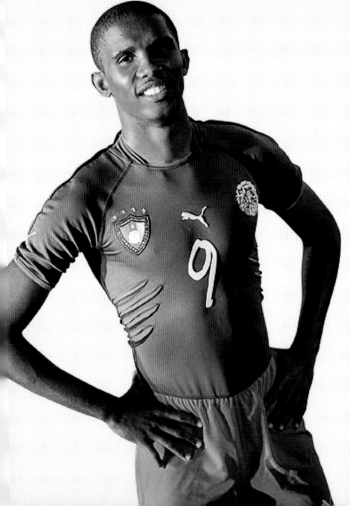

Brotherly war: in the 1920s, when Adolf Dassler (left) began making sports shoes with his brother, Rudolf, it was hardly predictable how things would turn out. Firstly, the high-tech 21st century footwear which footballers nowadays ply their trade in, was unimaginable at the time (above); and secondly, it was impossible to foresee the battle of the brands that would emerge, when Adolf (Adidas) and Rudolf (Puma) started competing against each other. A mere chapter in history: Puma's one-piece kit (aka Cameroon UniQT) for Cameroon, worn by Samuel Eto'o in 2004 (below), which was banned by FIFA. Eto'o's comment, "A totally absurd episode. If Adidas had designed our kit, nothing would have happened."

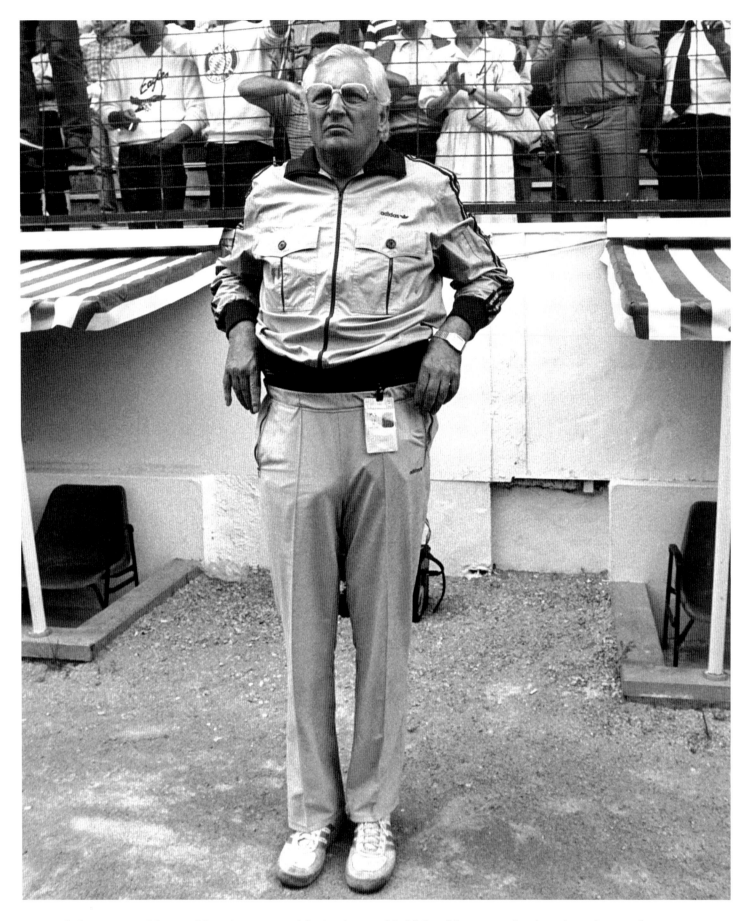

Dress code for managers: Manager Magazin *commented during the 2014 World Cup, "the manager's technical area has now become a catwalk". Well-dressed personalities like Pep Guardiola or Roberto Mancini (right) have set new style trends for the dugout. Back in 1982 Germany's manager, Jupp Derwall, also made quite an effort to ensure the correct fit of hair and trousers.*

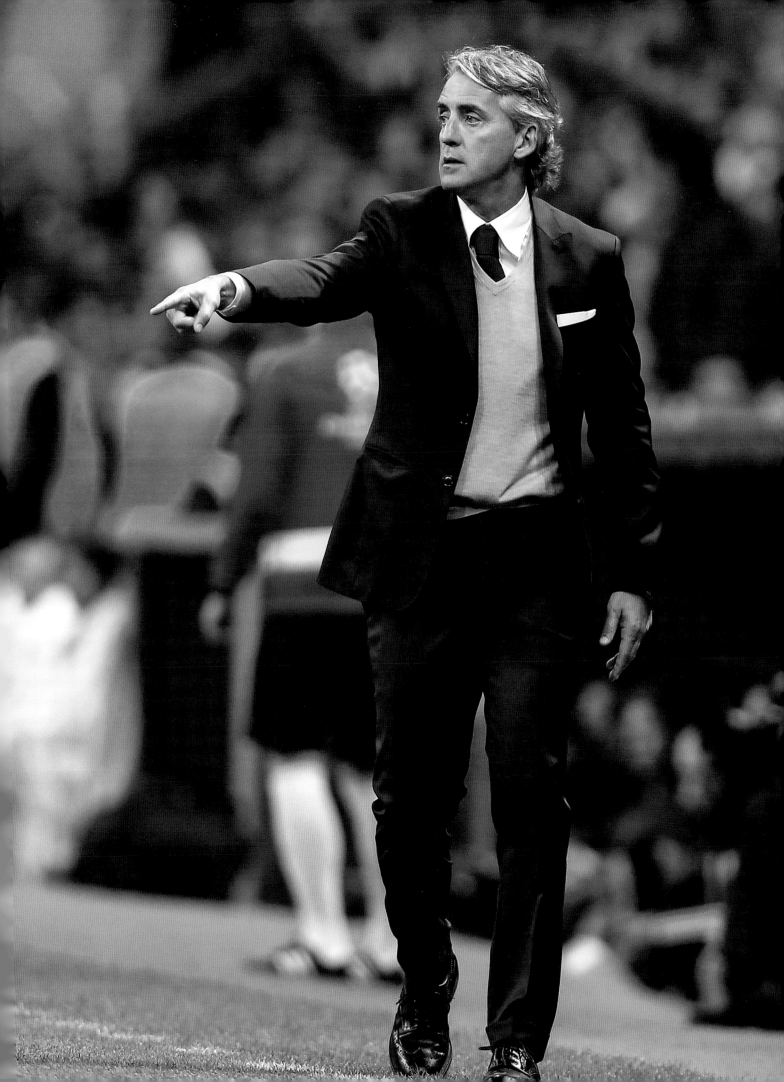

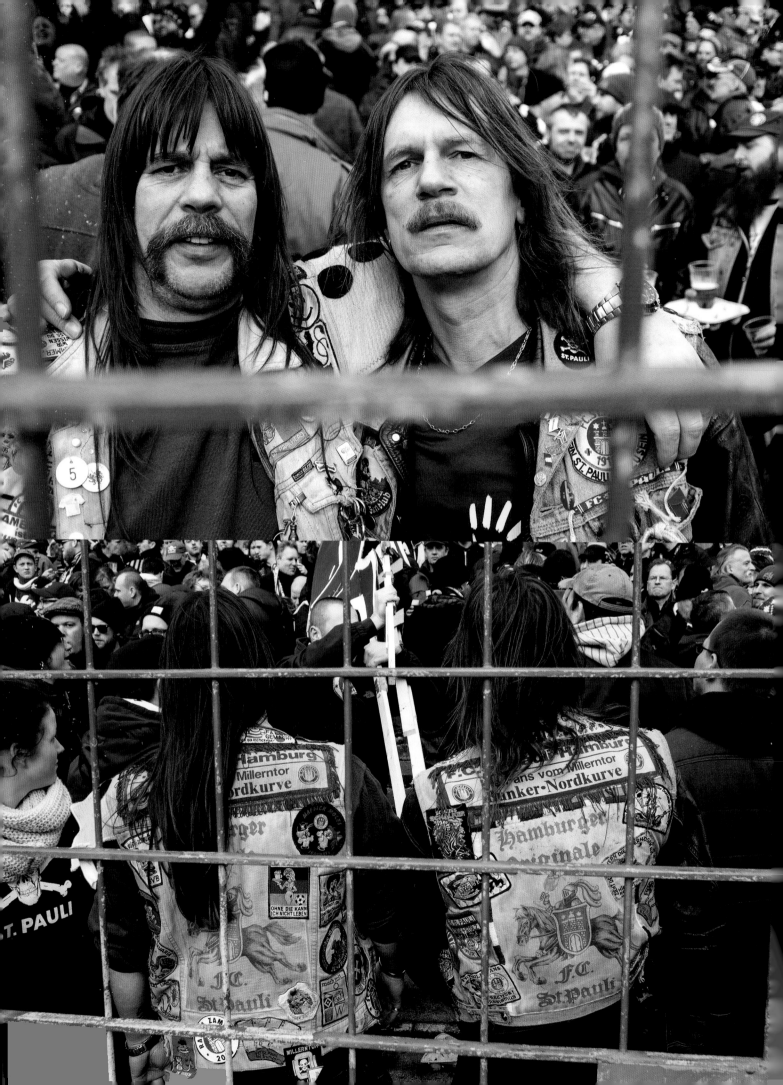

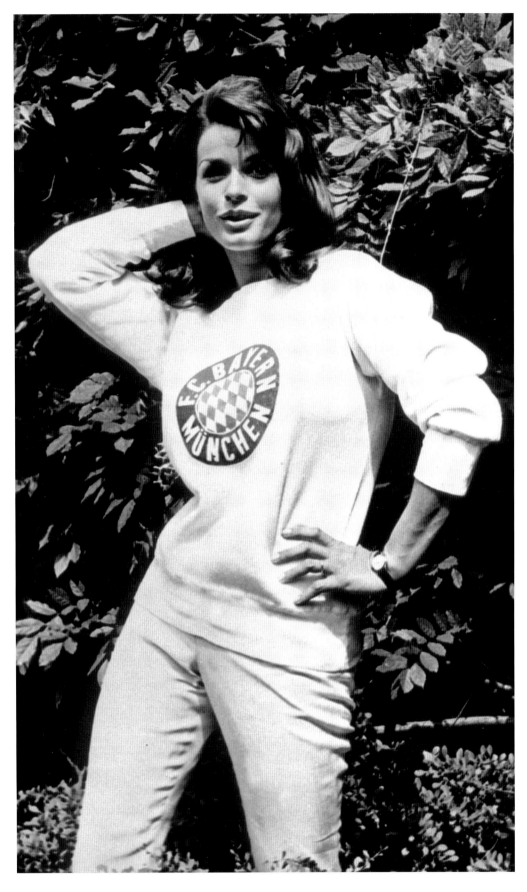

Dress code for fans: either in classic cut-off denim jackets (like the St Pauli supporters left) and with apparel from the club merchandise shop (like German actress Senta Berger above)…

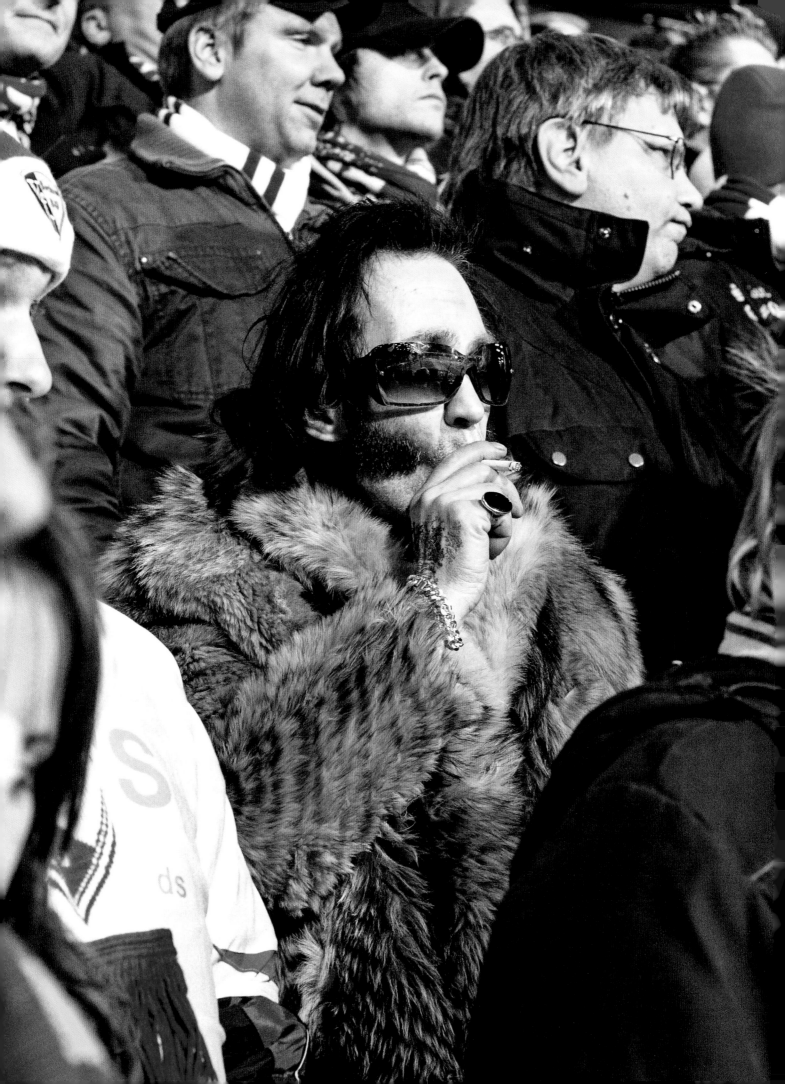

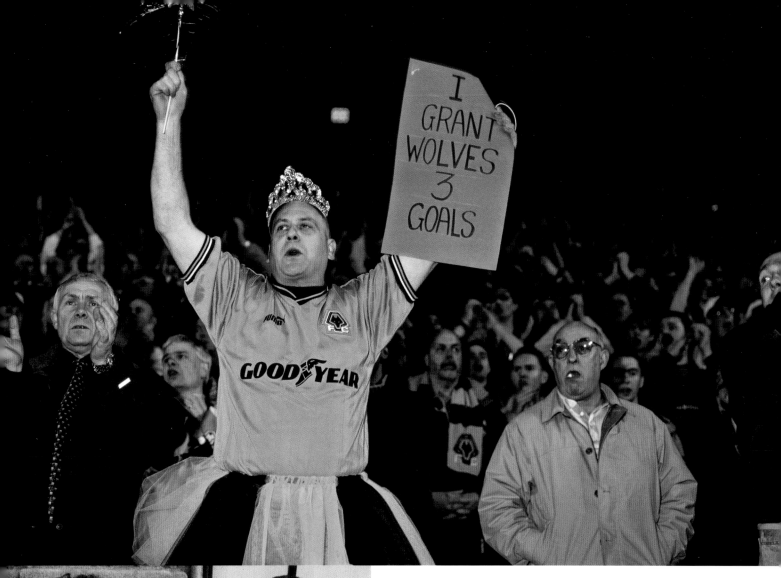

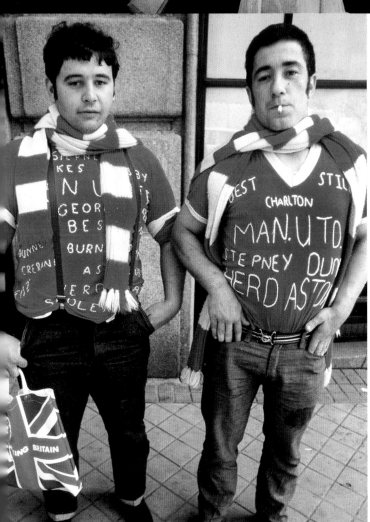

…or unconventional as an Elvis tribute act (left), as a fairy granting Wolverhampton Wanderers three goals (above) and with home-made team shirts (below); Gerrit Starczewski said of the Bochum "Elvis", "He often stood in the East stand. That evening Bochum was playing the derby against Schalke. Elvis stood still and smoked the whole time, but when Bochum scored, he positively exploded and danced in 'Jailhouse Rock' style."

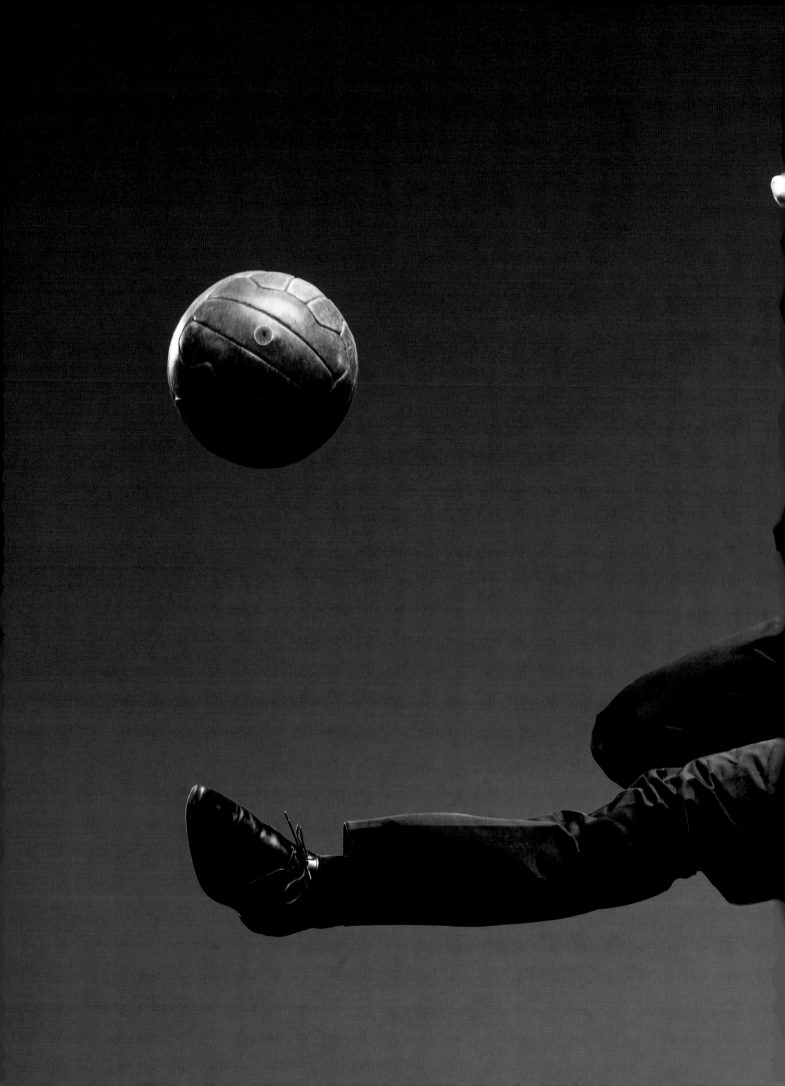

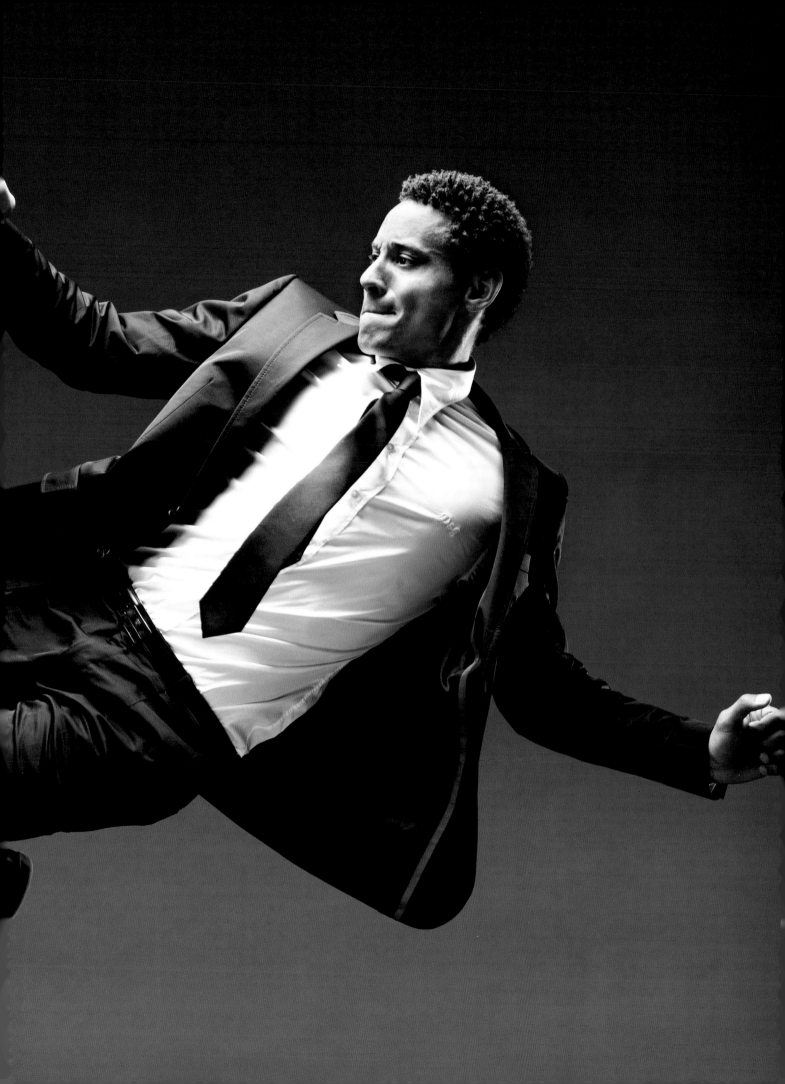

Calvin Klein
underwear

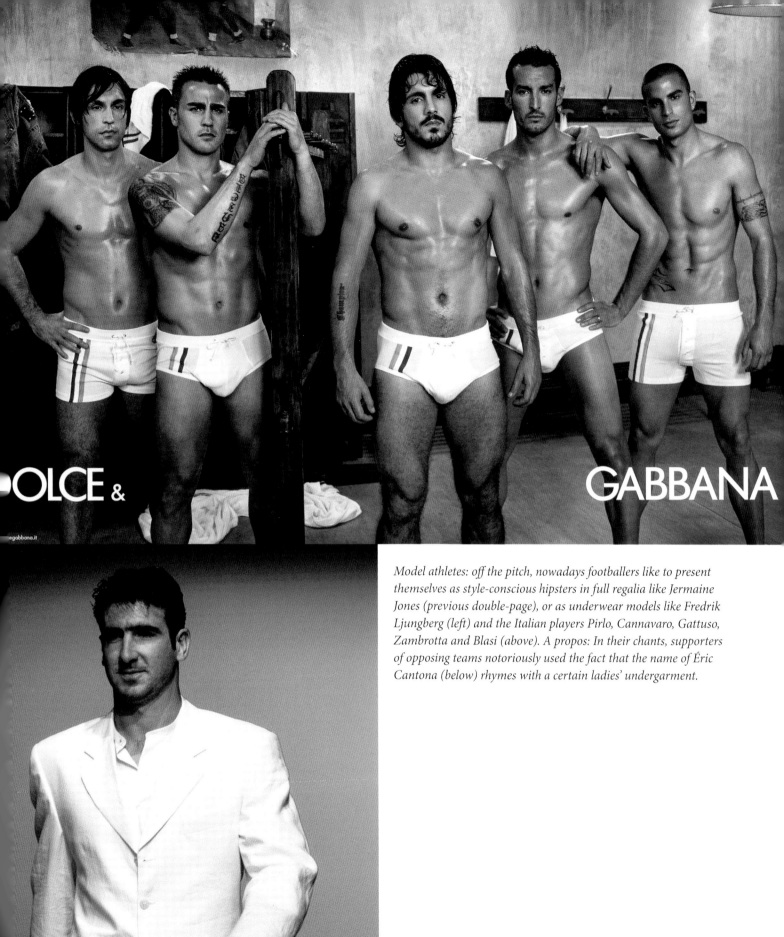

DOLCE &

GABBANA

egabbana.it

Model athletes: off the pitch, nowadays footballers like to present themselves as style-conscious hipsters in full regalia like Jermaine Jones (previous double-page), or as underwear models like Fredrik Ljungberg (left) and the Italian players Pirlo, Cannavaro, Gattuso, Zambrotta and Blasi (above). A propos: In their chants, supporters of opposing teams notoriously used the fact that the name of Éric Cantona (below) rhymes with a certain ladies' undergarment.

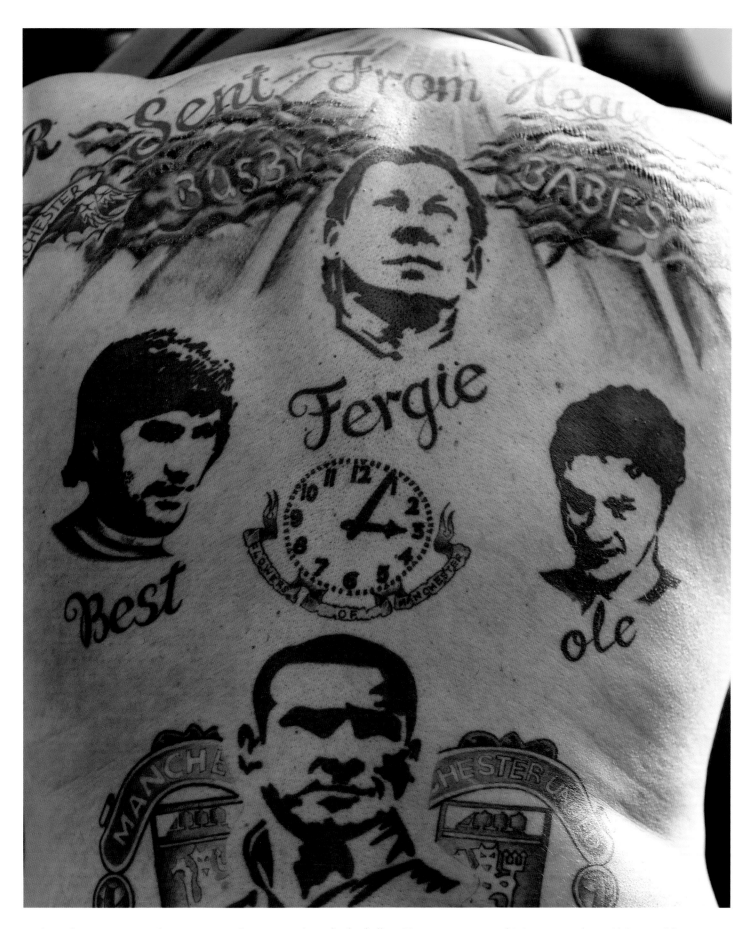

Body art bestows wings: today, tattoos are almost compulsory for footballers. Not everyone turns this into an aesthetic celebration like Frenchman Djibril Cissé (right). While Cissé's back shows him in the guise of an angel, the Manchester United fan above honours club legends like Alex Ferguson and Ole Gunnar Solskjær as heavenly messengers by tattooing their images on his back.

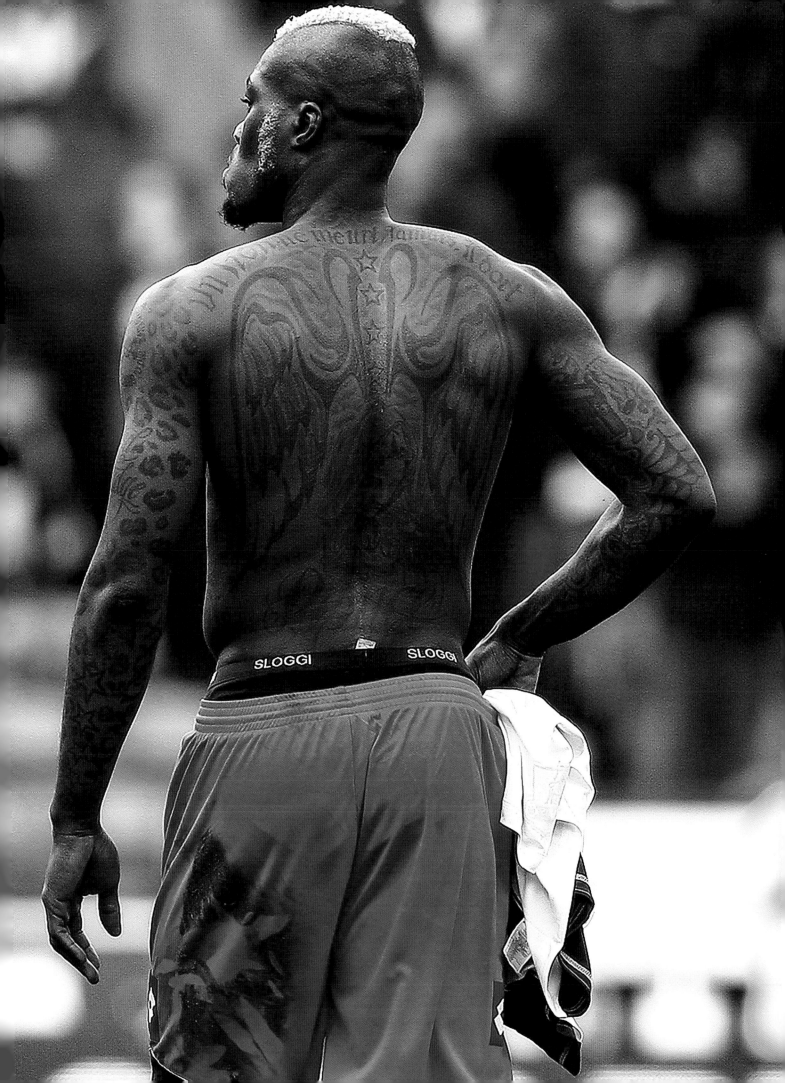

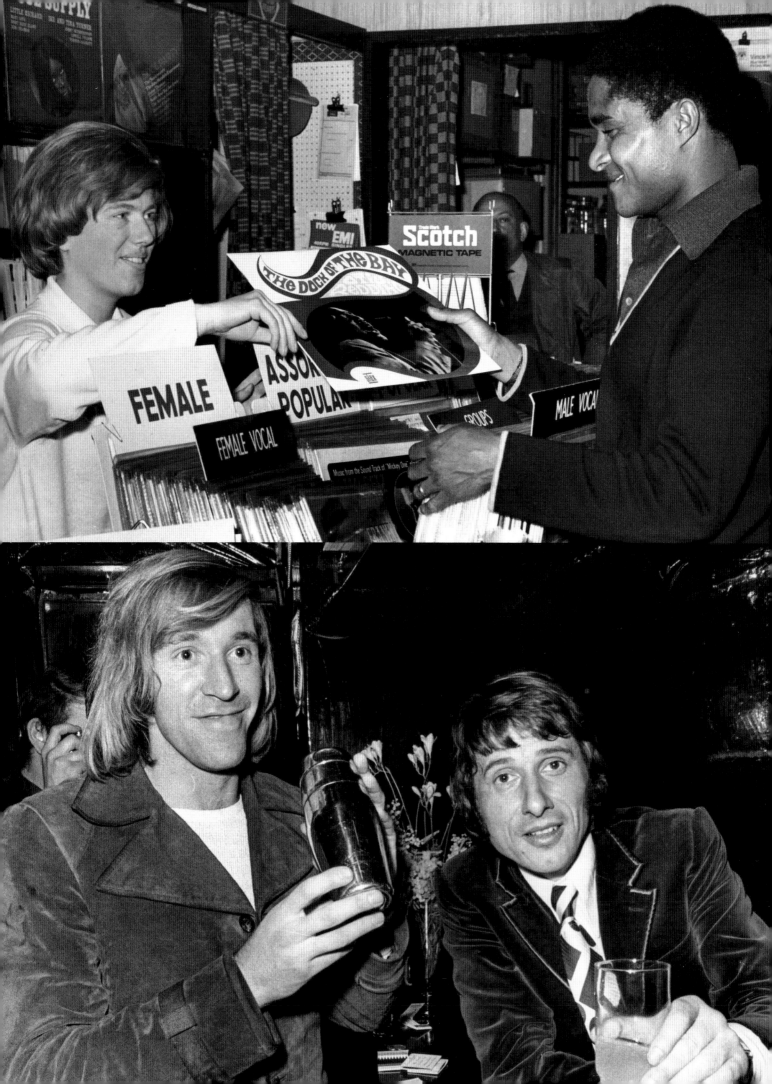

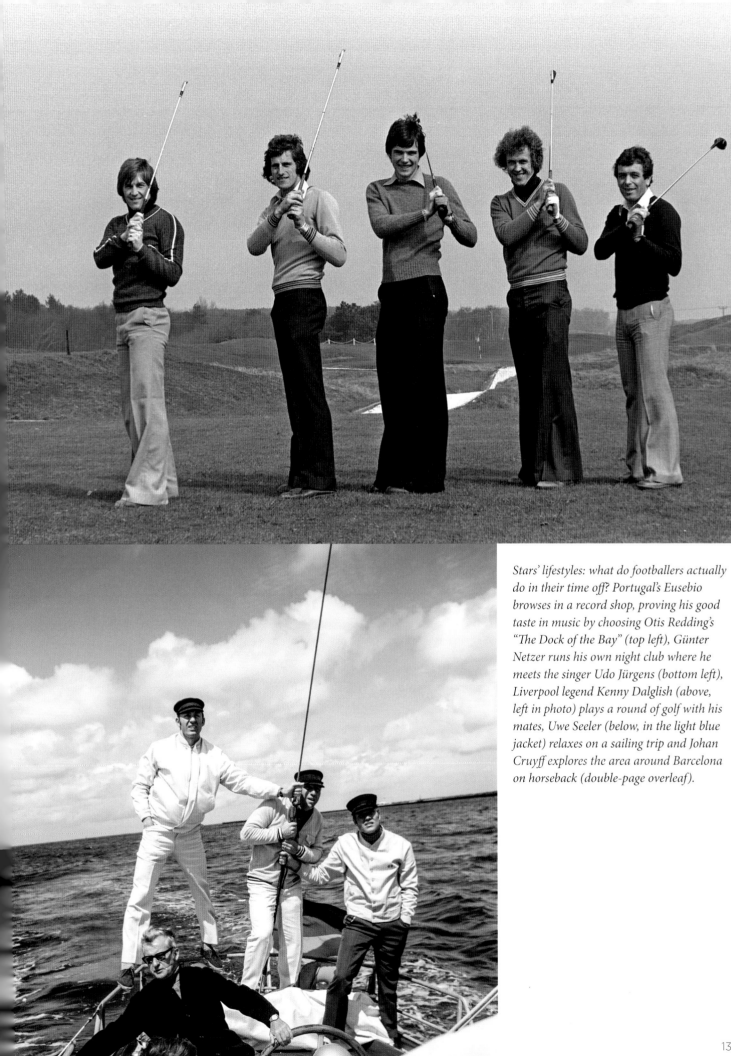

Stars' lifestyles: what do footballers actually do in their time off? Portugal's Eusebio browses in a record shop, proving his good taste in music by choosing Otis Redding's "The Dock of the Bay" (top left), Günter Netzer runs his own night club where he meets the singer Udo Jürgens (bottom left), Liverpool legend Kenny Dalglish (above, left in photo) plays a round of golf with his mates, Uwe Seeler (below, in the light blue jacket) relaxes on a sailing trip and Johan Cruyff explores the area around Barcelona on horseback (double-page overleaf).

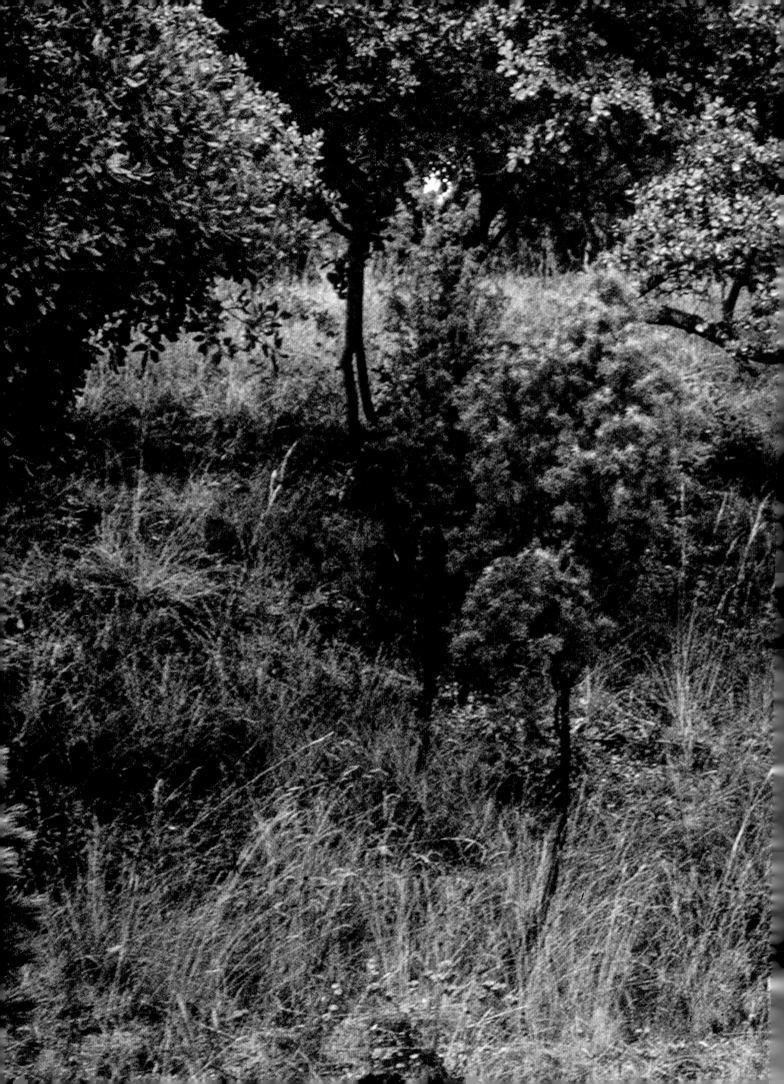

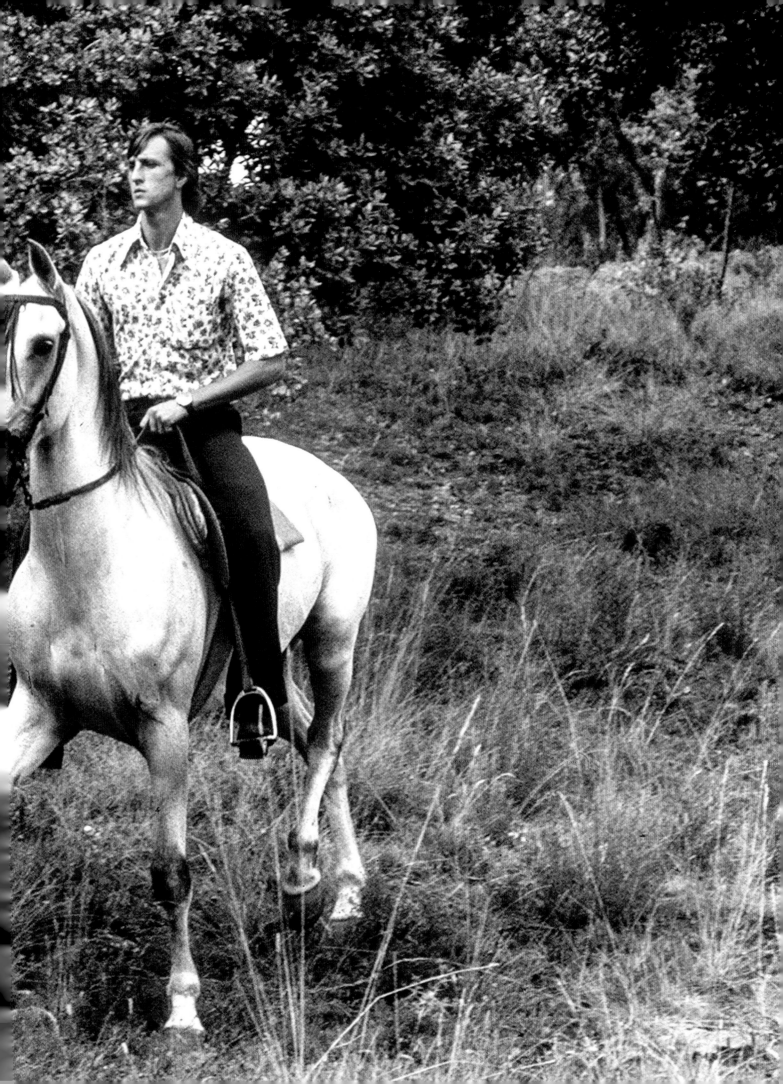

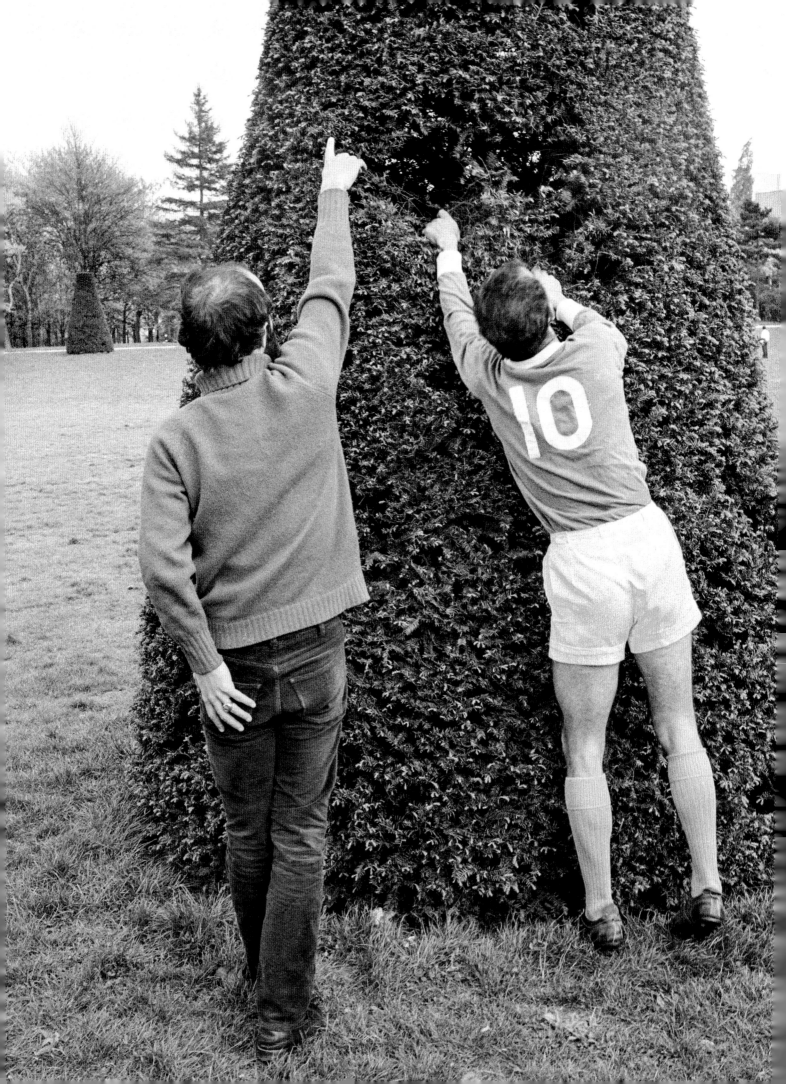

ART

The legendary manager of London's Arsenal football club, Arsène Wenger, once said, "Football is an art." It's not surprising that so many artists were mesmerized by this sport. The French philosopher and writer, Albert Camus, famously played in goal for his college club, Racing Universitaire Algérois. He coined the beautiful phrase, "All that I know most surely about morality and obligations, I owe to football." Russian composer Dmitri Shostakovich passionately supported Zenit Leningrad. In 1929, Shostakovich composed the score for the ballet *The Golden Age* about a Soviet football team's journey to a Western city. Shostakovich, who even invited players from his favourite team back home for dinner and entertained them by playing the piano, regarded life without football as unimaginable. He once made the telling remark that, "Football is the only place in our country where you can say what you think of what you see." Also, in the era of players like Günter Netzer and Berti Vogts, one of the leading contemporary artists, Markus Lüpertz, was not merely a passionate supporter of Borussia Mönchengladbach. In 1966, he created a work called *Fußball* (*Football*).

The fine arts also played an important role in a number of World Cups. A series of posters commissioned for the 1982 World Cup finals in Spain revealed 15 designs overall, each created by different artists, and reflecting the individual venues. Joan Miró designed the famous official poster entitled *España*. Incidentally,

Raising the profile: famous photographers and artists have different ways of interpreting football, effectively improving its social standing. On the left, Magnum photographer Richard Kalvar gets this small selection started with a photograph taken in 1972.

Salvador Dalí paintings were awarded to three players during the 1982 World Cup. The tournament's top goal scorer (Italy's Paolo Rossi), the first goal scorer of this world cup (Belgium's Erwin Vandenbergh) and the player scoring Spain's first goal of the championship (Roberto López Ufarte), were each presented with an artwork by the surrealist painter in honour of their achievements.

Football and art also played a stylish one-two during the 2006 World Cup in Germany. André Heller's design of a Football Globe became a flagship for advertising the official artistic and cultural programme that was worth millions. A visitor pavilion housed countless film evenings and readings over a three-year period. A smaller version of the multimedia space with large displays and interactive touchscreens also toured the metropolises of Tokyo, Madrid, Milan, London and Paris. During the tournament the artist Harun Farocki also devised the remarkable documenta video installation, entitled *Deep Play*. On twelve screens, arranged so that real visualization alternates with abstract displays to showcase the Berlin World Cup final between France and Italy, the artist and filmmaker interpreted the well-known events of 9 July 2006 in an entirely innovative way. Pictures from the live feed cameras in and around the Olympic Stadium, diagrams of the players' movements and sequences from the game make the World Cup final a vivid experience of art.

The close rapport between artists and professional footballers has gradually evolved since the 1970s. During their time at New York Cosmos, Franz Beckenbauer, Pelé and Carlos Alberto frequented the city's most popular club, Studio 54, where they mingled with painters, rock stars and actors. Yet, they refused Andy Warhol's invitations to his legendary studio, The Factory. With hindsight, Franz Beckenbauer explained this as follows, "Art and football in those days had little in common. Art has a long history, but at that time football was just emerging on this world-class level." Nevertheless, in the years that followed Warhol created several works of Pop Art depicting Beckenbauer and other footballers.

Football's portrayal in film also gathered pace in the 1970s. The first footballer in a starring role was a Northern Irish legend, in Hellmuth Costard's film *Football as Never Before* (1970). In fact, for a full 90 minutes George Best merely had to do what he excelled at – namely, play football. During that time, eight 16-mm cameras constantly followed his every move. Best is the film's sole protagonist. Subsequently, numerous players like Uwe Seeler, Pelé, Bobby Moore, Roberto Boninsegna or Franz Beckenbauer appeared in cameo roles, until one *enfant terrible* of the professional game made the career switch from football to acting properly. The film *Looking for Eric* (2009) produced by British director Ken Loach pays homage to Manchester United's star Éric Cantona. The entertaining film is an extraordinary marriage of football and art.

Star photographers: Thomas Hoepker and Elliott Erwitt, also with Magnum, are among the most respected photographers of our time. Hoepker's photo (pp. 144/145) shows children in 1963 playing with a football on the western side of the Berlin Wall. Erwitt's photograph (pp. 146/147) was created in 2005 in Bahia, Brazil.

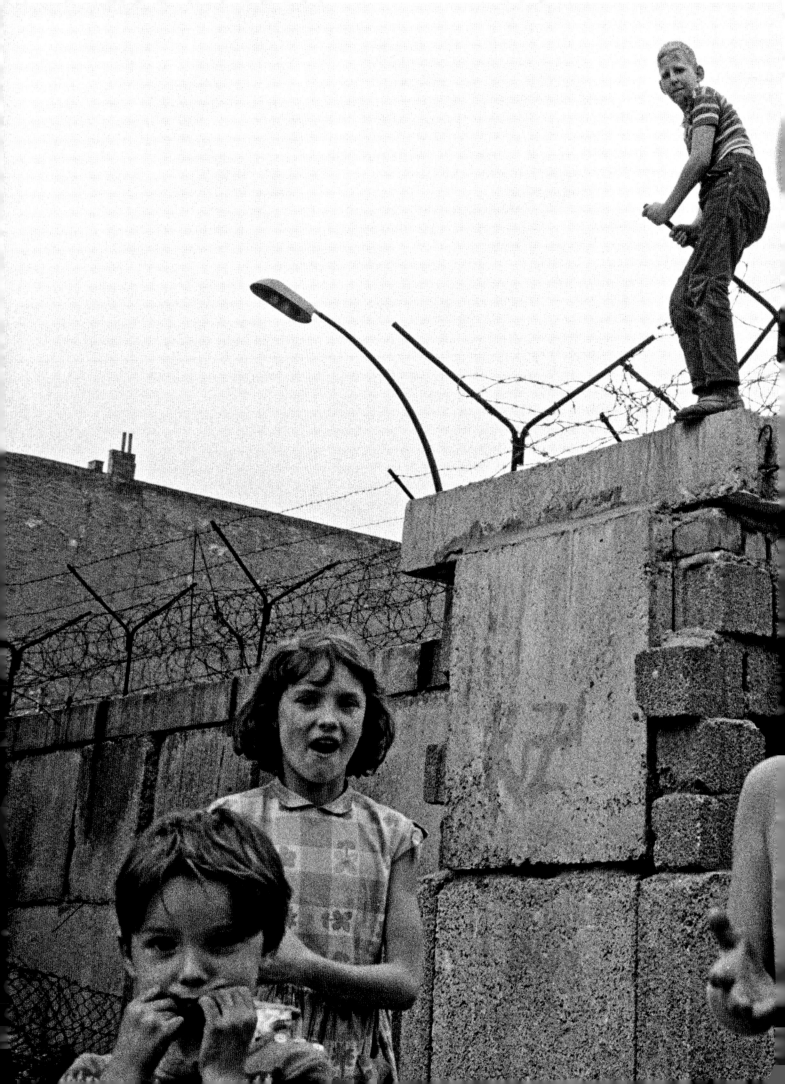

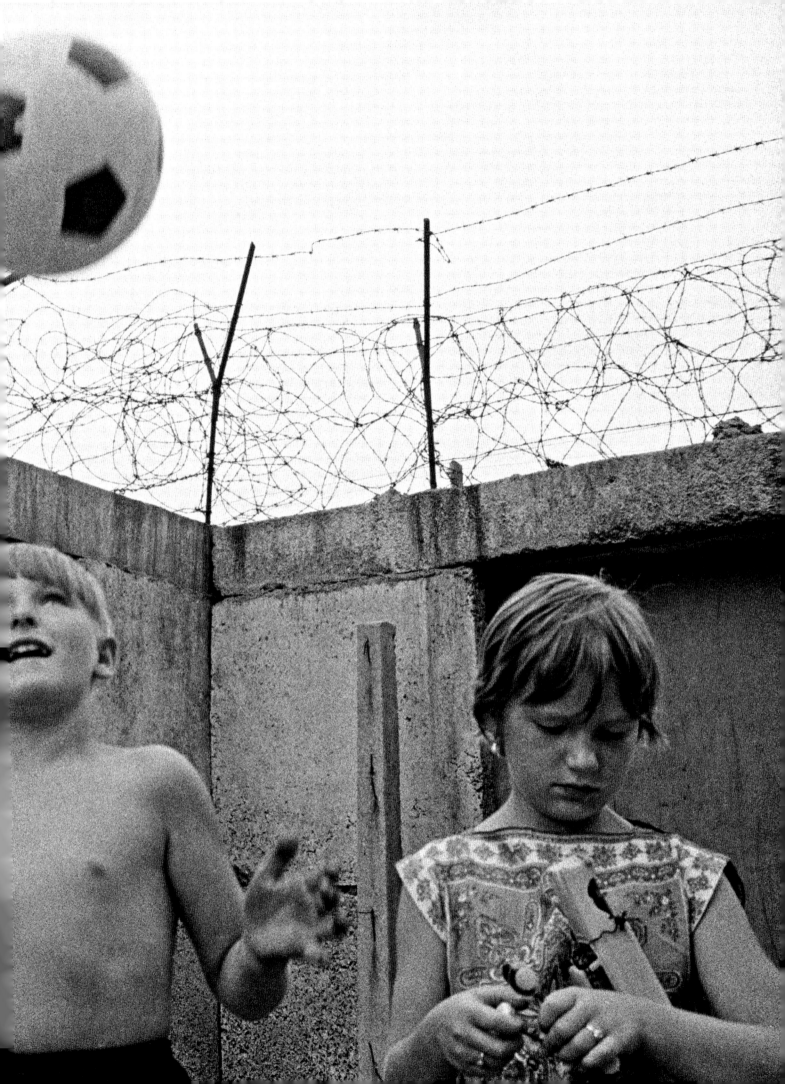

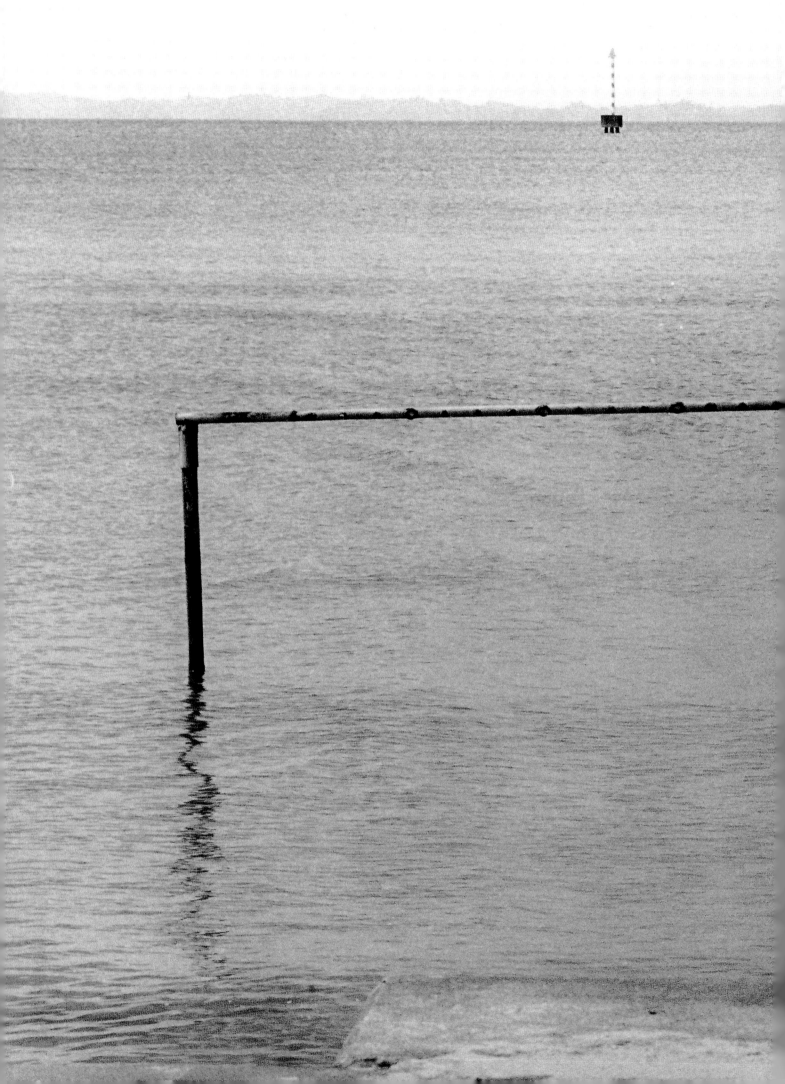

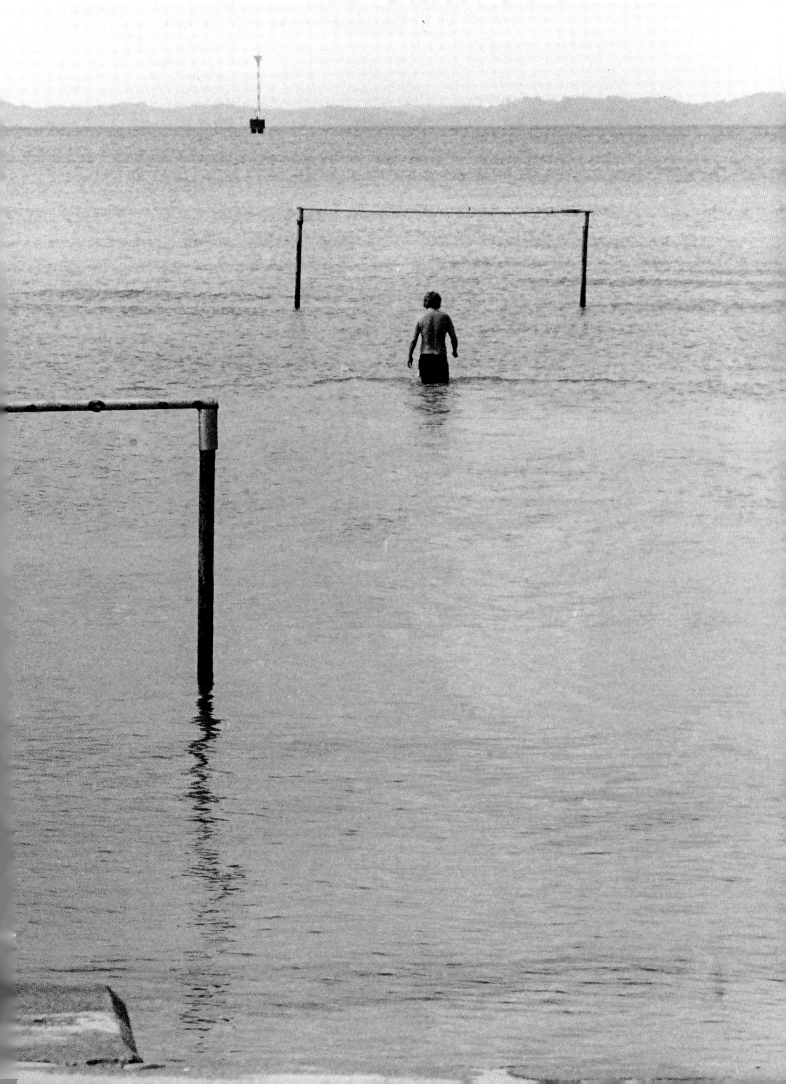

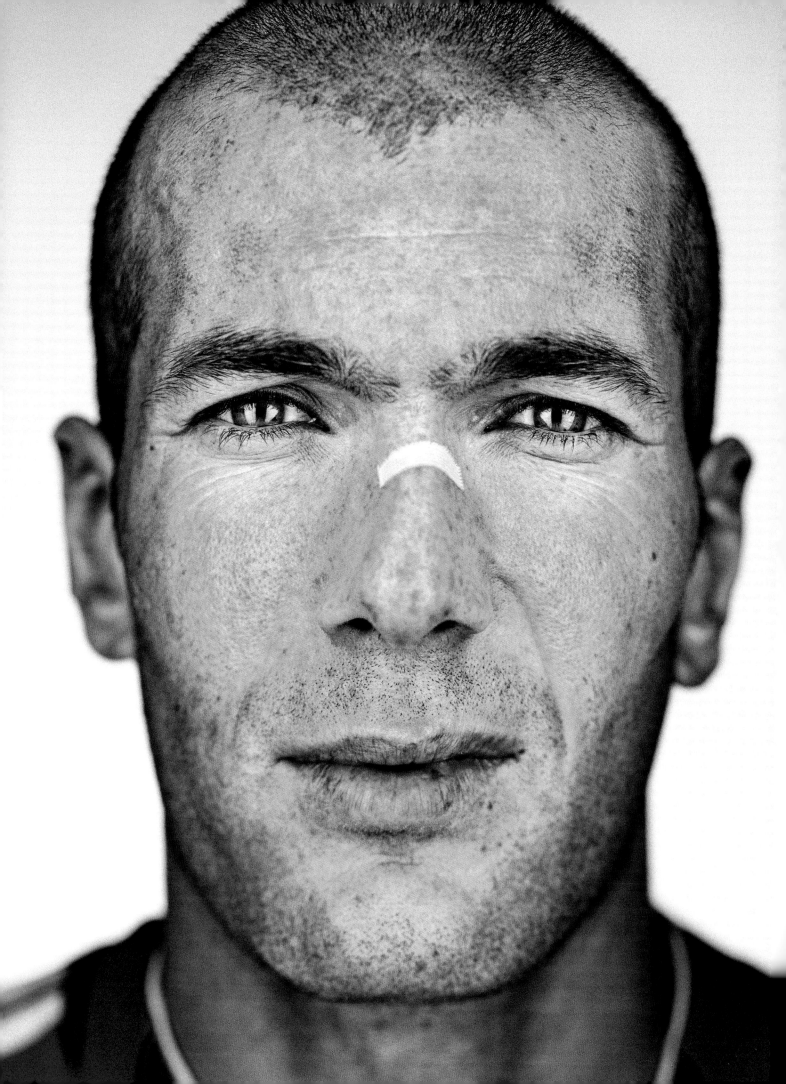

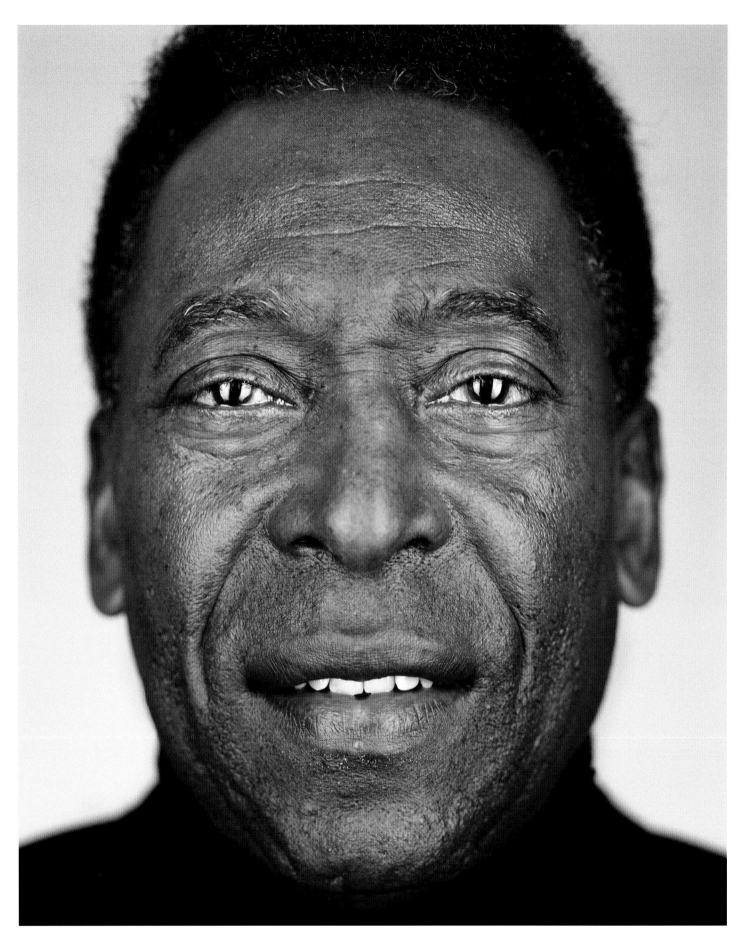

Close-up and wide shot: Martin Schoeller is mainly famous for his striking portraits of famous people, including Zinedine Zidane (left) and Pelé (above). Hans van der Meer photographs football venues across Europe, from Knippla, Sweden (2004, pp. 150/151) to Marseille, France (2004, pp. 152/153).

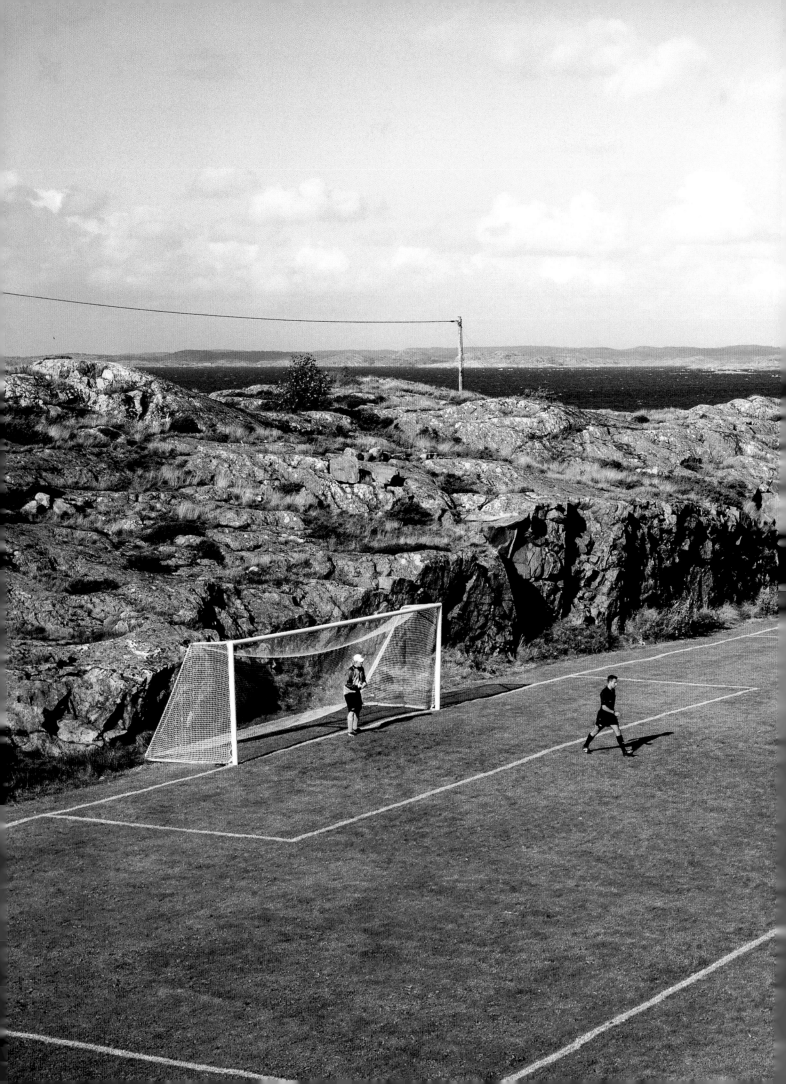

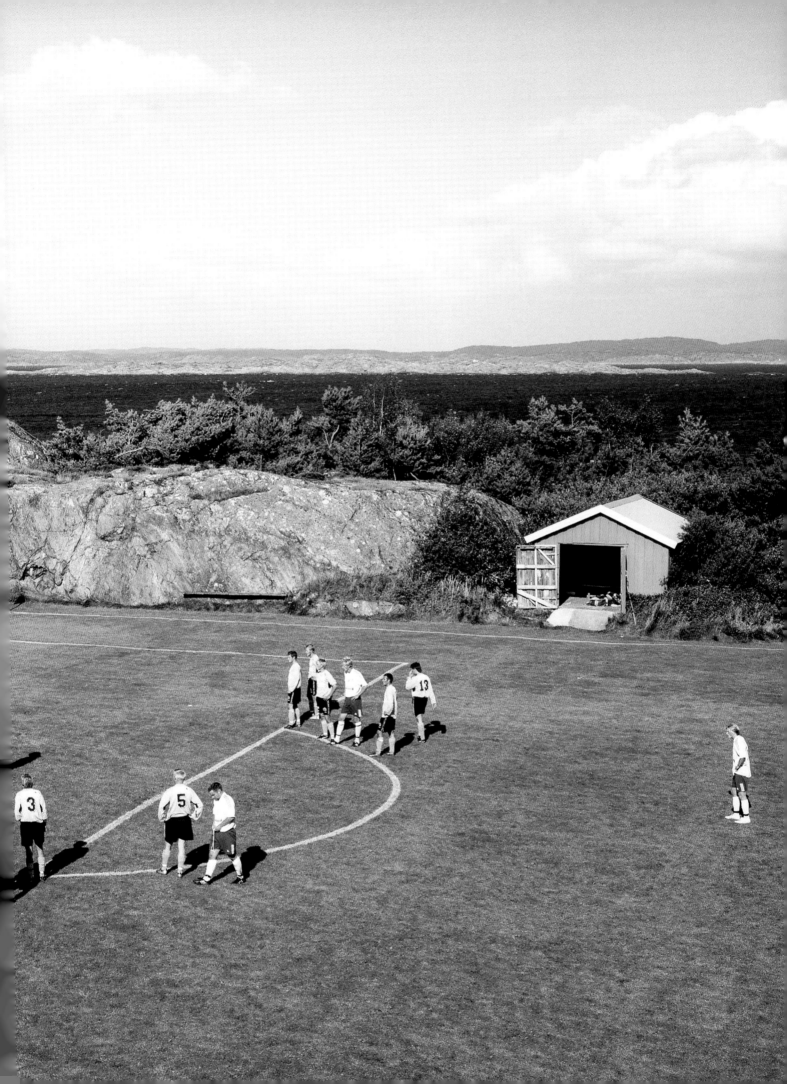

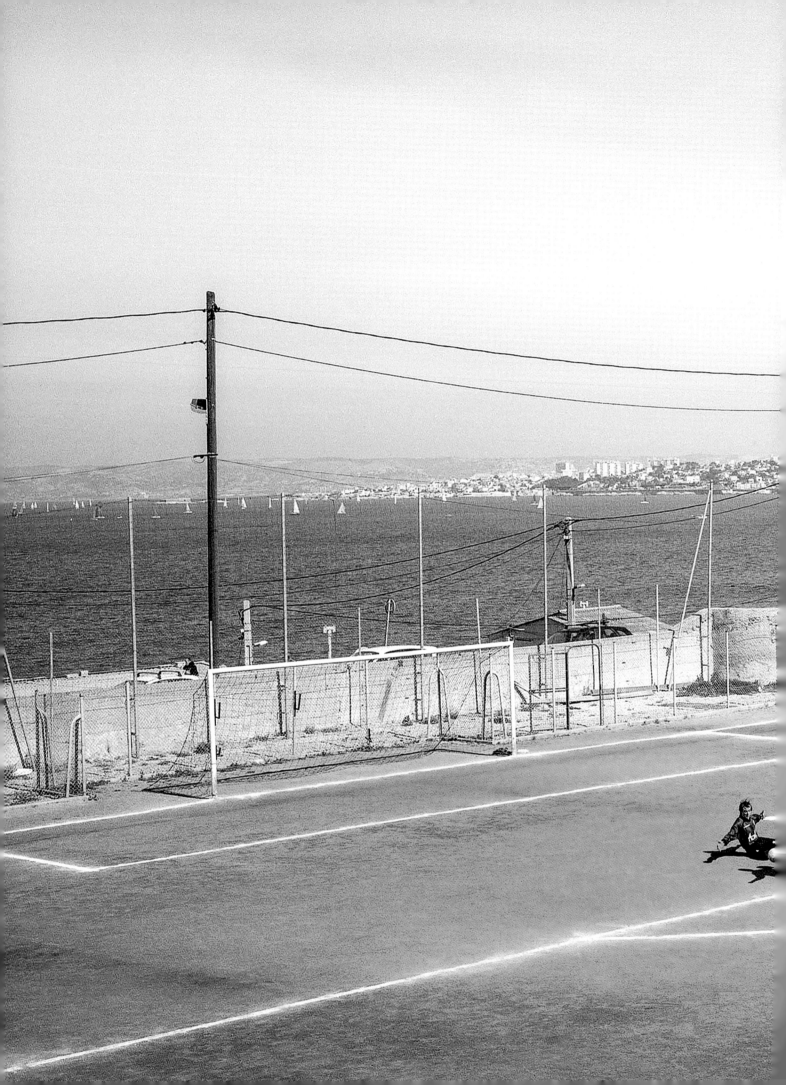

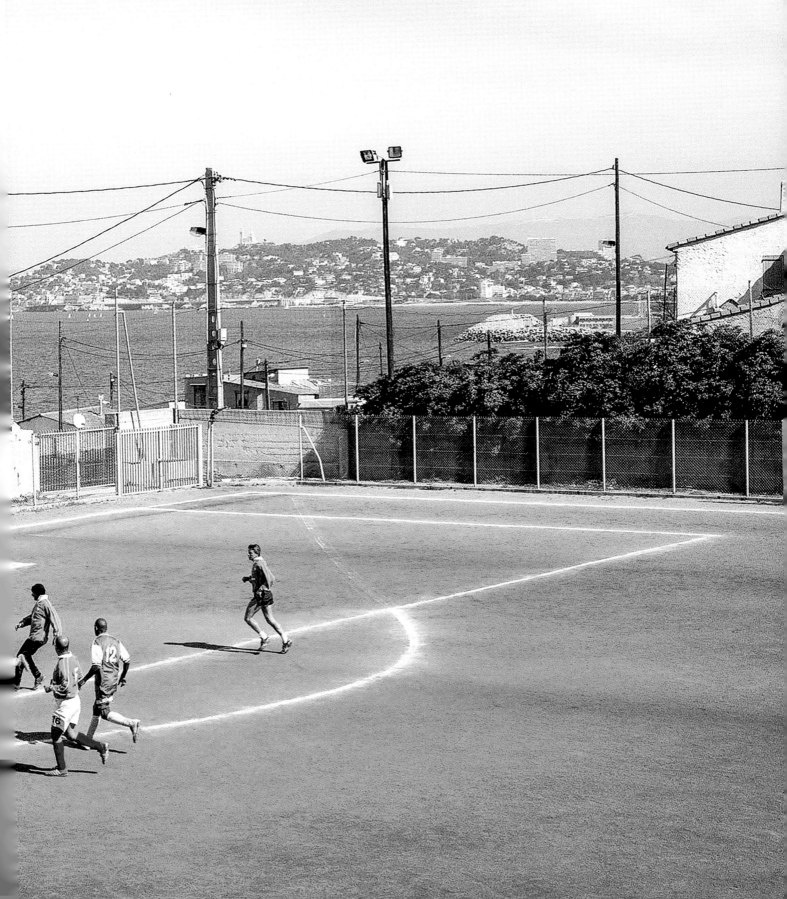

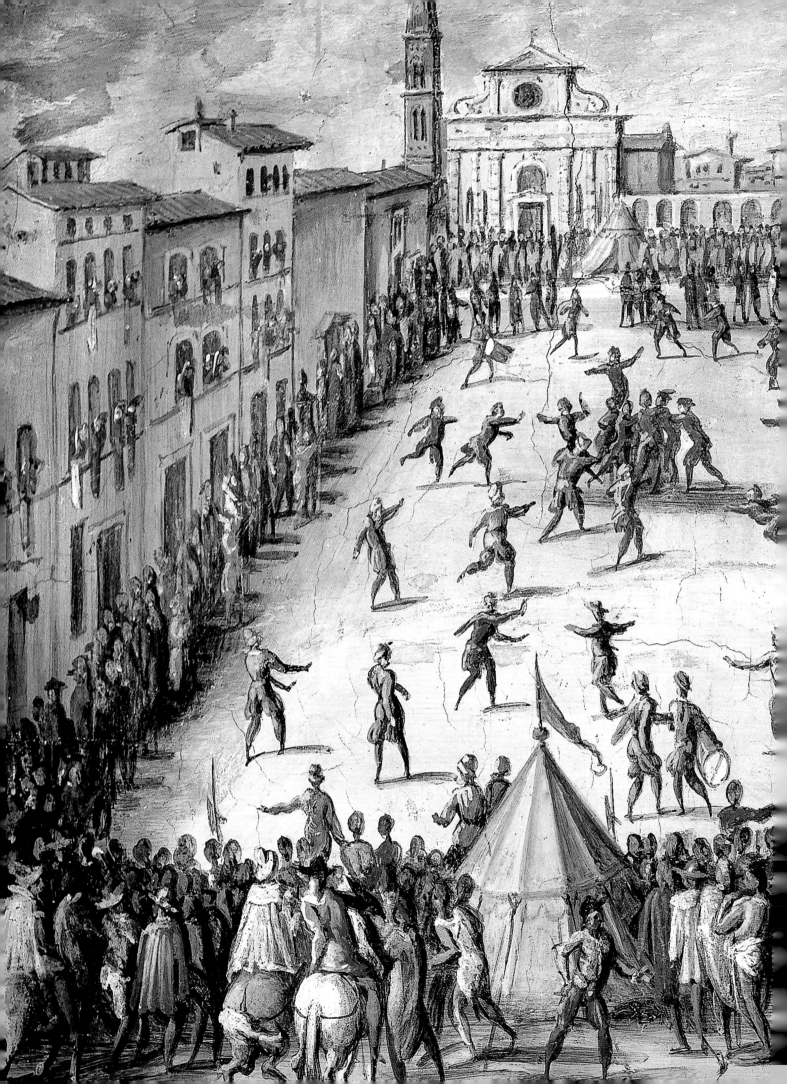

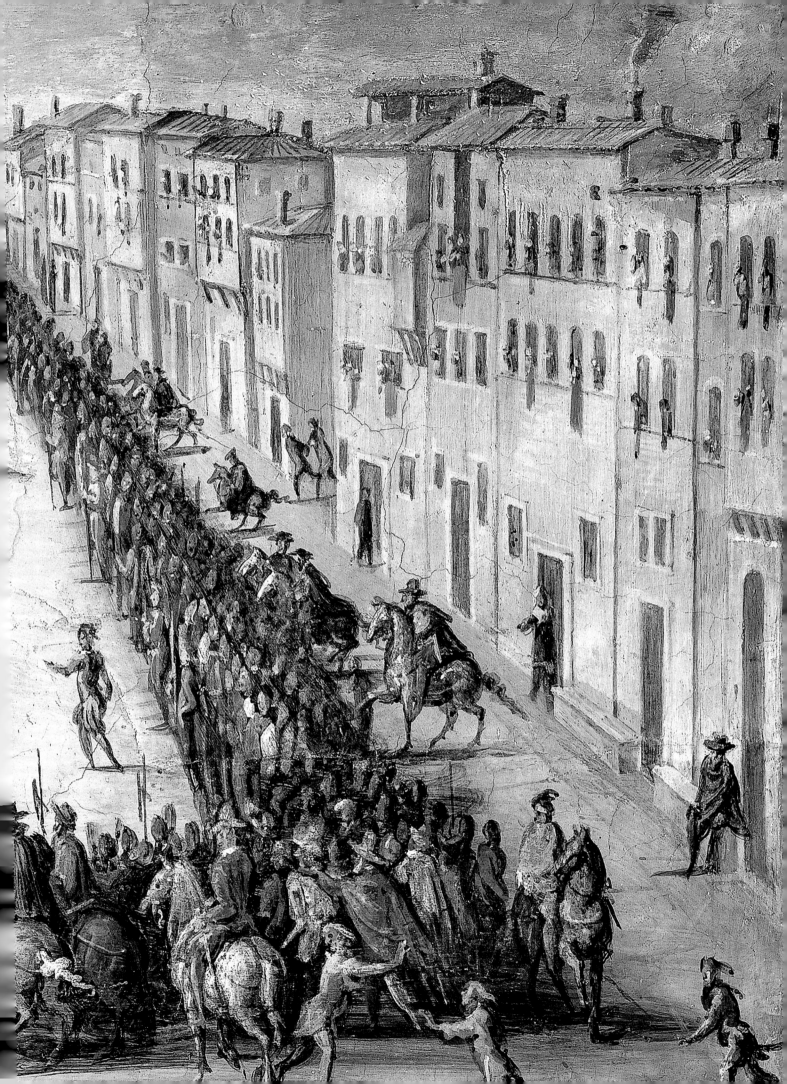

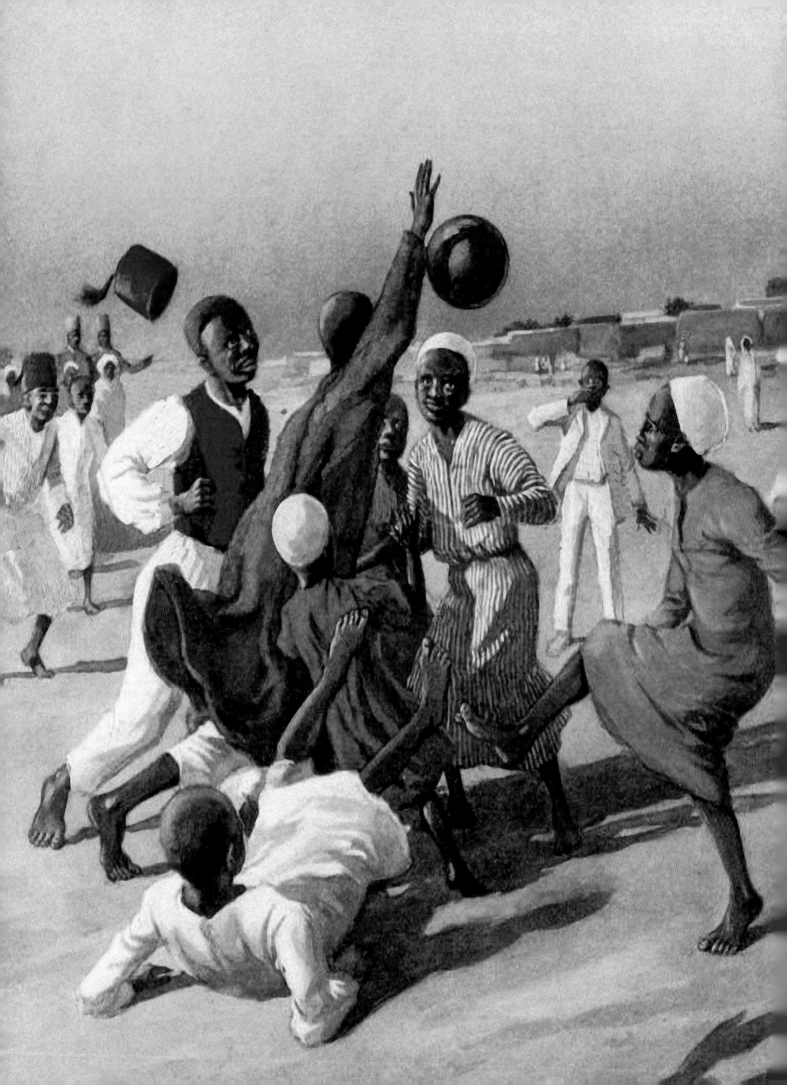

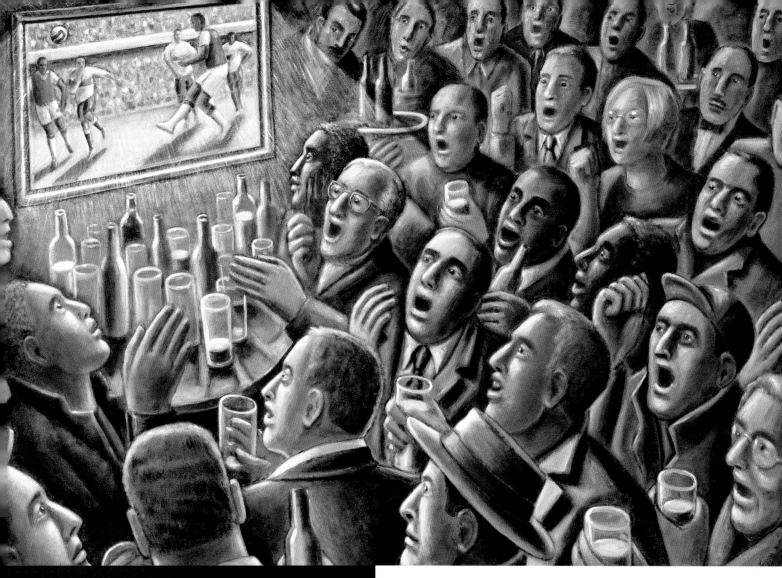

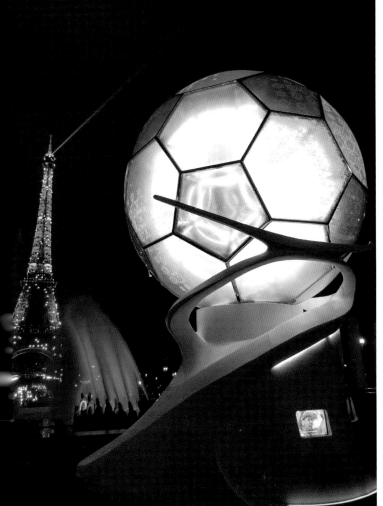

Cultural treasures: examples of football in art exist throughout the various epochs: from Jan van der Straet's 16th century painting that depicts a "Calcio" game on the square in front of Santa Maria Novella Church in Florence (pp. 154/155) to the illustration of a version of football from Sudan during the first half of the 20th century (left) to PJ Crook's work The Adoration from 2006 (above). Nowadays, a cultural programme is staged alongside the World Cup finals; André Heller's Football Globe was also exhibited in Paris during its overseas tour in 2006 (below).

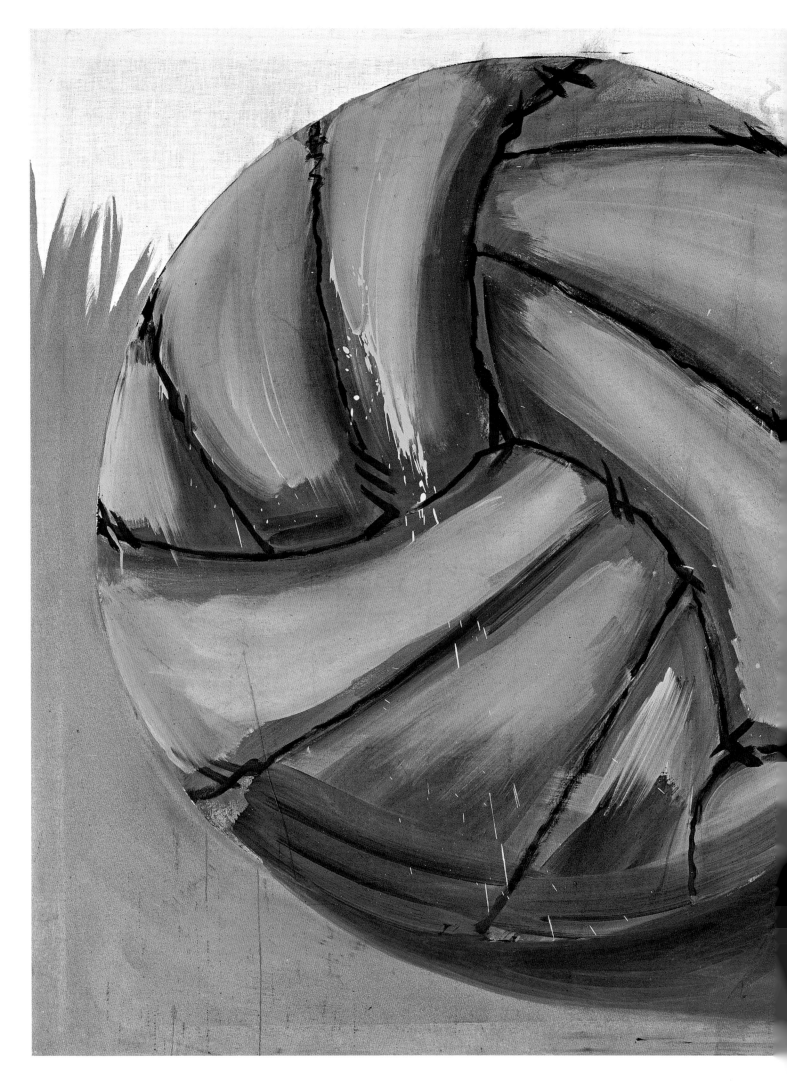

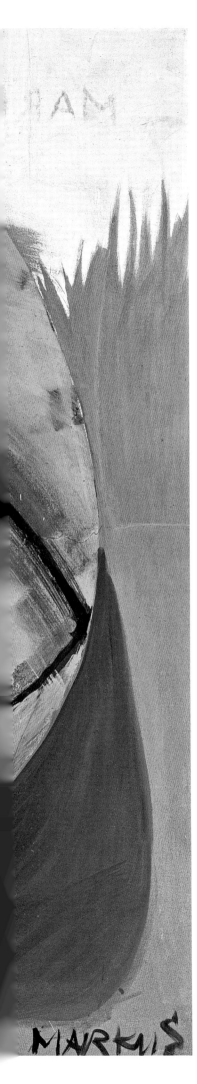

Markus Lüpertz
Fußball *(Football), 1966*
Distemper on canvas
149 x 151 cm

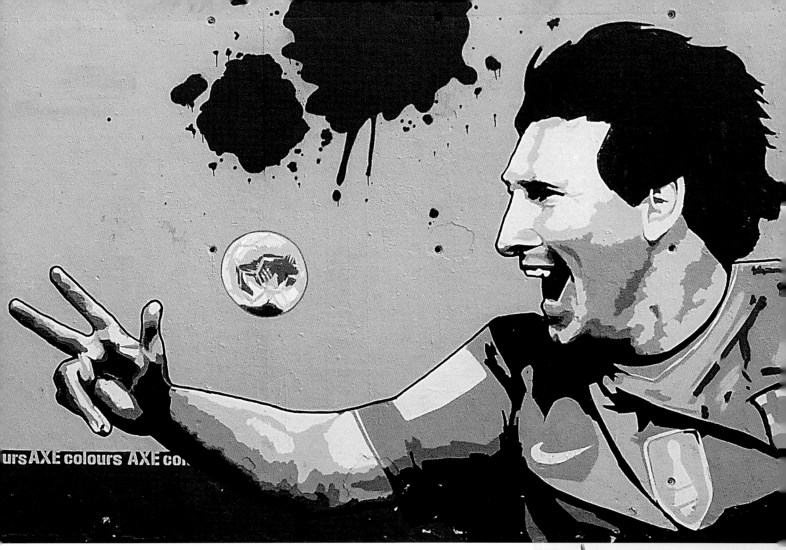

Versatile forms: there are endless genres for interpreting football in art. They range from a poem by Peter Handke which consists simply of the Nuremberg teamsheet for the game on 27 January 1968, to a sculpture of Zidane's headbutt against Materazzi. There are graffiti, sculptures and paintings showing stars like Leo Messi (above), Manchester United legends Best, Law and Charlton (below) or Franz Beckenbauer (top right: presentation of a portrait by the artist Annelies Štrba). Conversely, footballers have also become artists like Rudi Kargus, the former Hamburg goalkeeper (bottom right).

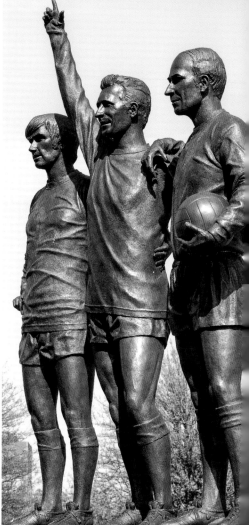

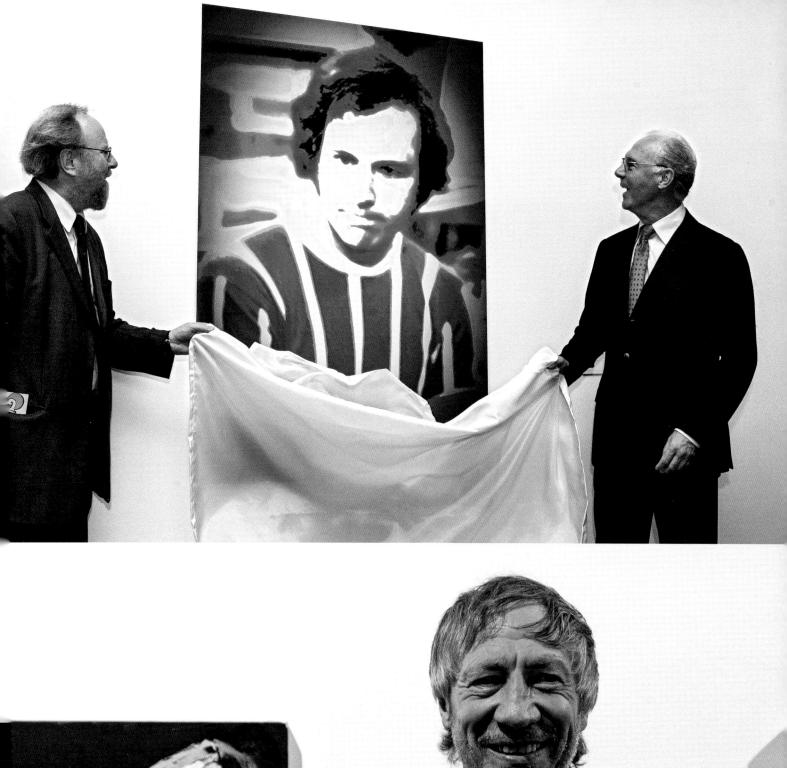
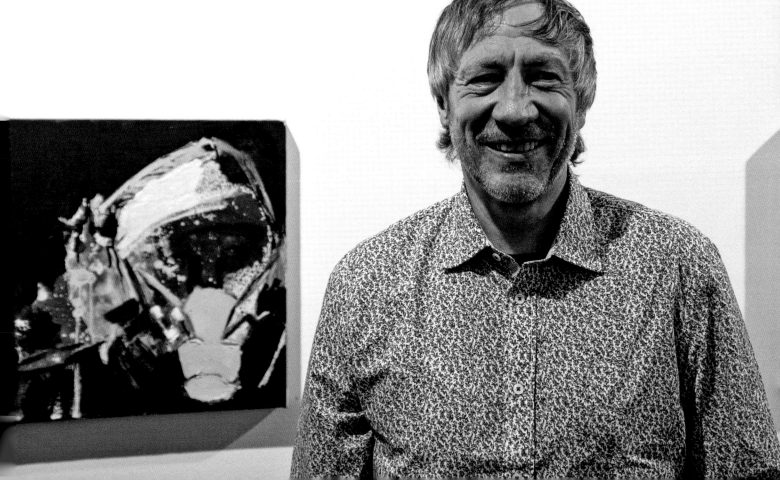

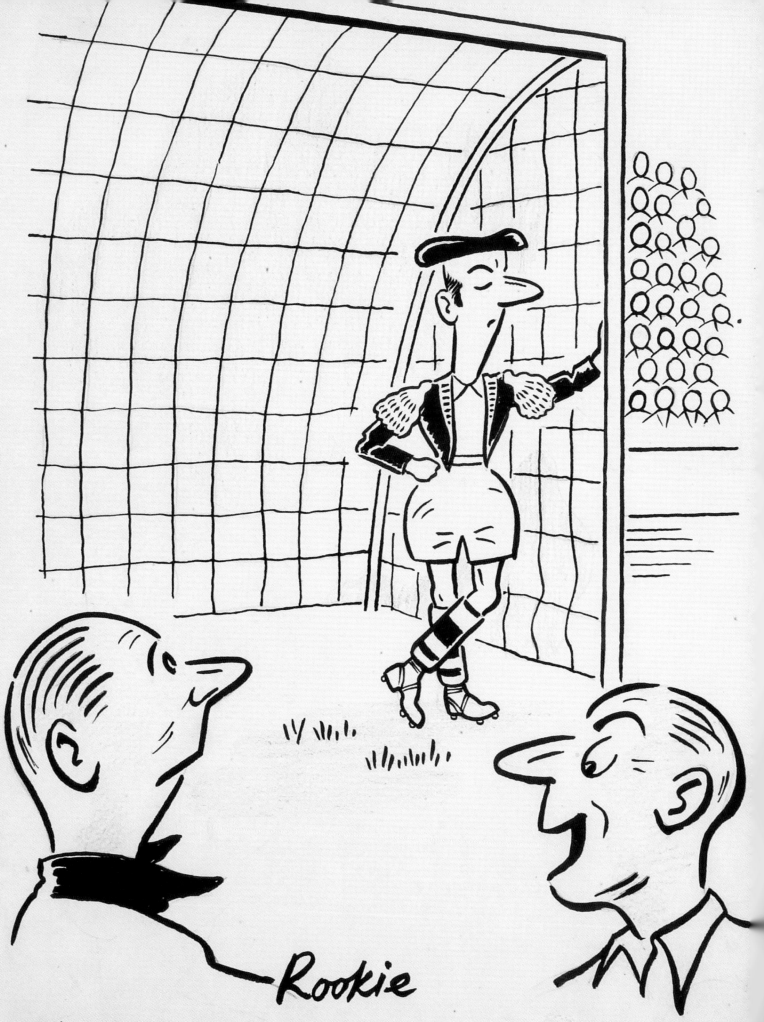

Rookie

"HE'S TRYING TO GET AN OFFER FROM A SOUTH AMERICAN CLUB"

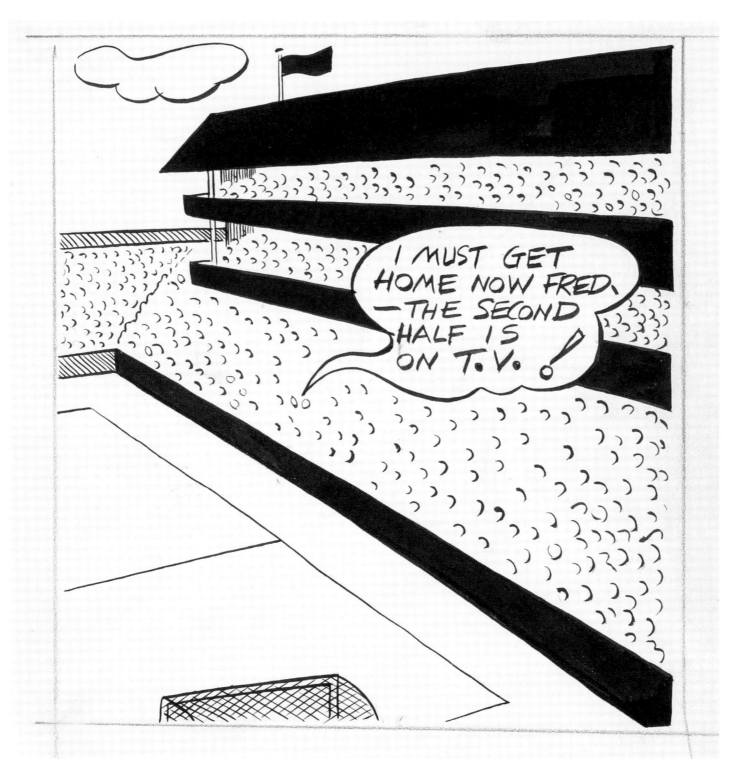

Comic-strip art: even cartoonists are football devotees. Here, two examples show how themes like commercialization or football's portrayal in the media were trending as early as in the 1950s.

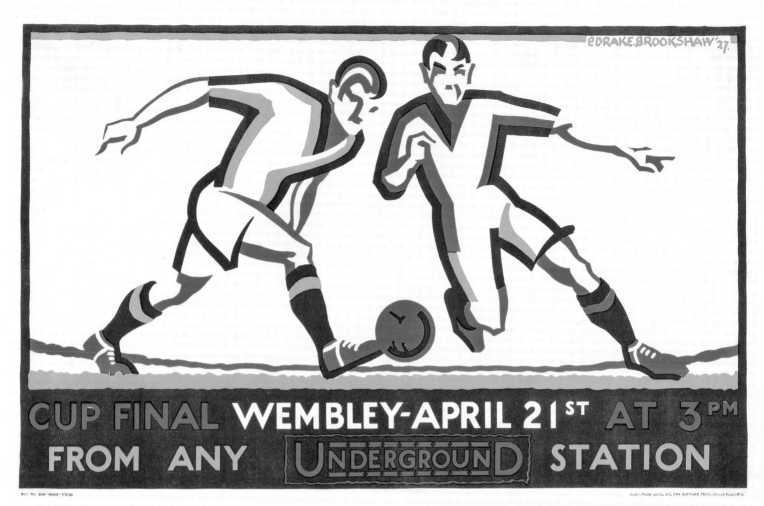

Zeitgeist: match day posters or advertisements for major tournaments also reveal contemporary tastes. Here, the promoted events are the 1928 FA Cup Final in London (Blackburn Rovers vs. Huddersfield Town, above), the 1943 Central American Cup in El Salvador (below) and the 1982 World Cup in Spain (right).

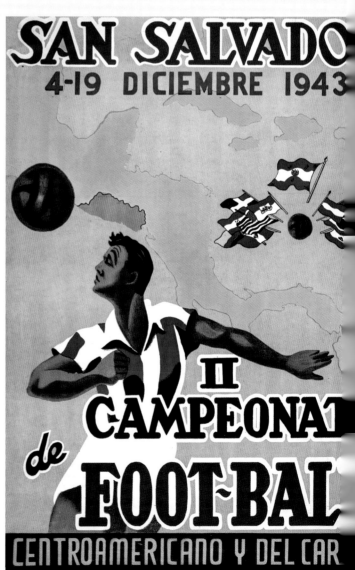

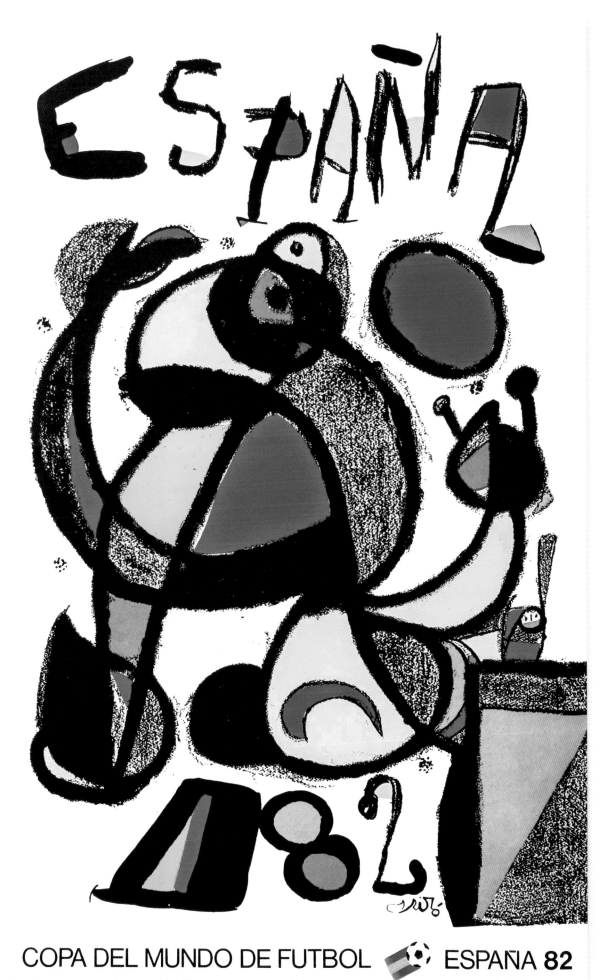

COPA DEL MUNDO DE FUTBOL ⚽ ESPAÑA **82**

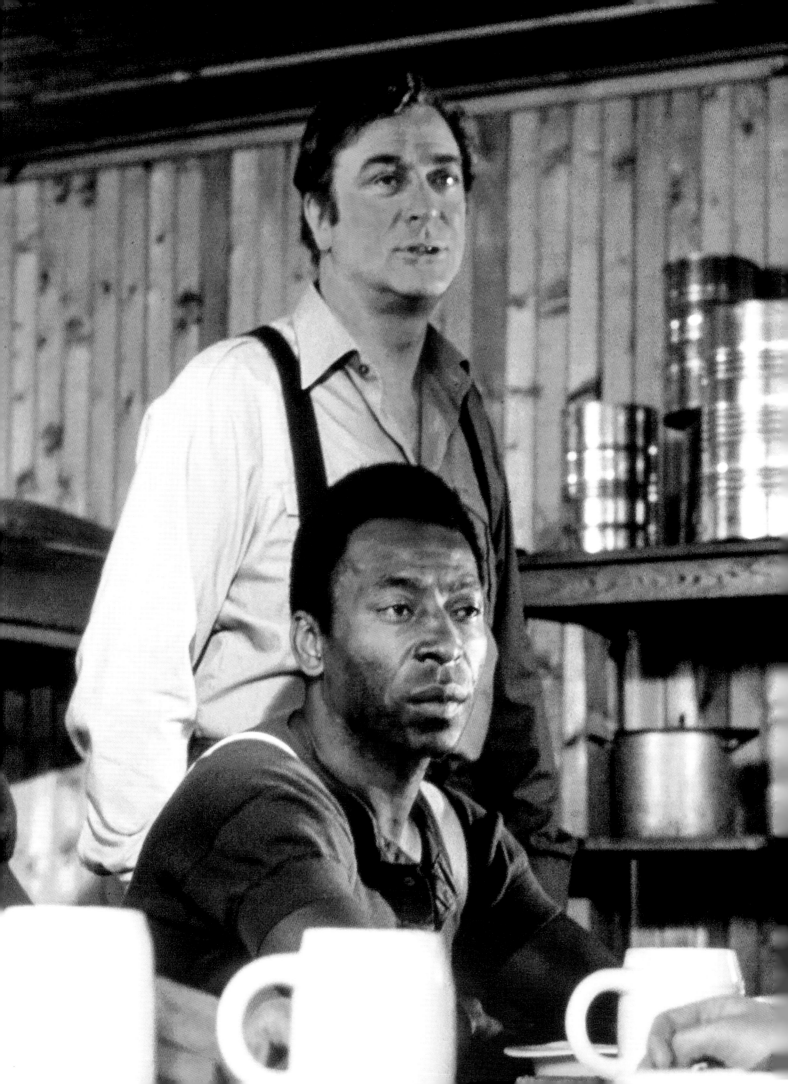

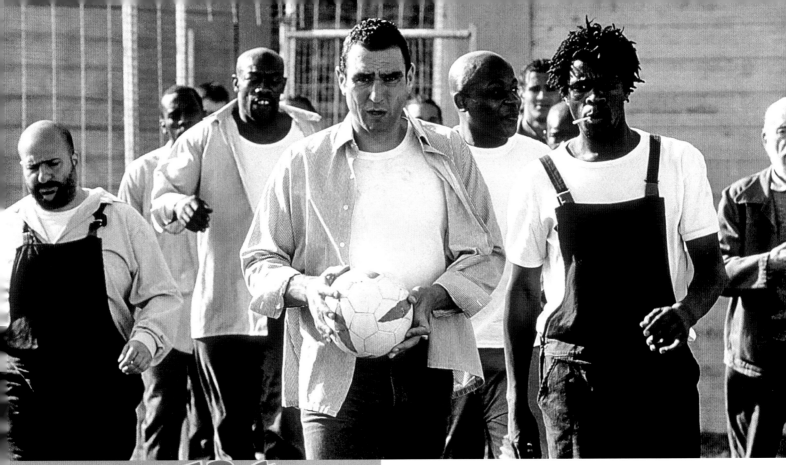

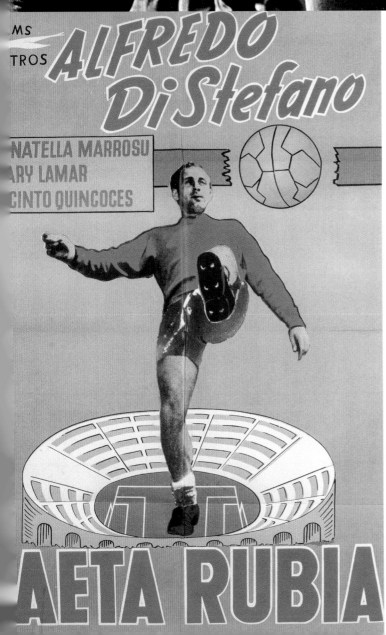

ALFREDO Di Stefano

MS
TROS

NATELLA MARROSU
ARY LAMAR
CINTO QUINCOCES

AETA RUBIA

"Play-acting!": this would pass as an insult in football grounds, but would be welcome praise for certain players. While Pelé (left, in Escape to Victory *alongside Michael Caine*) or Alfredo Di Stéfano (below) had cameo roles on screen, Vinnie Jones even achieved success in Hollywood. His first film: Lock, Stock and Two Smoking Barrels. *The director and ex-husband of Madonna, Guy Ritchie, later commented on football and film's bad guy, "If there were an apocalypse, a number of things would survive... Vinnie Jones would be one of them."*

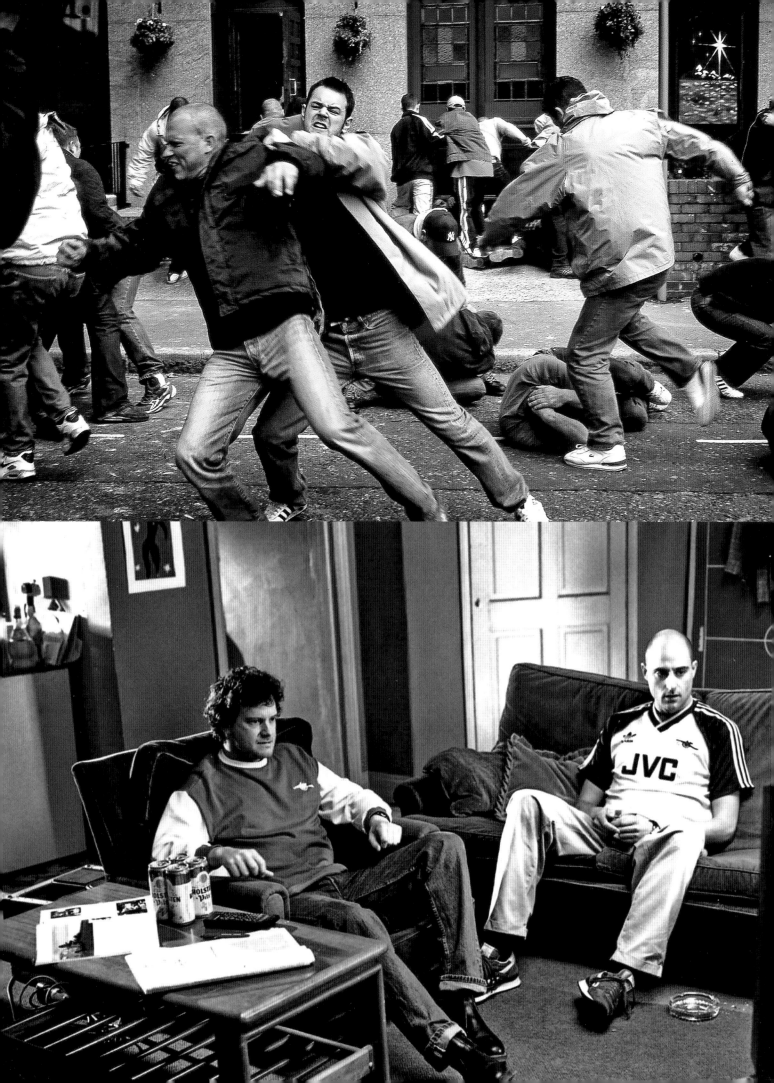

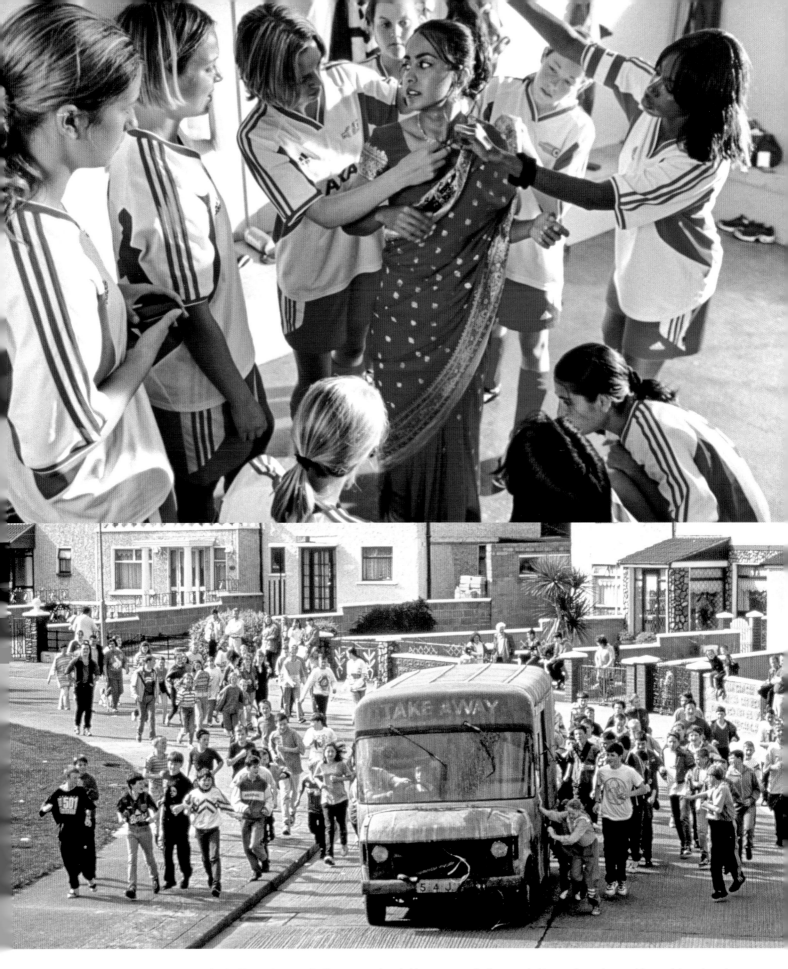

Among the countless movies about football are The Football Factory *(top left),* Fever Pitch *(bottom left),* Bend it Like Beckham *(above) and* Fish n' Chips *(below). A synthesis of the two – footballers as actors and films about football:* Looking for Eric *starring Éric Cantona (double-page overleaf).*

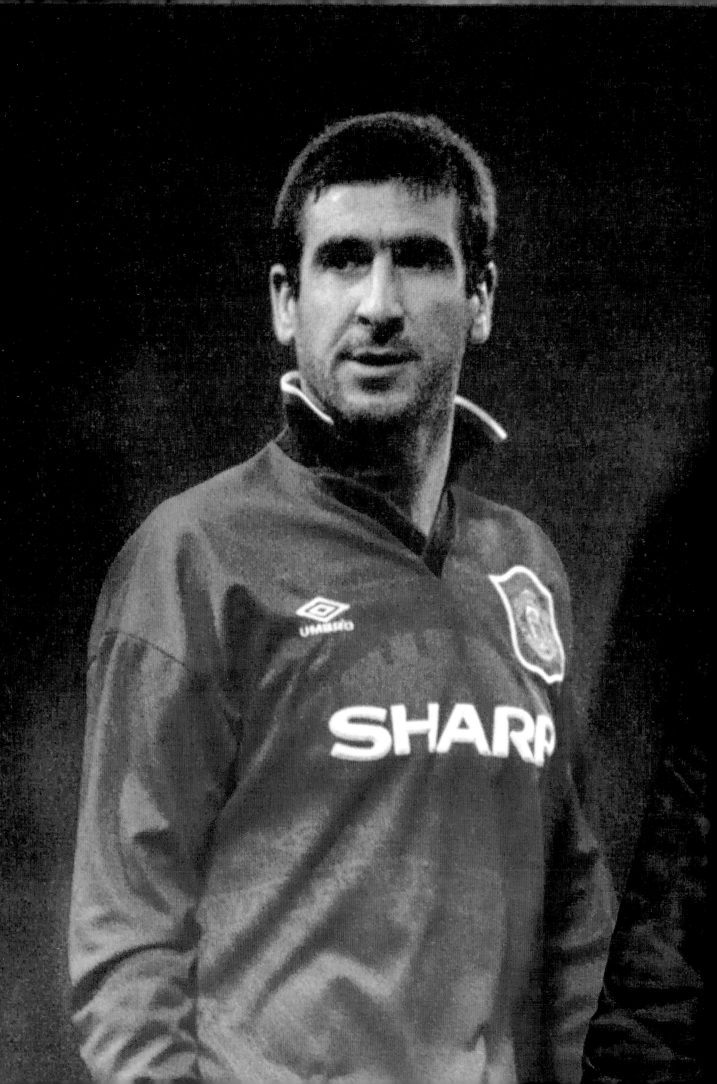

GLORY, GLORY MA
DOUBLE

PHOTO CREDITS

More than a thousand words: the Spanish writer Javier Marías gives a wonderful account of his passion for football in Salvajes y sentimentales *(*Savageness and Sentiments: Football Letters*). For him, it's among the few things that "today awaken the same reactions – exactly the same – in me as when I was ten: week in and week out, a true recreation of childhood." The power of words is one thing, but the gaze of the young Argentinian fan on the right (photographed by Gerrit Starczewski at the 2006 World Cup in Germany) maybe offers an even better explanation of the fascination of football.*

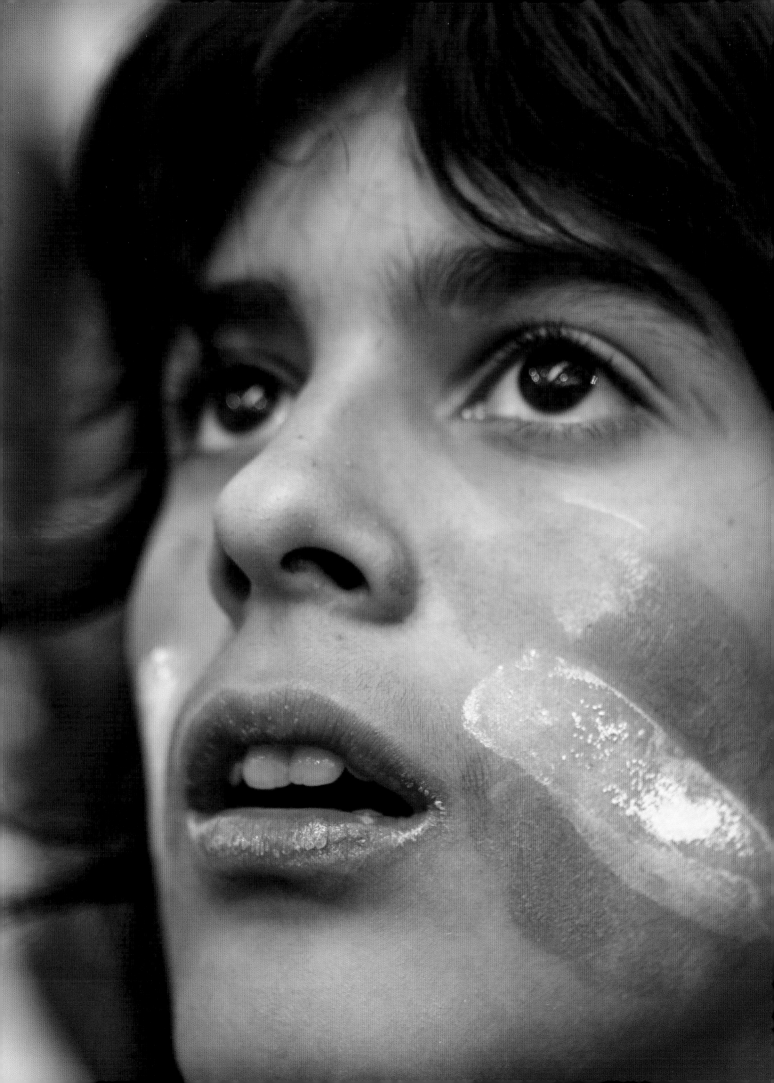

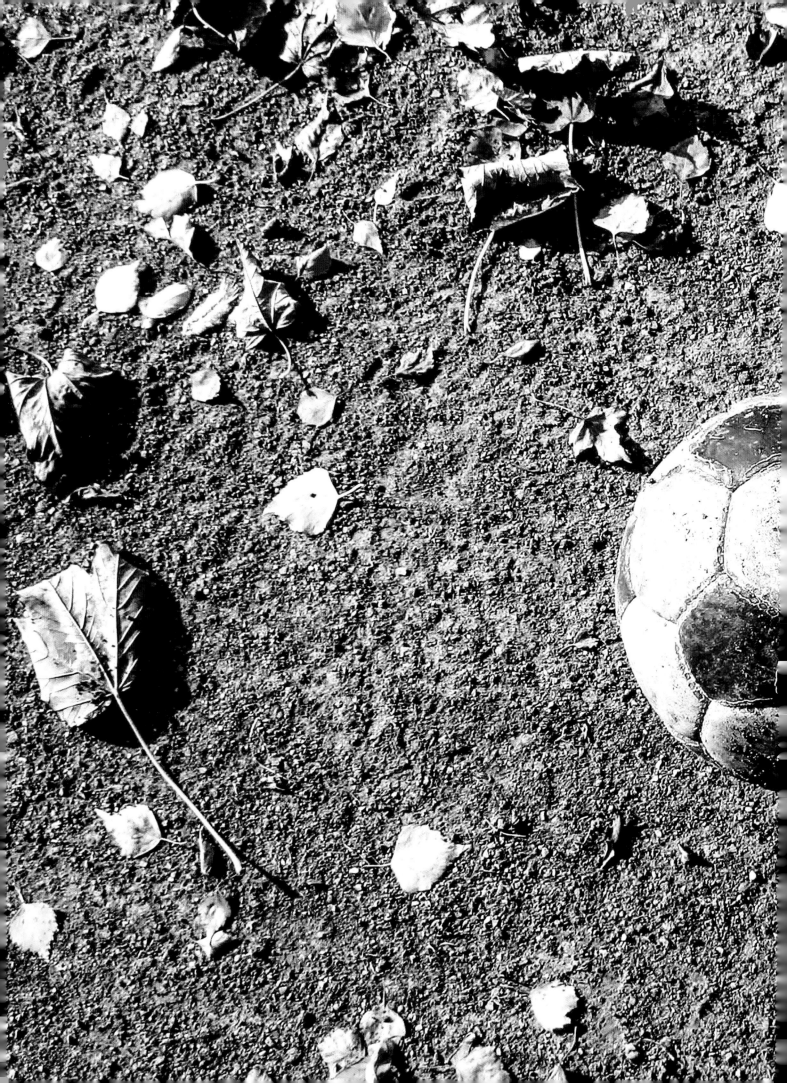

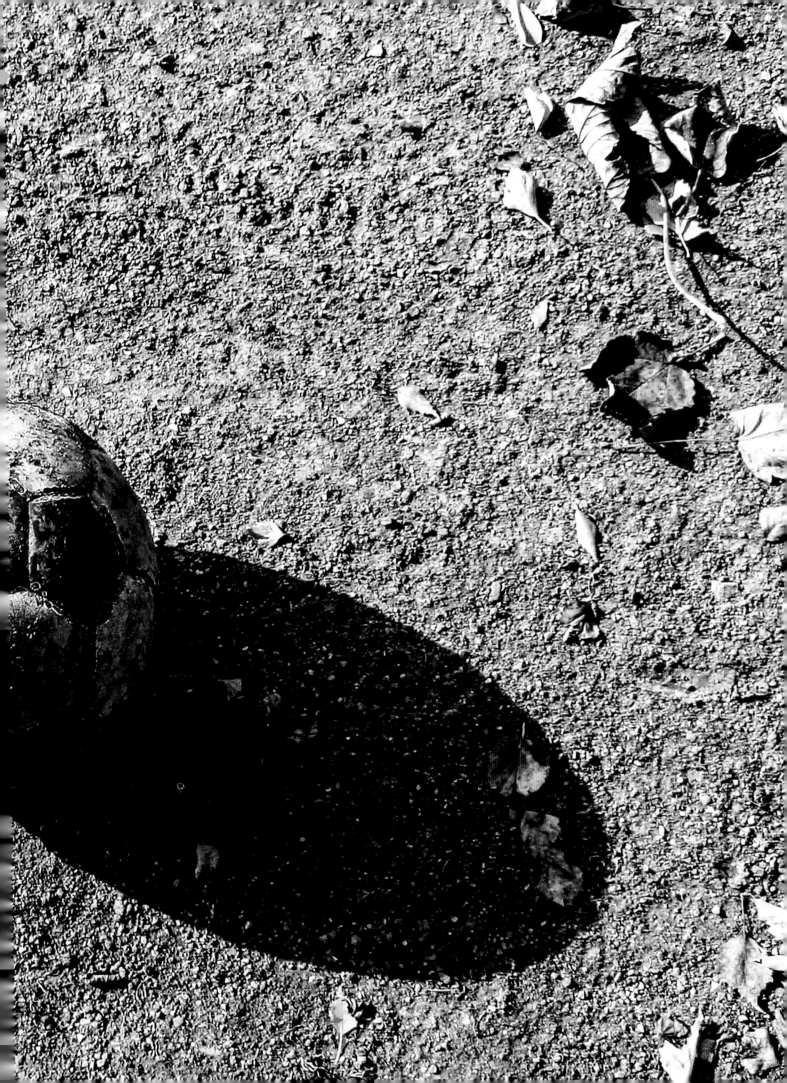

The Stylish Life: Football
© 2015 teNeues Media GmbH + Co. KG, Kempen

Introduction by Jessica Kastrop
Texts by Ben Redelings
Captions by Pit Pauen
Translations by Suzanne Kirkbright, Artes Translations
Design by Jens Grundei
Editorial coordination by Pit Pauen
Production by Dieter Haberzettl
Color separation by MT-Vreden, Vreden Germany

Published by teNeues Publishing Group

teNeues Media GmbH + Co. KG
Am Selder 37, 47906 Kempen, Germany
Phone: +49-(0)2152-916-0
Fax: +49-(0)2152-916-111
e-mail: books@teneues.com

Press department: Andrea Rehn
Phone: +49-(0)2152-916-202
e-mail: arehn@teneues.com

teNeues Publishing Company
7 West 18th Street, New York, NY 10011, USA
Phone: +1-212-627-9090
Fax: +1-212-627-9511

teNeues Publishing UK Ltd.
12 Ferndene Road, London SE24 0AQ, UK
Phone: +44-(0)20-3542-8997

teNeues France S.A.R.L.
39, rue des Billets, 18250 Henrichemont, France
Phone: +33-(0)2-4826-9348
Fax: +33-(0)1-7072-3482

www.teneues.com

ISBN 978-3-8327-3222-6

Library of Congress Number: 2014958709

Printed in the Czech Republic.

Bibliographic information published by the Deutsche Nationalbibliothek.
The Deutsche Nationalbibliothek lists this publication in the Deutsche Nationalbibliografie; detailed bibliographic data are available in the Internet at http://dnb.d-nb.de.

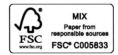

teNeues Publishing Group
Kempen
Berlin
London
Munich
New York
Paris

teNeues